Reality Bites

Rhetoric and the Circulation of
Truth Claims in U.S. Political Culture

Dana L. Cloud

THE OHIO STATE UNIVERSITY PRESS · COLUMBUS

Library of Congress Cataloging-in-Publication Data
Names: Cloud, Dana L., author.
Title: Reality bites : rhetoric and the circulation of truth claims in U.S. political culture /
    Dana L. Cloud.
Description: Columbus : The Ohio State University Press, [2018] | Includes bibliographical
    references and index.
Identifiers: LCCN 2017044861 | ISBN 9780814213612 (cloth) | ISBN 0814213618
    (cloth)
Subjects: LCSH: Political culture—United States. | Rhetoric—Political aspects—
United
    States. | Truthfulness and falsehood—Political aspects--United States. | Fake news
—United States.
Classification: LCC JA75.7 .C62 2018 | DDC 320.97301/4—dc23
LC record available at https://lccn.loc.gov/2017044861

Cover sculpture and photograph, "Bleeding," by Guy-Olivier Deveau.
Cover design by Regina Starace
Text design by Juliet Williams
Type set in Adobe Minion Pro

For Hugo, always at my side, ready with the comic corrective

CONTENTS

ACKNOWLEDGMENTS

AN ASTONISHING thirty years ago, I took graduate seminars in rhetorical theory and public address with John Lyne at the University of Iowa. It wasn't until I was reaching the end of writing this book—connecting epistemology, the rhetoric of science, and the rhetoric of the American Revolution—that I realized the degree to which I had internalized what he shared. Thank you, John, for your deep and lasting influence on my thinking. I offer thanks also to another intellectual ally in the case for rhetorical realism: Rick Cherwitz at the University of Texas, Austin. I spent twenty-three years at Texas and am extremely grateful for my colleagues and friends there. I miss you very much.

At the same time, I am very glad that two years ago my colleague Chuck Morris lured me to Syracuse University, a place where I am thriving intellectually. The culture you have built in the Department of Communication and Rhetorical Studies deserves a great deal of credit for nurturing me through this project. I offer thanks to all of my colleagues for their interest and support.

The graduate students here in the Department of Communication and Rhetorical Studies are outstanding intellectuals and teachers. I am deeply indebted to two of them, Ryan Bince and Carla Gaynor, for their help with the treasure hunt involved in chasing down my sources for my footnotes. Thank you for this effort and for all of the ways you have helped me over the past two years. To my first advisees at Syracuse: Ryan, you are a fine intellectual and colleague and an inspiring teacher. I'm proud to have been part of your journey. Logan Rae, thanks for bringing the fire. I admire your commitment to rigorous scholarship connected to social justice.

I don't know how to begin to express my pride in, admiration of, and gratitude for the graduate students I have had the honor of mentoring over the past twenty-four years. I am fortunate that there are too many to list—but know that your voices and work are core to my own. Thank you.

Writing is a fairly lonely undertaking. I am grateful for my developing network of neighbors, friends, and activists (and activist friends) here in Syracuse. Thank you, Claudia Klaver, Jennifer MacCauley, Carla Dias, Peter Calvert, Michael Schoonmaker, Diane Wiener, and Sharon Schoonmaker. I offer profound gratitude to Editor Tara Cyphers at The Ohio State University Press for her confidence in and advocacy of this project. Thanks also to Michelle Hoffmann and the whole team at the Press for your patience, generosity, and talent.

I offer loving thanks to my daughter Samantha Cloud Baxter, her husband James Baxter, and their son Keith, who have been a source of delight and a reminder of the urgency of changing the world.

To my mother, who, on a long car ride a few years ago asked me: What is your next book about? I answered: "Reality." She said, "That's not big." Thanks as ever for your humor and love. My father also has been a source of wisdom and generous support. Thanks, Dad.

My colleagues and dear friends across the country have been listening to me talk about this book for several years. Sonia Seeman, Karin Wilkins, Joshua Gunn, Mary Triece, Ashley Mack, Bryan McCann, Angela Aguayo, Kristen Hoerl, Amy Young, and so many others: Thank you for your work and the dialogue that fed my thinking and confidence. I am smarter with you than without you. Michelle Rodino-Colocino offered very helpful advice. I offer special thanks to Katie Feyh, whose thinking about the concept of fidelity in our collaborative work is very important here. I am grateful for Cindy Rigg, my longest-time friend: Thanks for cheering me on. And to Nina Lozano-Reich, superstar scholar, activist, and friend, the words "thank you" don't really do justice to my gratitude for your help, encouragement, ideas, and support.

My comrades in the International Socialist Organization are key to my political life and my understanding of the mediation of consciousness and struggle. The organization is a vital source of the kind of knowledge we need to struggle—and win.

To Rosa Eberly, my cherished friend, your deep concern for the common wealth is an inspiration. Your work on teaching as a proto-public site of citizenship training and your thinking on how cultural texts prompt the formation of publics in controversy resound on every page.

And in the memory of James Arnt Aune, Bruce Gronbeck, and Michael Calvin McGee, whose intellectual voices also resonate here.

Facing Reality in the Trump Era

I WROTE the bulk of this book before (what many thought to be) the unthinkable happened and Donald Trump was elected president of the United States. Its subject matter extends beyond Trump as an example of a challenge to truth telling in American politics. However, his election is something of a watershed moment.

In addition to widespread horror and lamentation among liberals and progressives, the already fervent panic over what people are calling the "post-truth" era exploded. The explosion of the post-truth frenzy represents what Stuart Hall calls a "moral panic": a whipped-up discourse about social disorder that ideologically places the blame for social crisis on the target of the panic. He indicted British news-induced panic in the 1980s over "mugging."[1] Like that panic, the alarm over "fake news" serves some ideological functions: It relegitimizes mainstream, commercial news media as guardians of the truth (with the *Washington Post* declaring on its masthead: "Democracy Dies in Darkness") and positions the Democratic Party, clearly located inside the business establishment, as "the resistance." Progressives and critical scholars who once dissected the complicity of the Democrats and the news media with the imperatives of capitalism have been encouraged to see those organizations as the valiant defense against "real" untruths. Erstwhile critics of state power have become champions of the Federal Bureau of Investigation in its efforts to investigate Trump's abuses of power. Moreover, the "post-truth" panic diverts attention away from the very real economic crisis that hit in 2008 and rendered the lives of many Americans precarious. In other words, if we can blame "fake news" for the suffering of citizens, we need not challenge the economic system for producing that suffering.

Former champions of ordinary people have scapegoated disaffected working class Americans themselves for Trump's election. The implicit argument behind calls for intensified fact-checking, viral lists of "fake" news sites,[2] and warnings about the "echo-chambers" of Facebook and other social media[3] is that it was willful ignorance among the U.S's rural, working class, white citizens that produced the debacle of a Trump presidency.

My argument in this book challenges the elitism of assumptions that rural and working class people are necessarily ignorant and backward as an explanation for Trump's victory. The capacity of a misogynistic, racist, xenophobic, Islamophobic, anti-immigrant, billionaire demagogue to win the allegiance of, if not a majority of the popular vote, then the requisite number of electoral-college votes, is indeed appalling. However, as a number of astute political analysts have pointed out, Trump's base was not primarily among the working class but among the relatively well-off class of the self-employed. His appeal to industrial workers in the rust belt notwithstanding, it was this layer of the middle class, including many women, steeped in racism and sexism, who propelled Trump into office.[4]

These voters were not motivated by ignorance. They listened to Trump's rhetoric (as inept as it was—one need only think of the nonword "bigly"[5] or the bizarre Tweet "Despite the constant negative press covfefe"[6]) on a level transcending the mere fact. As a friend of mine put it recently, Trump supporters took him seriously—they did not need to take him *literally*. His language is keyed to produce a feeling rather than make a convincing argument. The *New York Times* interviewed conservatives about what they regarded as truth, as opposed to "fake news," and learned that political frames and emotion guide the reception of information as credible or not. Part of being credible is resonating with the lives and struggles of one's audience.[7]

Parts of the Left, on the other hand, were so obsessed (and remain obsessed) with holding him to a literal standard that they failed to take him seriously until it was too late.[8] If we had a time machine and could go back to the primary election season, what would it have meant to take Trump seriously? For one thing, it would have meant that progressives would not have mocked and belittled potential Trump voters as Hillary Clinton did, calling them "deplorables." It would mean that, instead of building an enormous, Rube-Goldberg-esque fact-checking machine, we might have listened to the substance of his appeal to disaffected and alienated Americans, some working class and suffering, others precarious and afraid.

It might have meant taking more seriously the candidacy of Bernie Sanders—who did understand populism, but from the Left, with earnest answers to address human suffering and anxiety—rather than purging him and his ideas from the Democratic mainstream. It would have meant the realization that a Democratic candidate who was the most pro-corporate and establishment candidate who has ever run for office was not the right choice. Indeed, the Democratic Party, in its ever more desperate efforts to secure power, has mistakenly moved to the right since the last term of Franklin Delano Roosevelt ended. We see what relying on the lesser evil has gotten us: the greater evil, and in spades.

For as Trump fills his Cabinet and other positions, it is increasingly clear that his presidency contains proto-fascist elements, not in the casual way that some activists throw the word *fascist* around to mean everyone from the National Security Agency to their boss. What we are facing is the possibility of a more sustained assault than we have seen in two generations on human rights, freedom of assembly and expression, and progressive policies (such as they are, after decades of neoliberal cuts); we are witnessing racist thuggery emerge from out of the shadows with the implicit if not explicit support of Trump's advisers, one of whom is the alt-right (white supremacist) figurehead Steve Bannon. Anti-Semitic, racist, anti-immigrant, and antigay assaults and vandalism are escalating in number and severity. Trump has promised, with ominous references to the productivity of Japanese internment camps during the Second World War, to institute a registry for all Muslims in the United States. He has threatened regular U.S. Immigration and Customs Enforcement (ICE) raids on workplaces across the nation, with the aim of sending millions of working people across the U.S.-Mexico border and imprisoning them behind a wall. If Trump is deposed, his equally rabid but exponentially more competent vice president, Mike Pence, will carry on the president's agenda.

Each new week witnesses errors of varying magnitude in Trump's administration such that advisers and pundits keep predicting that the emperor of falsehoods will fall. Instead of failing, however, Trump's administration has begun the rollback of what few civil rights and environmental protections U.S. citizens have benefited from. He has pulled the United States from the international climate accord, keeping not just the United States but the planet hurtling toward meltdown. His leadership has emboldened all manner of racist, sexist, Islamophobic, and homophobic thuggery.

The question becomes, then, about how best to respond to these attacks. Specifically, I am concerned with how a section of the Left has defined the problem as a problem of truth rather than of power. Instead of responding with fact-checking, we should speak and write in ways that motivate resistance in the full acceptance that knowledge is partial and partisan. Fact-checks of Trump's presidency run on continual loop. The *New York Times* has, for example, published a fact-check of his first 100 chaotic days.[9] Here is a partial list: Trump lied about a fictive rising murder rate; about contacts and communications with international leaders, especially those representing Russia; about the numbers of his supporters at various events; about his investments in jobs; about the causes of economic crisis. He overestimated job loss to other countries; manufactured a fictive terrorist attack in Sweden (defended by spokesperson Kellyanne Conway as simply "alternative facts"); contradicted his own record on racism and anti-Semitism; misrepresented Obama administration legislation, including the Affordable Care Act; exaggerated the number of crimes on the U.S.-Mexico border; underestimated U.S. military forces; accused the Obama administration of "wiretapping"; inflated numbers of jobs that could be restored to the U.S. workforce; lied about the pricing of airplanes; denied his own prior statements; defended his overall truthfulness; and attacked the mainstream news media for propagating "fake news." And, of course, he claimed against all evidence that his inauguration drew the biggest crowds in U.S. history. One could spend countless hours opening up the little windows of this advent calendar of mendacity. I'd argue, however, that knowing about every single lie as presented in a simple list does not galvanize citizens in the same way that the recognition of broader political and social injustice does.

With this basic argument, I hope to reach five overlapping audiences. The first consists of communities of progressives and liberals who, I believe, have put too much blame and too much attention on mere facts or the deficit of them. The second set of audiences for this work includes journalists and political communication scholars who have embraced fact-checking as a democratizing practice. My third audience consists of academics with whom I have argued over the past few decades about the implications of poststructuralist relativism for political judgment and action. They have made a persuasive case that Marxist scholars and critics in general should get past representational or correspondence-based theories of truth. My position is that it is possible to construct a sophisticated realism that does not give ground to relativism while recognizing the rhetorical character (i.e., mediation) of all knowledge. Fourth, I address educators inside and outside of formal schooling: You are among the most important mediators of knowledge. Finally, I hope that this book is interesting to activists and others who are not necessarily scholars, teachers, or journalists.

We need a reality check. A sober look at history reveals what happens when good people fail to rise up in mass and in force against a demagogue. Only a mass movement, unified across differences in identity, economic status, and belief, can confront the unfolding assaults. We cheer when the mythic heroes of blockbuster films go up against evil. Luke and Leia knew that it would take a war, not just Jedi mind tricks, to defeat Darth Vader. Even the cute Ewoks got on board. Katniss Everdeen knew, in the *Hunger Games* trilogy, that a war—with brutal battles and steep casualties of all kinds—was needed to take the Capitol city down. The pacifist Ents, in *Lord of the Rings*, uprooted themselves to crush the empire of Isengard. Hell, even Harry Potter knew, in *Harry Potter and the Order of the Phoenix*, that individual magic—like individual action of any kind—would not win against the fascist regime of Dolores Umbridge. It would take the soldiers of "Dumbledore's Army," trained in combat and willing to put their young lives on the line.

We are smarter at the movies than in "real life." The communication of science needs science fiction. The minutiae of fact-checkers cannot fathom reality at the system level as well as what we believe to be fiction can do. Our attempts to hold fast the grains of sand we think are truths are folly.

Let's think big. Our lives depend upon it. Trump's presidency is not a fantasy. The reality is that we have to fight. And that reality does, indeed, bite.

Toward a Rhetorical Realism

I COME to this project with the frustration of being a progressive critical scholar of political discourse who has been forced to recognize something uncomfortable: There are a number of claims circulating in political culture with no basis in reality that are persuasive nonetheless. They are largely impervious to challenges based on empirical evidence. Meanwhile, the Left traffics predominantly in the assertion of truths against (what we think should be) obvious falsehoods controlling political knowledge, for example, regarding creationism and climate change denial. The Left, armed with science, history, and buckets full of facts, attempts to "speak truth to power."[1] In other words, we assume that in any controversy, the person who has the truth on their side will eventually win the day. Here's the uncomfortable part: This assumption is just not true. The truth does not necessarily set us free; indeed, the powerful often control the circulation and authority of what counts as truth.

Infamously, in 2004, President George W. Bush aide Karl Rove called a journalist who questioned administration statements about the Afghan and Iraq Wars part of the "reality-based community," which he defined as people who "believe that solutions emerge from your judicious study of discernible reality." He added,

That's not the way the world really works anymore. We're an empire now, and when we act, we create our own reality. And while you're studying that

> reality—judiciously, as you will—we'll act again, creating other new realities, which you can study too, and that's how things will sort out. We're history's actors . . . and you, all of you, will be left to just study what we do.[2]

This statement has proven to be shockingly accurate. U.S. wars in Iraq and Afghanistan persist despite their basis in untruths about weapons of mass destruction and the causes of terrorism. These wars proceed according to sketchy motivations and in spite of indeterminate (at best) success.

Rove was right: We in the "reality-based community" are left to study, deconstruct, analyze, and correct historical actions, but in a certain real sense, the actions of the powerful do create the truths of dominant common sense. As Jason Hannan argues in his collection *Truth in the Public Sphere*, truth is the first casualty of American politics.[3] It is also, ironically, its first product.

In this book, I argue that the rhetorical strategies of the "reality-based community" are limited by commitments to rationalism and too-simple understandings of truth. At the same time, relativist stances that suggest that there is no foundational reality independent of subjective perception are impoverished by the inability to make moral and political judgments about competing accounts of reality and truth. Here I try to chart a middle way with the idea of "rhetorical realism," or the idea that there is a reality—but none of us can know it except through frames of mediation, or interpretation by politicians, activists, pundits, and the mass media. The necessity of mediation means that we cannot simply put "facts" in front of audiences and expect them to respond in a meaningful political way. Instead, the Left should take up some of the compelling rhetorical mediation tools that the Right has long embraced: emotion, embodiment, narrative, myth, and spectacle. Successful mediation is what takes "facts" and turns them into beliefs and, ultimately, common sense.

I am late to this party. Along with many other critical rhetoricians and activists, I have clung to the strategies of what James Arnt Aune called "the culture of critical discourse" (CCD).[4] The CCD is where you will find poor, former vice president Al Gore with his charts, pointer, and ladder, explaining to the viewers of *An Inconvenient Truth* why their beliefs about global warming are just plain wrong. The only people viewing, however, are those who already agree with him. The CCD is where you find the journalistic fact-checkers dutifully researching each narrow political claim without touching the bigger truths that organize our social and political lives.

LIMITS OF THE REALITY-BASED COMMUNITY

We on the Left are mired in the epistemic. By this claim I mean that activists and scholars in the "reality-based community" rely too heavily and uncritically upon *facts*: observations, examples, statistics, transcripts of historical events, and so on. But there is another set of truths, those of common sense or *doxa*, which win adherents because they are packaged in terms of established beliefs and values along with meaning frames—schemes of interpretation that selectively include, omit, or emphasize features—that cultivate belief. In other words, if you, like 95 percent of the world's population, believe that there is a divine creator with at least some influence on unfolding events, it makes sense and is reasonable to believe that such a creator cultivated life on our planet. If you believe that people should be loyal first and foremost to their nation-state, it makes sense and is reasonable to believe that any costs are justifiable in the conquest of external enemies.

Furthermore, cultivators of the status quo—politicians, mainstream media, schools, churches, museums, families, and so on—operate in a number of different rhetorical modalities, or strategies of communication, whereas members of the CCD prize most highly the well-reasoned and evidenced argument. The rhetorical modalities of the Right include arguments, too, but what else do they have? They have narrative, myth, embodiment, affect, and spectacle. They enjoin people's bodies and emotions in narratives about living alongside dinosaurs. They tell compelling stories about our origins and destinies that foster deep identification and commitment. They have the whole chicken—and the duck and the turkey. They have the whole turducken and we in the reality-based community become so much chopped liver.

I recognize the massive creativity of the Left in culture, literature, and sport, as well as the profound resonance of dance, singing, theater, puppetry, and other arts in protest movements around the world.[5] In no way am I arguing that we on the Left never serve up the three-meat platter of rhetorical strategies. Even so, the idea of a simple "speaking truth to power" has extensive reach and appeal.

The "debate" over global warming brings the tragic contours of this problem to the fore. A May 2013 article published in *Environmental Research Letters* surveyed thousands of scientific studies, concluding that more than 97 percent of them not only establish the reality of global warming but also confidently locate the cause of that warming in human activity.[6] Although at the time of this writing, the majority of Americans believe that global warming is a real phenomenon (largely due to personal experience of weather-related disasters), only 42 percent believe that it is driven by human activity.[7] Massive evidence here fails to inform common sense. Like the full weight of the scientific community, Al Gore was mired in the epistemic, and the result was one of the most boring and ineffective pieces of scientific rhetoric in modern history. The truth in this case is not just inconvenient; it is made to be unintelligible and uninteresting. Moreover, it does not help to mock citizens who refuse to identify with Gore or who fail to register scientific information in itself, without careful thought to rhetorical framing and the winning of popular assent. This failure to reach U.S. citizens in large numbers with messages about the profundity, causation, and urgency of this crisis will be literally devastating.

In the context of the impending environmental cataclysm, we cannot keep slogging through the swamp of epistemology: Let us consider, as George Lakoff does, adopting the strategy of crafting frames of moral commitment and belief that can carry our truths out of the glades and into glorious, plain view.[8] Along with Lakoff, I will suggest that progressives should think more carefully about the multiple modalities involved in the construction of one's identity and social being: affect, embodiment narrative, myth, and spectacle. There are three problems with such an effort, however.

PROBLEMS WITH RHETORICAL RELATIVISM

The first is ethical: Do we want to engage in rhetorical strategies that are suspiciously manipulative?

The second is practical. It has been established in social movement studies that groups challenging the terms of existing social reality cannot avail themselves of exactly those terms. At the same time, refusal to engage the reality frames of the powerful and the common-sensible renders activists unintelligible and boring at the best of times and profoundly terrifying at the worst (facts, facts, police murders, facts, violence against women, facts, oppression, facts, global annihilation, facts). How does one trouble blind patriotism in favor of internationalism when these frames are mutually unintelligible? How might we credibly alert people to their own oppression and exploitation when structural thinking is not the norm—and when, understandably, the person sitting next to you at the bar probably would not welcome a lecture on her own oppression?

The third problem is theoretical. Followers of the postmodern turn have troubled any easy resort to something that could be identified as "true" or "real." Power on this view is the capacity to constitute "truth regimes" that govern populations not by repression but by inculcation in prevailing common sense.[9] Rhetoricians since the debates between the Sophists and Plato recognized the role of rhetoric as "epistemic," that is, integral to all processes of human knowing, even if one can posit a reality outside of the human interpretive (and therefore rhetorical) encounter with it. Friedrich Nietzsche famously stated, "There are no facts," arguing instead for the primacy of human interpretation.[10] I am going to argue that there are no facts without interpretation, which is a very different case.

Poststructuralist critics follow Nietzsche in disparaging reality-based critique as naïve; therefore, such scholars approach truth regimes descriptively without employing an economic or political "reality" standard to evaluate political claims.[11] Similarly, theories of rhetoric as itself alone constitutive of a community of "the people" tend toward relativism. Ernesto Laclau, for example, describes all populist rhetorics (appeals to "the people") as basically equal, without differentiation or evaluation in terms of fidelity to any particular group's experienced reality.[12] In contrast, I advocate a perspective from which to perform criticism in the service of demystifying power and enabling the formation of public consciousness faithful to the insurgent knowledges of the oppressed and exploited.

Such antifoundationalism defines theoretical and critical practice across the humanities today. However, while I question both the effectiveness and desirability of the Left's resolute and unpleasant wading through the epistemic swamp, in antifoundationalist thought, all political commitments become relative without any anchor at all in something we can call reality. Why critique rape culture unless we can say surely that women are oppressed, that consent should be a precondition for sexual engagement, or that violence against women is wrong? Why organize a movement against police murders if we can't really know that the historical structures of racism condition those crimes? How do we criticize the American Dream unless we know that there is, really, an American Nightmare?

TOWARD A RHETORIC OF BELIEF

Hence the present project, one aimed at a defense of realism and recognition of the epistemic, but in rhetorical terms: a rhetorical realism. Characteristics of a rhetorical realism are first, that it identifies and deploys epistemic resources, that is, "scientific" knowledge alongside lived experience; and second, that it mobilizes knowledge in rhetorical modalities in a way to succeed in throwing one's claims over the transom of the epistemic to circulate in the doxastic, in common sense. Third, however, a rhetorical realism does not concede all grounds for truth claims to the operations of power. A rhetorical realism should try to establish the fidelity of a commonsense construct to the interests of the exploited and oppressed, whose experiences, in reality, are the conditions of possibility for alternative realities and rhetorics based upon them.

To the end of defining a workable rhetorical realism, *Reality Bites* explores the status and importance of truth claims in contemporary U.S. political rhetoric. It does so in the face of widespread skepticism among both politicians and communication theorists regarding the utility, ethics, and viability of an empirical standard for political truths. Appeals to the truth often assume a transparent relationship between reality and the rhetorical representation of that reality, an assumption that is fundamentally flawed. Even so, the possibility of anything like a democratic society requires public accountability to reality and the critical ability to separate lies from truths.

A definitional note is in order at this point: "Truth" and "reality" are imbricated but not interchangeable concepts. For present purposes, I define "reality" as the existing world of nature, social arrangements, and the experiences of people living in them. "Truth" here is the exhibition of a claim, narrative, or other symbolic form's fidelity to "reality," in the full recognition that reality itself is subject to rhetorical constitution and therefore contingent on history and social position. I do not believe that pursuing questions of ontology, or the question of reality outside the capacity to perceive and interpret it, is productive. Even if there were ever an original "state of nature" in which humans encountered the world afresh, from that day forward, human symbolic framing and interpretation would have been ever present.

Rather than pursuing questions of ontology, I aim to establish a rhetorically nuanced analytic of social truth, that is to say, of *belief,* one grounded in classical rhetorical theory and the Marxism of Georg Lukács and Antonio Gramsci.[13] In Stuart Hall's terms, it may be more important to discover and analyze what is true in what people believe than to expose what is "false."[14]

Such an approach recognizes that the fidelity of discourses to reality is contingent and perspectival. Rhetoricians Richard Cherwitz and James Hikins have made a compelling case for a perspectival, but not relativist, concept of reality and truth.[15] Likewise, Mary Triece's study of the welfare rights movement demonstrates how women mounting resistance to oppression and exploitation engage in standpoint-based "reality-referencing," in which the truths proffered have particular experiential bases.[16] Exploring the deployment of knowledge by divergent groups with divergent interests is dialectical, emphasizing how systems of ideas and the development of knowledge correspond to epochs in history, and how processes of social contradiction generate transformative struggle and emergent knowledges. In other words, there is no single ahistorical truth but rather dialectically evolving systems of ideas and regimes of knowledge that correspond to the imperatives of particular historical moments. Furthermore, the development of subjectivity and consciousness, a rhetorical process, diverges along lines of exploitation and oppression such that the experience of sweatshop workers could generate a collective counter-knowledge to corporate propaganda.

Through a series of case studies, I will explore how divergent experiential knowledge (*episteme*) is transformed in a process of political, rhetorical mediation such that competing regimes of common sense (*doxa*) emerge in the political public sphere. In turn, prevailing common sense influences the further filtering and organizing of epistemic knowledge (i.e., the process flows both ways).

From this conceptual foundation, I am guided by the following questions: How do rhetorical processes of inclusion, exclusion, and ordering delimit what counts as fact? How do prevailing ideas governing social reality emerge, circulate, and become naturalized in the service of the hegemonic power of a particular class? What epistemic resources are available to subordinated groups, and which rhetorical affordances benefit those invested in the status quo? What are the various forces of mediation (not only actual communicative media but also political organization and rhetorical interventions) that condition the emergence of public knowledge? Ultimately, what are the conditions of possibility for radical contestation for hegemony on the terrain of *doxa*, or mass circulated political awareness?

In answer to those questions, I will argue that there are empirical bases for epistemic knowledge, including the concrete experience of human beings. The most powerful political discourses emerge when epistemic knowledge is mediated by explanatory and justificatory political frames. When political actors become mired in information without making the transition to explanation and rationalization, they lose the possibility of their facts becoming common knowledge. On the other hand, when political actors construct common sense without reference to experiential and scientific knowledge, they risk ethical breach and the alienation of their base.

Moreover, it is in the mediation of information in the transition to the public domain where rhetorical intervention may translate knowledge and situate it in sensible interpretive frames. Such rhetorical intervention may take conservative form when corporate media and interests control that mediation; however, when social struggle and alternative political organizations mediate collective experience (as during the Black Lives Matter movement), the resulting contestation between a set of beliefs that are true only for elites and the organized experiential knowledge of ordinary people enables critique and social transformation. If dominant reality "bites"—in its being oppressive and exploitative—an oppositional "reality-based" community can "bite back." This book explores when and how such democratic contestation over reality occurs.

To this end, chapter 1 argues that understanding how widespread adherence to commonsense ideas is accomplished in rhetoric is important. This chapter begins by making an Aristotelian distinction between *episteme* (knowledge or justified belief) and *doxa* (prevailing common sense).[17] I reject the elitism inherent in the Aristotelian distinction between enlightened and common knowledge, and I recognize that *episteme* can never be composed of a priori facts outside of rhetorical invention. Instead, I believe that we can posit a version of *episteme* as experiential knowledge requiring rhetorical shaping to become *doxa*. The power of these two categories lies in their ability to help theorize how rhetorical work organizes and transforms social knowledge in generalizing particular experience. This chapter will require some discussion of publics and counterpublic spheres, noting the existential tie of counterpublics to local experience and the costs of generalizing that experience in the broader public domain. In a structured social and economic context, rhetorical invention takes up experiential knowledge and mediates that knowledge's appearance in society as commonly accepted truth (*doxa*) in a process that is always partial and invested with class interests. Here, Lukács is important to understanding how class consciousness emerges from a rhetorically mediated experiential reality; his account of class consciousness is supplemented with insights about the complexity of social truths from other Marxists.

For example, political philosopher Raymond Geuss writes,

> Humans' beliefs and desires are in constant flux, and changes in them can take place for any number of reasons. Transformations of specific sectors of human knowledge are often accompanied by very widespread further changes in worldview and values.[18]

In emphasizing the process of change in knowledge and ideas, a realist standard for political ethics, and a call to action in the context of global crisis, Geuss influences my thinking in this chapter. His discussion of the ebb and flow between historically situated knowledge and the broader cultural imagination corresponds to my distinction between *episteme* and *doxa*. Bourdieu's distinction between "ortho-doxy" ("correct" "doxa" aligned with dominant common sense) and "hetero-doxy" (the pluralization of common senses enabling democratic contestation over the future direction of society) likewise suggests the rhetorical and historical contingency of knowledge production and circulation.

Chapter 2 lays out definitions and examples of what I call the "big five" strategies of mediation: affect, embodiment, narrative, myth, and spectacle (including image and celebrity). I acknowledge that both Left and Right have historically availed themselves of these techniques. However, in our "post-truth" political moment, progressives have typically answered with a barrage of facts. We should rediscover the power of the "big five" strategies and use it for our side.

Chapter 3 explores the limits of fact-checking and debunking. I argue that journalistic fact-checking as currently practiced is an inadequate tool for evaluating political accountability to reality due to narrowness of focus, hyper-thoroughness, and naïve empiricism. I recommend "frame-checking" as an alternative mode of critique.[19] There has been an explosion of efforts to "fact-check" political rhetoric, starting with those of the *Tampa Bay Times'* PolitiFact project and the fact-checking blog of Glenn Kessler at the *Washington Post*. These ostensibly noble efforts are frustrated by a number of factors, including (1) rampant bipartisan political manipulation of truths, (2) the apparent inattention paid by consumers of political information to questions of fact, (3) the demonstrated power of the elites to determine what information circulates as truth in mass media environments, and (4) the critical limits of efforts attempting to document myriad falsehoods without taking on the values frames and political perspectives that set the conditions for the productions of "truths."

Thus, fact-checkers are mired in the epistemic. As Kenneth Burke argues about "debunking," "The typical debunker is involved in a strategy of this sort: He discerns an evil. He wants to eradicate this evil. And he wants to do a thorough job of it. Hence, he becomes *too thorough*"[20] in "an avalanche of arguments . . . a snowing under, a purely quantitative mode of propaganda."[21] Resorting to a narrow empirical baseline, these fact-checkers miss the point: It's not about what's in the box but who gets to decide its boundaries and shape.

In response to these challenges, I argue for a depth hermeneutics approach that goes beyond fact-checking to "frame-checking." I build upon the work of Raymond Geuss, whose distinctions among different kinds of falsehood help us to understand interest-based criteria for truth, and Mary Triece, whose concept of "reality-referencing" in political discourse is both straightforward and theoretically rich.[22] This materialist project that situates political claims historically and economically and theorizes the concepts of truth and false-hood in complex ways while retaining the critical importance of reality to both critique and activism.

I pursue these arguments through two case studies: the 2015–16 Planned Parenthood "selling baby parts" scandal and the success, baffling to rational-ists and fact-checkers, of the 2016 presidential race. In both cases, progres-sives have failed to respond meaningfully to the values frames and emotional resonance of these phenomena. Instead, they claim victory—and it is a hollow one—in the narrow struggle over empirical truth.

In the book's fourth chapter, I explore the complexity of political truths in the case of Chelsea (formerly Bradley) Manning, a freed soldier convicted and jailed for releasing classified military secrets to WikiLeaks in 2008. I contrast the political framing of her story to the framing of that of Edward Snowden, who leaked a similarly large amount of classified information. The chapter first describes how the "information dump" of military knowledge via WikiLeaks is a politically weak mode of truth-telling.[23] (The circulation of the torture photographs from Abu Ghraib is another example of masses of information never coming into mass circulation.) At the same time, Man-ning's sexual orientation and gender identity became subjects of political speculation. The emergence of knowledge of one's own or others' gender identity and sexual orientation are complex, process-governed revelations situated in subaltern discourse communities with access to political frames for understanding that process.

Thus, this chapter contrasts the relatively simple but politically ineffica-cious exposure of military secrets against the complex and partial discovery of gender identity. The latter takes place in the particular politicized space of LGBTQ* rights and liberation, one generally without the agency to mediate that knowledge so that it becomes intelligible in the broader public.[24] In other words, knowledge of Manning's gender and sexual orientation is grounded in the epistemic moment of discovery. On this basis, this case study demon-strates the difference between exposure of truths in the epistemic as opposed to the doxastic mode. This distinction is made clearer in a comparison with the revelations of former National Security Agency (NSA) contractor Edward Snowden, whose leaks were mediated by journalists who could craft compel-ling narratives about his experience.

The knowledges of counterpublics are confronted with the dilemma of sacrificing generalized public circulation of truth, necessarily mediated by dominant interests, for fidelity to the experiences of a localized community. In Foucault's terms, Manning's is a case of "subjugated knowledges . . . a whole set of knowledges that have been disqualified as inadequate to their task or insufficiently elaborated: naive knowledges, located low down on the hierarchy, beneath the required level of cognition or scientificity."[25] What Foucault describes is a set of experiential knowledges that need cognitive organization and circulation; that goal requires an insurrection.

Chapter 5 describes the rhetorical strategies of the Right that reach beyond epistemology into *doxa,* or common sense. In this chapter, I will examine appeals to science made by advocates of the integration of creationism or "intelligent design" alongside evolution as a theory of creation and the emergence of humankind. I consider research on the Creation Museum and the rhetoric of intelligent design as a credible theory of the world's development.[26] I develop a contrast between the Right's use of the "big five" strategies and how they are employed in the 2014 Fox series *Cosmos,* hosted by celebrity scientist Neil deGrasse Tyson.

Producers Seth MacFarlane and Ann Druyan make this objective explicit. In the miniseries, physicist Neil DeGrasse Tyson hosts a spectacular journey in a "spaceship of the imagination." The labeling of the program as a "spacetime *Odyssey*" indexes the attempt to tell the story of science in the form of a grand, mythic narrative. The show thus employs two of the rhetorical resources dominated by the Right: myth and spectacle. There is an attempt at embodiment in the person of deGrasse Tyson, who strides across the cosmic calendar and peers underwater as life forms first began to develop eyes. Like its forebearer in 1980, the 2014 *Cosmos* develops an intriguing contradiction between stating key pieces of scientific knowledge as *fact* while exposing its own efforts at mediation.

The chapter then turns to a discussion of scientific education in the public schools. While creationists have failed in their attempts to integrate their beliefs into public school curricula, their efforts point to the need to theorize the educational domain as a key site of mediation of knowledge in a democratic society.

Chapter 6 begins with an analysis of Thomas Paine's *Common Sense.*[27] As a number of scholars have noticed, the document is an excellent example of a rhetor's bringing complex issues and information to public attention in such a way that her arguments make "common sense."[28] I situate the document in the history of the American Revolution, a situation that gave expression to the demands of a rising mercantile class, employing the media of newspapers and pamphlets to organize information suited to meet those interests. Paine's text demonstrates how the resources of affect, identification, embodiment, narrative, myth, and spectacle aligned with a revolutionary historical moment in which the "insurrectionary knowledges" of a rising social class began to make sense.

After this analysis, I explore the possibility of multiple mediation of epistemic knowledge in the promotion of subjugated knowledges. As a case in point, I analyze the rhetoric and effectiveness of the Black Lives Matter movement as a challenge to common sense that succeeds in a struggle over the interpretation of police violence in the political arena. Although a dominant class controls the mass mediation and circulation of information framed to suit its own interests (which are themselves sometimes contradictory), there is a massive layer of working class and poor Americans whose experience contradicts the orthodoxy rationalizing austerity, war, and environmental catastrophe. What sort of mediation is required to throw the epistemic knowledge of ordinary people over the transom of power and mass consciousness? Returning to the example of Paine, who played that mediating role, I argue that political organization and the use of alternative social movement media may be the affordances of the 99 percent, which came to voice briefly in the 2011 and 2012 Occupy movement. These examples speak to the conditions of possibility of heterodox transformation, a transformation generally possible during times of broader social revolution—times where new truths can come before the people in compelling terms.

The book's conclusion reviews the conceptual achievements of each chapter and returns to how we might mobilize a rhetorical realism beyond fact-checking in a world dominated by the wealthy, whose words stand in as truth far too often.

Determining what is real—which claims sustain credible belief—against the ideological and understanding both the dominance and vulnerability of reigning common sense are extraordinarily complex tasks, given the inherent rhetoricity of all knowledge and the global proliferation of vast amounts of information. However, immiseration on a global scale, an unprecedented and growing class divide, and rampant racism, sexism, and other oppressions all prevail in contemporary capitalist society. All are justified and naturalized in the circulation of social truths. Denaturalization of oppression requires contact with the competing truths of ordinary people. The critical task of identifying such truths and the work they perform in public life is urgently necessary in the real world.

CHAPTER 1

Rhetorical Realism, or,
Theory in the Real World

THE IDEA that there is a reality outside of our heads may seem to most people like common sense.

Or maybe not.

There are signs in public culture of widespread cynicism about truth, especially in politics. In 2005, comedian and late night talk show host Stephen Colbert coined the noun "truthiness," which refers to the capacity of messages to seem true because of their resonance with common sense.[1] Truthiness is operating when an idea is repeated so often that people naturally take it to be true. Truthiness is also a feature of the rhetoric of the powerful. As Karl Rove pointed out, people in power create the terms of reality to which others are subjected and under which they must operate. Large numbers of U.S. citizens believe that politicians lie, but that there is nothing we can do about it.

Colbert hosted his satirical show *The Colbert Report* in the persona of a hardline, patriotic, pro-capitalist conservative. He performed truthiness in a way that was compelling because it actually tapped the public feeling that identity and truth are inherently unstable. In other words, although the idea of "truthiness" began in jest, it indexes a real anxiety. As the *New York Times* commented in August 2016, we ostensibly live in an age of "post-truth" politics:

> As politics becomes more adversarial and dominated by television performances, the status of facts in public debate rises too high. We place expectations on statistics and expert testimony that strains them to breaking point.

Rather than sit coolly outside the fray of political argument, facts are now one of the main rhetorical weapons within it.

How can we still be speaking of "facts" when they no longer provide us with a reality that we all agree on? The problem is that the experts and agencies involved in producing facts have multiplied, and many are now for hire. If you really want to find an expert willing to endorse a fact, and have sufficient money or political clout behind you, you probably can.[2]

In chapter 3, I will assess the work of fact-checkers to hold politicians accountable to their claims. They do valiant battle against truthiness. But it is clear that realism, or the idea that there is an empirical domain as a measure of political accountability, is in doubt today.

My argument in this chapter is that we cannot concede ground to post-truth forces. Our historical moment of rapid global warming, ongoing racism and police murders, misogyny, war, and the most significant economic inequality in U.S. history demands discourse that is accountable to reality. However, I will argue that there are two wrong ways of responding to the "reality crisis." One is to hunker down in the trenches of massive numbers of facts and hope that when these facts are brought to light, publics will engage in enlightened rational debate. The other is to give up entirely and embrace relativism, or the idea that there is no foundational reality, only the production in discourse of what "counts" as reality.

There is a third and better way, and that is to conceive of truth as standpoint-based and perspectival.[3] There are contending unequal groups in society with divergent vantage points on reality. The problem is that truth from the vantage point of elites circulates most often and most effectively as what counts as truth. Others struggle to articulate their experience, ideas, interests, and needs. Marxists are often charged with holding to a simplistic version of the idea of "false consciousness," or the position that people who believe ideas that are not in their better interests are mindless dupes of dominant lies and mystifications. Some adherents of the idea of false consciousness argue that there is an easy-to-identify "truth" behind the lies and mystifications.[4] I hope that I have been clear so far that while I believe that often people hold beliefs against their own interests (and no one among us is immune), the category of "falsehood" is quite complex. I will discuss in this chapter how it is better to assess whether a belief is "faithful" to someone's interest than whether it corresponds to a reality that we can point to as objective.

Stuart Hall's definition of ideology stresses that it is necessary to understand ideology as people's "truth," and not just as a set of false beliefs. Jorge Larrain has criticized this approach, arguing that Hall has given up a "negative" concept of ideology that Larrain finds necessary to the project of critique. Unless we can say that a belief is false, how can we go about producing or enabling "better" critical consciousness among scholars and activists?[5] My view is that one can regard ideological discourses as truths, but then ask, *whose* truths are they? Are they fitting for ordinary people? Why do people accept them? How can we challenge them without the elitism inherent in the idea of false consciousness?

Neither fact-checking nor truthiness can respond meaningfully to this problem. Hence, I am proposing a *rhetorical realism,* or the idea that communicators can bring knowledge from particular perspectives and experiences into the domain of common sense, and that we can evaluate truth claims in public culture on the basis of whether they exhibit fidelity to the experience and interests of the people they claim to describe and represent.

When all beliefs are in principle true and all truth is a matter of belief, there is no ground for judgment. Is one political party better than another? If we want, in a well-known formulation, to "speak truth to power," what are our resources for doing so? If every social order is just another regime, are not some regimes more justifiable than others? To respond to this problem, in this chapter I develop a rhetorical realist position that acknowledges the partiality of knowledge and the complexities of representation without giving up the capacity for political judgment that can guide action for social change.

I am not adopting the tenets of positivism or empiricism, nor am I claiming that claims about truth can or should correspond to and transparently represent an objectively observable reality. I take caution from the postmodern critiques of the Enlightenment, which brought with it a number of ideas that were both democratizing and oppressive, among them the virtues of scientific inquiry and observable knowledge. The ambition of positivism sought to explain the world in new ways, but also imposed ways of seeing and thinking on populations subjugated by colonial rule. Empiricism relies on the assumption that we can perceive objects in the world directly and accurately. This assumption, however, privileges the perspective of those who have the power to decide how reality will be described. Moreover, it is impossible to represent features of our world without language, and language always shapes perception. Where an industrialist sees profit and progress, a worker perceives an unrewarding daily grind. Where a king surveys his realm, he sees a range of resources and territory for his comfort. The peasant experiences vision bound to dirt and toil.

A version of realism that takes critiques of the Enlightenment into account is possible and useful; it is also ethically superior to relativism, or the suspension of belief when all beliefs are thought to be products of rhetorical fabrication. We need a position on reality that is neither naïvely empiricist nor relativist, but one that allows critics and theorists to make normative in addition to descriptive claims—to critique, not just describe. Realist arguments have been criticized for what is regarded as a theory of representation or correspondence, assuming that communication can actually represent reality directly and simply. Below I will discuss how scholars of the rhetoric of science replace notions of transparency, correspondence, and representation with an idea of rhetoric as *mediation,* as occupying the middle space between knowledge and meaning, inevitably shaping what can be known and how it can be known, as well as defining what counts as true and real. A view of rhetoric as mediation can move experiential and other grounded knowledge—*episteme*—into the realm of *doxa,* or public belief.

Ancient rhetoricians made a useful distinction between *episteme* and *doxa* (knowledge and common sense, or belief). In contemporary times, rhetoricians have engaged questions of epistemology or the production of knowledge. In the 1980s, debates about the role of rhetoric in creating, representing, and shaping reality exploded in the field of rhetorical studies. In the 1990s, rhetoricians began to explore how power, interestedness, and history influenced scientific discovery and reporting. All of these tendencies are resources for a rhetorical realism. At issue is the necessity of mediation—the intervention of human agents and all of their investments—in communicating and making meaning of experience.

At the end of this chapter, I will suggest that inflecting these insights with a Marxist theory of mediation generates a critical, realist, rhetorical theory. Marxist concepts of hegemony, interests, and standpoint are helpful to understand how differential class positions in society produce truths that differ in perspective. The idea of fidelity, or representativeness of a discourse to a perspective or standpoint, becomes a standard that privileges the standpoint of the oppressed. Speaking truth to power may not be a matter of "just the facts," but neither is it impossible or foolhardy, as many postmodern philosophers claim.

REALISM'S BAD RAP: STRUCTURALISM, POSTSTRUCTURALISM, AND POSTMODERNISM

There have been currents of relativist thought since ancient times, for example, among the Greek Sophists.[6] The Sophists were itinerant teachers of persuasion who coached elite men in how to become powerful politicians. Notoriously, according to the usual narrative, they suspended questions like truth and ethics in favor of effectiveness. Susan Jarrat, however, has argued that the Sophists did not lack ethical commitments. Foremost, they were committed to a critical pedagogy that encouraged pupils to critique social norms in ways that equipped them for democratic practice.[7] They challenged the idea of divine causality and disrupted other social norms. Importantly for my project, Jarrat describes how Sophists embraced the deployment of *mythos* (myth) and *pathos* (emotion) alongside *logos* (reasoning). For the Sophists, hard reality, or *physis*, is inaccessible to human knowing; instead, we perceive and interpret and shape the meaning of *nomos*, or social reality. This contrast between *physis* and *nomos* (reality/construct) is parallel to the distinction I am sustaining between *episteme* (knowledge) and *doxa* (common sense, belief).

My goal is not to discover whether social reality or common sense can or should correspond to some objective reality or fixed knowledge. Instead, I am interested in how rhetoric moves claims about reality and truth into the prevailing social constructs of reality and enables different groups' knowledge to register as common sense in the public imagination. How, when, and on whose terms does such entry into common knowledge happen? Can we enable marginal or oppressed groups' experiential knowledge to gain entry into what counts as true? The Sophistic recognition of multiple, perspectival truths troubled Plato, who, giving voice through his character Socrates, denounced the Sophists. His quest for absolute Truth through philosophy warranted an authoritarian model of power: the Philosopher King.

In modern times, this dispute has a parallel between Enlightenment thinkers and postmodernists. The most significant modern critiques of the Enlightenment turn have emerged since the 1960s in theories under the headings of structuralism and poststructuralism. Structuralism is an academic school coming out of critical linguistics and anthropology, for example, in the work of Ferdinand de Saussure. Scholars in this school, notably Louis Althusser,[8] posited a social world constituted in signs and symbols; language creates the world even though it cannot faithfully represent its "reality." Rather than being relativists, however, structuralists tended to hold that the system of language and meaning that constructs reality is tightly sewn together so that there is no outside to it. The powerful have determined the shape of society and won the consent of populations to it. There is no check on whether this symbolically constructed reality corresponds to anything like the truth.[9]

A good illustration can be found in the film *The Matrix*, where the protagonist Neo and other characters discover that their bodies are serving as batteries for a society of machines who have created a virtual social world for their minds: the Matrix.[10] Neo and his compatriots are liberated bodily from the battery tanks into a harsher, but real, world. Although the second and third films in this trilogy cast doubt even on that experience being real outside the ideological construct, the initial message is hopeful: People caught up in false ideas long to know what is real. Eventually they seek freedom and find an experiential world that defies and contradicts the sense of reality in which they have been raised. Neo's critical power depends on there being a reality as a critical check on ideology.

The second and third films in the trilogy, however, represent another feature of structuralist thought: Even what you thought was outside is still inside. Power has so carefully crafted a social world that it has included fail-safes for contradiction and opposition. Even when Neo thinks his mind is free, he is still on one or another level of the Matrix. The argument that humans are constituted in social worlds that constrain their thought and actions without there being an "outside" is called *antihumanism*. We all walk around thinking, like Neo, that we are living life according to our own free will, but according to structuralism, we have been raised up to accept and live according to the ideologies put in place by a generation of elites before us.

Poststructuralism carries these ideas into recent decades, but rather than seeing ideology as something created by identifiable elites in their own interests, this school argues that there is only power without center or will. Power, according to the poststructuralist thinker Michel Foucault, is constituted in knowledge. Power occurs in regimes of discourse that govern and discipline their subjects, without there being an "outside" to power. To speak of truth is already to exert power; to be the person in the know is to claim power. Therefore, scholars, citizens, and activists who want to hold politics to a truth standard are engaged in just another form of the exercise of power.

The institutions of medicine and imprisonment, for example, constituted what it means to be healthy or sick and criminal or innocent, justifying the institutionalization and incarceration of many thousands of people. The question of whether any one patient or inmate was truly sick or criminal misses the point: The definitions of illness and wellness are what govern us. Foucault's most accessible work is his *History of Sexuality*. In it he makes the compelling argument that there was no "true," primal sexuality repressed by Victorian antisex ideologies. Instead, Victorian regimes of discourse gave way to modern ones in which the idea that one must "come out" about one's sexuality, and the idea that freedom is inherent in open sexuality, just became the new structure of disciplining knowledge.[11] When we think we are expressing freedom through sexuality, we are participating in a society that is engaged in surveillance and governance of us and everybody else.

To many readers, these ideas may be old news, really depressing, or unhelpfully arcane. However, the importance of the critique of Enlightenment realism becomes clear when one considers how Western capitalist powers have exported "knowledge" to other societies, disrupting, uprooting, and annihilating not only local ways of knowing but also human lives. Atrocities such as the experiments on Jewish concentration camp inmates by Josef Mengele are driven by the desire to know, and therefore to control, others. The invention of nuclear weapons was driven by a desire for knowledge but resulted in devastating technology that its scientific inventors (most notably J. Robert Oppenheimer) lamented.[12] In the domain of reproductive health care, modernity produced a cadre of trained professionals, almost exclusively male, who undermined the authority of women, natural healers, and midwives. Declaring a certain kind of medical knowledge superior because of its basis in scientific research disempowered people with knowledges of their own based on experience. Indeed, until hand washing and, later, antibiotics became normal in modern hospitals, the old ways were largely safer than the new.

On the level of society and the state writ large, the degeneration of Russia's 1917 socialist revolution into a set of Stalinist atrocities and the failure of mass social movements in Europe in the 1960s bred further skepticism about any political movement that said it had the truth. Enlightenment thought is modern; hence the critique of the Enlightenment is a core tenet of postmodernism. Connected to poststructuralism, postmodernist philosophy declared such grand projects to be dead. Reacting understandably to the tragic ends of twentieth-century liberatory struggles, the postmodernists Jean Baudrillard and Jean-François Lyotard urged the refusal of any foundations in favor of recognizing the domination of spectacular realities constructed in language and culture.[13] Baudrillard also noted the inability of language and other symbol systems to represent "reality." Instead, he argues, we are bombarded by "simulacra," copies of copies of something in the world, but completely detached from any original.[14] Postmodernists underscore the impossibility of describing the world around us in language or images in a way that "reflects" or "corresponds with" that world.

Poststructuralist and postmodern thought have two merits. First, they seem, ironically, to *actually* (in reality) describe the social world confronting us today with politics of "truthiness" and spectacle. Second, they have pushed back usefully against the arrogance of oppressive and colonial knowledge that has been used to oppress and justify the killing of its subjects. They have challenged the arrogance of revolutionaries who, once in power, reproduce oppressive regimes of truth.

On the other hand, a number of philosophers and critics have enumerated the dangers and limits of the "posts," arguing that those committed to poststructuralist theory tend either toward cynicism about public engagement or the ironic participation in the issues of the day. They unnecessarily jettison extra-ideological standards for truth, or reality checks, such that a critic is left unable to distinguish between a better regime and a worse one, and for whom.

In addition, postmodern analysis is predicated on the idea that capitalist glo-balization has wreaked havoc on traditional lines of conflict: In other words, there is no more organized working class against the capitalist—and no class consciousness.

Postmodern theorists of globalization argue that the capacity to govern the globe no longer inheres in a single center. In other words, we cannot look to powerful nation-states (such as the United States) as targets of critique and activism. However, a number of sociologists, geographers, and others have called attention to how inaccurate or partial such an account is. Wars in Iraq and Afghanistan point to the ongoing centrality of U.S. foreign policy. In the United States, labor may be weak, but strikes have erupted across Europe over the last decade, challenging corporate and state power. We are witnessing a rise of radical ideas among young people around the world, many of them embracing the cause of socialism.

THEORY AND REALITY

I lay out these debates because there is a parallel duality in the actually exist-ing political world, between "truthiness" and the fact-checkers. This dualism also appears in the work of scholars in communication studies. Reacting to the post-Enlightenment crisis of truth, one camp retreats to defend positivism, empiricism, and/or rationalism in naïve terms. The other, as I have described, advocates a relativist stance without critical foundation or recourse to critique. In philosophy, this battle is most clearly articulated in a dispute between Fou-cault, on the one hand, and the philosopher Jürgen Habermas, on the other.

Habermas is a thinker in the tradition of the Frankfurt School, émigré theorists who insisted on the values of the Enlightenment against the fascist rule that they escaped. In response to the crisis of faith in reason, Haber-mas defined rules for rational deliberation among ideally disinterested and informed citizens. This argument can be described as procedural rationalism.

Foucault and others have observed that few actually existing publics engage in such a process. They also note the Kantian implications of his claim that individuals and groups could and should set aside their interests and opinions in the process of deliberation. Kant, an Enlightenment thinker, advanced this idea as the "categorical imperative." It was, as critics both mod-ern and postmodern have noted, a key idea to justify the rise of capitalist soci-ety in which the ideas of a new ruling class could pass as being in everyone's interest equally. Hence the new class could rule through consent by putting into place organs of deliberation and representation while asking participants to leave their problems and needs at the door. Only those without problems or needs can actually be advantaged by this situation.[15]

This battle is not just academic. For Habermas, just substitute fact-checkers and their busy optimism. For Foucault, just substitute . . . Karl Rove. The two responses to a reality crisis in both theory and popular politics are to try mightily to resurrect an uncomplicated Enlightenment or to give in to the idea that the powerful create reality and all of the rest of us are stupidly living in the (modernist) reality-based community. Theories of reality operate in all domains of experience. Where experience and theory intersect, I would submit, is in the idea of rhetoric. Scholarship in rhetorical studies offers a third way of thinking about realism. We might be able to construct a critical realism that is flexible, contingent, and cognizant of power and perspective, yet still affording us some place from which to make a critique.

RHETORIC AS A RESOURCE FOR A CRITICAL REALISM

Earlier I mentioned the Sophists, a school of wandering teachers of speech and politics in Ancient Greece. In a number of dialogues by Plato, Socrates (taking the stand of the hard realist) mocks and defeats in argument the characters of the Sophists Gorgias and Phaedrus.[16] The Sophists taught rhetoric, which Plato believed to be the skills of manipulation and deceit.[17] For Plato, rhetoric could not serve the common good if, as the Sophists taught, one could learn to argue either side of a case equally well. However, as Haskins and Jarratt have recently argued, the Sophists were not advocates of an amoral practice. Isocrates, who famously invented the system of arguing both sides of an issue (*dissoi logoi*) as a form of pedagogy, also wrote the treatise *Against the Sophists*, in which he sought to distinguish himself from the other Sophists. He believed that rhetorical training could promote vigorous democratic life, at least among propertied men.

Likewise, Plato's student Aristotle defended the rhetorical crafting of *doxa*, or common sense. Plato opposed *doxa* to true, knowledge-based belief, or *episteme*. For Aristotle, doxastic ideas supported by argument and winning persisted, and widespread usage counted as an important form of knowledge—the knowledge that rhetoric has a hand in making and shaping.[18] Aristotle and other rhetoricians have been interested in how we can theorize *doxa*, or self-evident belief, with reference to truths, or *episteme*. Aristotle argued that persuasion cannot be a matter of facts alone; rhetors construct common ground based on audiences' values and identities in a form of reasoning he called the *enthymeme*. As a side note, it is no accident that Foucault called his governing discourse formations particular to a given era "epistemes." For him, there is only *episteme,* or knowledge, not counterpoised to *doxa* since there is neither truth nor mere opinion, only discursively constructed belief.

In contrast, I am sustaining a dichotomy between *episteme* and *doxa,* not to dismiss the latter but rather to ask how rhetors with particular epistemic knowledge can turn that knowledge into commonly held belief. In other words, from the perspective of someone seeking redress of oppression, one task is to make that oppression widely known and understood. Effectiveness in mobilizing "truth from below" is an urgent concern. Twentieth- and twenty-first-century work in rhetoric offers additional helpful concepts in this regard.

In more modern rhetorical theory, the debate over realism exploded upon the publication of R. L. Scott's essay, "On Viewing Rhetoric as Epistemic."[19] Scott's argument was essentially an Aristotelian or Isocratean one defending rhetoric's place in establishing shared knowledge. He was not arguing that rhetoric was the source and site of all truths, but rather the domain of justifying and spreading them. The idea that rhetoric shapes and circulates public knowledge is core to the rhetorical tradition.

In response to this essay, scholars took variously relativist and realist stances.[20] Scholars such as Barry Brummett and Edward Schiappa maintained that "rhetoric is epistemic" means that we cannot have recourse to certain knowledge and ought to privilege the place of language and symbolic action as sites of socially produced and shared knowledge. Michael McGee had long been arguing along similar lines.[21] On the realist side, Richard Cherwitz and James Hikins challenged the relativist position as lacking an ethical standard for judgment. However, they defended not a universalist realist perspective, or the idea that there is a single, discoverable truth outside of its rhetorical constitution. Instead, they argued that truths are perspectival.[22] In other words, we can recognize the partial perspective different groups have on the truth and argue that the theorist or critic should hold rhetoric accountable to realities that are not universally shared but rather mutually debated. This position resonates with my own.

There were many additional salvos in the rhetoric and epistemology debates. The next round occurred partially in response to my own work in an essay where I defended both realism and materialism. Materialism is the idea in philosophy that the embodied practices and social organization of humans drive changes in ideas rather than the other way around, which corresponds with the label "idealism." Marxist thinkers developed a materialist stance more particularly, in response to Hegel's (Platonic) idealism. For Marx and subsequent Marxists, it is the basic social organization that people form to meet their human needs—or mode of production—that gives rise to past and future regimes of ideas. When new classes rise up into power, their ideas get universalized as *doxa,* or ideology. Thus, the expanding colonial powers and rising merchant class of the seventeenth and eighteenth centuries corresponded to new ideas about science, knowledge, and reason—and devalued established, arbitrary divine and aristocratic power. Those conditions gave rise to numerous scientific advances that were more "accurate" than previous models, say, of the solar system.

I charged several rhetoricians—most importantly the critical ones who should be indicting inequality and injustice—with being simultaneously idealist in situating rhetoric as the driver of social reality and relativist in denying any exterior reality to which rhetoric could be held accountable.[23] In response, Ronald Walter Greene brought Foucault and other poststructuralist and postmodern thinkers into the field to defend a "new materialism," which basically meant a materialism of ideas, or idealism renamed materialism in a kind of sleight-of-hand. (Again, Michael McGee had already moved in this direction.)[24] Both positions were taken up by Raymie McKerrow in his signal essay "Critical Rhetoric: Theory and Practice."[25] McKerrow argued that we could engage in a materialist way in the critique of domination while at the same time recognizing that we must critique what counts as freedom, in a Foucauldian mode. This attempt to reconcile incommensurable philosophical stances has been influential and has brought numerous rhetorical scholars to critique oppressive and exploitative social relations. At the same time, scholars in similar fields across the humanities were grappling with the problem of relativism and realism. The first is without ethics or politics, but the second is often naïve.

I have taken the time and space to survey these debates in rhetorical studies because they are still crucially important conversations. The urgency of the discussion is made clear in recent studies of rhetoric in the human sciences. On the one hand, we must find cures for AIDS and cancer and prevent plague, malnutrition, death in childbirth, diabetes, and so on. Yet rhetoricians necessarily point out that while scientists take on the discovery of scientific knowledge, they also build and circulate doxastic knowledge that has ideological and discriminatory effects.

To an extent, we must have faith in the possibility of science to discover and circulate knowledge. How can we know which scientific claims are "better" or "worse"? Global warming is the most urgent example of this point. Given imminent global climate disaster (the heat index in Iran on July 30, 2017, was 164 degrees (Fahrenheit), we need not only to understand how truths about the climate are political but also to assert that some claims are better than others, and on what grounds.

THE RHETORICAL STUDY OF SCIENCE: UNDERSTANDING MEDIATION

A story in *Slate* recently exhorted scientists to stop thinking about science communication as the effective laying out of facts. More important, argues author Tim Requarth, is to appeal to emotion: "spending time on why [science] matters to the author and why it should matter to the reader" and working to establish trust with one's audiences.[26] Science historian Al Coppola notes that 2017's marches for the climate and for science are reminders that science is inherently political and shifts in scientific common sense were products of controversy and movements. In addition, he observes how science has always needed "theatricality and performance" and the fabrication of experiments that others could observe; that is to say, science has always needed rhetoric.[27]

Beyond the recognition that scientists could be better persuaders, a number of social theorists have pointed out that what we have regarded as "facts" are social constructs that aid the powerful in the exertion of their interests. For example, Mary Poovey gives us a history of "the modern fact," which, she discovers, became the norm in early capitalist bookkeeping as a way of warranting the legitimacy of commercial enterprise. Paula Treichler and Bernice Hausman, likewise, have shown how the rhetorics of science seek, create, and use data in ways that are always political. Alongside these thinkers, philosopher Richard Bernstein rejects the ideology of "scientism," or the idea that "science is the only measure of what counts as knowledge and reality."[28] Bernstein notes Thomas Kuhn's insight that there are paradigm shifts in scientific inquiry that are connected to shifts in technological capacity and systems of rule.[29] Not only are knowledges matters of perspective, they are also historically variant and specific. Thus, critical work on the rhetorical production, interpretation, and critique of scientific knowledge is connected to a broader philosophical conversation in the philosophy of science.

Paula Treichler's perspective on the interaction of language, meaning, and scientific truth is that, with regard to HIV/AIDS, "our knowledge of the virus and other natural phenomena is inevitably mediated through our symbolic constructions of them."[30] In chapters exploring the cultural discourses of homophobia, gender difference, and the character of AIDS in the Third World, she argues that culture—from biomedicine to television news and

women's magazines—shapes our perception of scientific information in ideological and coherent engagement with the material world.[31]

Alan Gross helpfully surveys scholarship in the rhetoric of inquiry.[32] All of
the scholars in his taxonomy of research directions posit rhetoric as a form of
either *mediation* or *persuasion* (or both). By mediation, I mean the process
of making sense of information through symbolic action, in which choice of
words, meaning frames, justifications, and articulation of local knowledge to
general discourses of power all influence the uptake, circulation, and understanding of that knowledge. The process is never neutral, since one cannot
directly represent reality. The process of mediation is also persuasive, or
strategic in winning the conviction of audiences. There can be serious consequences of the frames scientists cultivate and abide in the production of
knowledge. For example, as Charles Bazerman explains, the standard style of
social scientific writing cultivates an attitude toward humanity of behavior-
ism.[33] In other words, the contributors to the subfield of the rhetoric of science
recognize scientific knowledge as always political and invested with power.
Michael Shapiro therefore encourages theorists and critics to take seriously
their social responsibilities.[34]

Most rhetoricians of the sciences would not argue that there are *no* facts
outside of rhetoric's intervention, even if knowing them is always a process of
rhetorical mediation. The efficacy of hand washing, vaccines, and antibiotics
is not subject to dispute. However, the implementation of their use varies in
ways that are strategic and invested with power. There are few hard realists
among rhetoricians of science. The point of the work in total is that rhetorical invention is necessary to convey—or create—scientific truths. Among the
scholars of the rhetoric of science, a complete relativist is also somewhat difficult to find, however, since these rhetoricians are dealing with bodily concerns
that are matters of life and death.

An exception appears in a 1980s collection of essays from a symposium on
the rhetoric of human sciences, in which the authors argued that the "rhetoric
of inquiry turns away from modernism and foundationalism in the philosophy of science."[35] At the same time, the contributors do not reject the idea that
we could posit a reality outside its symbolic constitution, but rather the idea
that there is a single version of reality and a single set of rules for evaluating
scientific claims; in other words, they challenge the idea that we should seek
absolute certainty when engaging science.

The rhetorical realism I am advocating is likewise perspectival; it acknowledges the multiplicity of lived experience, methods of seeking knowledge, and
the diversity of bodies of knowledge. There are still standards to which claims
might be held, which I will explore throughout this book. As Leff argues, we

ought not collapse the scientific into the rhetorical.[36] Richard Rorty advocates a pragmatism that regards science as solidarity, in other words, asks for science to be cognizant of the knowledges it makes possible and to recognize the multiplicity of stances of observation, methods of study, and collective needs.[37] He writes, "Inquiry is a matter of continually reweaving a web of beliefs rather than the application of criteria to case."[38] Reflexivity about how science can colonize, appropriate, discredit, and wipe out alternative cultures and peoples is a crucial dimension of the critique of the rhetoric of science, anthropology being the textbook case of these problems.[39]

Scholars in the rhetoric of science are interested in how communicative mediation persuasively influences what is known, how it is known, how knowledge circulates, and to whose benefit and harm. As Gross explains, it is important to acknowledge rhetoric's role in describing and defining knowledge, constructing the questions to be asked, determining what is in the purview of any particular study, positing relations of causation and comparison, and generally working to establish what counts as fact, train publics in how to evaluate scientific claims, and suggest policy directions. Gross writes, "While our sentences about the world are caused by objects and events in the world, it is we and not the world who attribute meaning to those objects and events."[40] Scientific theories must be "argued into place" and are achievements of rhetorical craft. Moreover, knowledge is never a matter of individual experience or observation but is fundamentally collective and social.

Critics in this current have performed close readings of texts, with an emphasis on the constitutive and persuasive nature of scientific rhetoric. Noticing that scientists employ rhetorical strategy, this group argues that it is not the science but the way that it is conveyed that is rhetorical. For example, Leah Ceccarelli has argued that the sociobiologist E. O. Wilson failed in his anti-Darwinist campaign because he refused the tools of persuasion.[41] More recently, Ceccarelli charts the metaphor of science as "frontier."[42] The image of the frontier carries mythic connotations, she argues. It is a "terministic screen" or metaphorical frame that

> shapes our understanding of science in America, it narrows our perception of who is qualified to undertake scientific research (ruggedly individualistic men), the motives that guide scientists (progressive), the means and proper actions they take to achieve their goals (competitive and exploitative), and the setting in which they work (uncharted territory).[43]

The metaphor is both a rhetorical or persuasive tool for scientists and a more subvert set of meaning frames that constrain both scientists and their knowledge and shape popular belief. The deployment of this metaphor has serious consequences when, for example, leaders of the Human Genome Project regard the human body as wilderness and the scientist's mission as manifest destiny.[44]

Scholars in the rhetoric of science faced a challenge from relativists in the field of rhetorical studies more broadly. For example, Dilip Gaonkar charged that rhetoric is unsuited to the analysis of science.[45] Arguing that we can no longer expect communicative acts to correspond to or accurately reflect some external reality, Gaonkar urged the description of regimes of knowledge rather than the evaluation of a scientist's persuasive accomplishments. Gross responded that the realism of the rhetoric of science is not naïve; rather, the scholar explores how scientists produce more and less coherent accounts of an object or event that, "as far as we know," resemble them in a way that affects what counts as knowledge in the public domain. Objectivism is illusory, and a rhetorical account can dispel the illusion and open received knowledge up to critique, reevaluation, new questions, and new discoveries.

Occupational medicine is a strong example of a rhetoric of science motivated by elite interests, according to Gross. That subfield constructed workers as objects and machines in ways that used knowledge to justify exploitative capitalist social relations. Exposure of the illusory claim of such science to disinterested objectivity opens the way for challenge:

> Workers must turn social stasis into social drama; they must remake a moral order that has forced a coincidence of purpose between the biomedical model of disease and industrial imperatives. They much create a new moral order based on a different model of disease, the ecological, in which the environment itself can count as a pathogen. They must do so by creating a breach in the existing moral order, and, by means of a rhetoric of talk coupled with a rhetoric of action, they must redefine human health in a way that serves their interests.[46]

In other words, the rhetoric of science facilitates critique and resistance when it exposes given knowledge as partial, interested, and rhetorical—that is, subject to contestation. While scientific knowledge has been used to discipline and punish, the generation of controversy is one positive feature of historical scientific rhetoric.

Work in the rhetoric of science is a resource for a rhetorical realism, one that is not naïve about our capacity to represent anything like an objective truth while remaining committed to the idea that, in spite of the necessity of rhetorical mediation, there are better and worse scientific claims and better and worse regimes of knowledge.

MEDIATION IN PUBLIC SPHERES

The process of mediation takes place in publics and counterpublics. Although Habermas's rationalism has limits, as I noted above, his work has been crucial to how we understand how publics—groups of people in civil society, outside the state's direct influence—form, deliberate, and make decisions. He took as his model the eighteenth-century coffeehouses in Europe, which, at a moment of historic transition from aristocratic rule to mercantile capitalism (also a subject of chapter 6), became hotbeds of political and cultural conversation.[47] Feminists and other scholars have criticized Habermas's vision because it calls for people to suspend their personal needs and interests in the process of deliberation. Women, workers, the oppressed, and the poor need deliberation to be specifically about their needs and interests. Moreover, the division in modern society between public and private spheres has excluded women, defined in terms of their private sphere (familial) role, from political participation.[48]

These criticisms led scholars and activists to posit the existence of oppositional "counterpublics" in the form of minority communities and activist groups who challenge and resist dominant relations of power and the discourses that justify them. Michael Warner and Rosa Eberly have helpfully observed how publics form around rhetorical acts—speeches, books, news, films, videos, social media, games, and other discourse—to deliberate over the issues and controversies raised there.[49] Thus, the appearance of controversial abortion videos, news coverage of government whistleblowers, a science documentary, or a revolutionary pamphlet can be the occasion for widespread engagement in controversy and struggle. Those texts mediate not only our experience of reality but also how we identify with social groups and causes. As with every rhetorical act described in this book, publics and counterpublics are expressions of different groups with divergent amounts of economic and social power and cultural representation. When considering public spheres, we must ask, whose public is this? On whose terms is it organized? Whose interests does it represent? These are the questions of critical theories of society, including Marxism.

The knowledge I am interested in understanding in this book is the knowledge of ordinary people about the meaning of their lived experiences. Overall, I am arguing in this book that dominant groups manage for their partial versions of reality to become common sense and to thus cultivate cooperation with the status quo. I ask the question, how might ordinary people who suffer oppression and exploitation make those realities intelligible in common sense?

Marxism, as a critical social theory particularly attentive to the realities of exploitation and oppression, also looks to mediation to explain how rhetoric influences what appears in common sense to be true.

MARXISM AS A RESOURCE FOR RHETORICAL REALISM

Marxism, like Enlightenment philosophy in general, is much maligned for what critics see as its crude theories of truth, ideology, and mediation. Indeed, rhetorician James Aune charged Marxist theory with being "anti-rhetorical," because, he argued, it had no theory of mediation. (This he called Marxism's "nuclear contradiction.") However, not only in the writings of Marx and Engels themselves, but especially in the work of the theorists Antonio Gramsci and Georg Lukács, we find a pronounced sensitivity to the role of symbolic action in the constitution and (non-correspondent) representation of realities and consciousness of them. The method of critique in Marxism is historical materialism, which is a way of seeing human identity, purpose, and reality in the contexts of shifting material, or economic, conditions, understood broadly as the ways in which humans collaborate to transform nature to meet their basic needs in varying kinds of societies. Class society, most recently and currently capitalism, features the structural antagonism between economic elites and the interests of working people.

Hegemony

Gramsci is often given credit for amplifying this dimension of Marxist theory in his writings on fascist politics; the need for workers to struggle for cultural, political, and economic hegemony; and working class education.[50] His interest in the hegemonic process is, first and foremost, a critique of how a ruling class wins the "consent" of ordinary people against their own, real, class interests. Gramsci argued that ordinary people have an abstract *interest* in overcoming their exploitation, which requires education and political discourse to win workers to political organization and struggle. Thus, in "Working-Class Education and Culture," he explains that workers are not dupes, though they may require education conducted by and for them to "truly understand the full implications of the notion of 'ruling class.'"[51] For Gramsci, real working class education must debunk "ideologies aimed at reconciling opposing interests" in favor of "the expression of these subaltern classes."[52]

The Working Class

Classical Marxism has often been accused of economic reductionism and the displacement of human agency by economic determination of reality. But far from relying on automatic class consciousness and economic action to turn the wheel of history, Marxists have argued that "the moment of politics," or a moment of rhetorical mediation, is crucial in cultivating collective consciousness and action. The experience of being an industrial worker, as Gross notes, is that of being reduced to an object and a machine. While this experience is real for the worker, it takes rhetoric to interpret that experience and define it as exploitation and as a situation to be challenged. Unions and labor parties may perform this mediating role. Independent groups of workers may form and generalize their experiences, building theoretical knowledge about their condition, its causes, and its remedies. Marx calls this moment the turn from being a "class in itself," a group without self-knowledge, to a "class for itself"—a group that has used communication to define itself and its reality. This distinction itself points to how Marx saw communication as being central to the formation of knowledge, identity, and action.

In other words, simply existing—as a worker, a woman, a person of color, a Muslim, a lesbian, a poor person, and so on—is not enough to establish those persons' realities in public life. One may have the bodily experience of suffering, but it is not understandable as "exploitation" until communication names it so. Thus the reality of exploitation inheres not only in direct experience but also in its naming and interpretation. What this means for rhetorical and cultural theory is that class belonging and lived experience compose only an epistemological potential. It takes communication in collectivity to establish the reality of exploitation as common sense among workers and then to circulate it as viable knowledge more broadly.

In Marxist thought, class is a shared *relationship*, and only potentially an identity. The working class thus comprises the vast majority of humanity worldwide (of every gender, race, religion, sexual orientation, and nationality), including most students, industrial and service workers, the poorest, and the better off (including most people who consider themselves "middle class").[53] All members of this class, whether automatically cognizant of it or not, share a fundamental interest in changing their relationship to production to one in which the fruits of their labor and control over their daily lives are their own.

Rhetorical Mediation of Class Consciousness

Mediation has several related meanings in the Marxist tradition. Marx's writings explore how the commodity—the product of human labor turned into something that can be bought and sold—mediates workers' experience in capitalism. In other words, we understand ourselves and our relationship to society through the production, buying, and selling of commodities, which take on an almost magical "aura" in capitalism.[54]

In addition, however, political organizations, events, and our own collective experience can foster a different and more critical understanding of our society. Mediation, for Marxists, refers to any text or activity that makes sense of immediate experience in more general terms. In other words, mediation helps us to understand our local immediate experience, which is disconnected from others and from explanation, in terms of a broader explanation that connects us to other people. Mediation provides a linkage sustaining relationships among people in society. For example, a fast-food worker knows that her work is hard; she works long shifts and goes home to try to support herself and her family, returning again the next morning. However, when a group of activists in the "Fight for $15" campaign greet her after work one day, she begins to understand that she is not alone in her immediate experience. Rather, she is connected to others who recognize that they are overworked and underpaid. In getting involved in the movement for a fifteen-dollar minimum wage, she becomes linked to others in common cause and has a new understanding of reality in capitalist society. In this example, the organizers are the mediators who generalize her immediate experience and make the big picture visible in a particular way.

While class interests can be the real foundation upon which an anticapitalist politics can be built, their mere existence is insufficient to the task. It's not automatic that a fast-food worker would recognize that she is exploited without talking to others, and the mass media work to convince her that her suffering is her own fault. There are many forces blocking radical mediation in favor of interpretations favored by elites in society: The commercial media industry and its advertisers circulate versions of reality that lionize capitalism and discredit its critics. Marxist theorists in the Frankfurt School called attention to the importance of consciousness and subjectivity. It's not enough that a society is built upon exploitation and inequality.[55] Critics must get involved in persuading people about the nature of the system, or changing their consciousness. In other words, in addition to *objective* reality, we must engage *subjective* experience. This process is the definition of mediation.

Lukács, among others, rejected the idea that class consciousness is an automatic response to proletarian existence. However, he argued that political organizations can interrupt mainstream conservative mediation processes. Oskar Negt and Alexander Kluge explain in *Public Sphere and Experience* that interests, grounded in lived experience, are the basis for but not the realization of a proletarian public, which is organized in discourse.[56] In Marxist theory and socialist practice historically, the role of rhetorical catalyst is played by the political party or organization, which, emerging out of the working class itself, proceeds to recruit members, circulates ideas interpersonally and in media, and attempts to win adherence to a particular world view and course of action.[57]

Lukács adds other crucial components to a critical rhetorical realism: the ideas of reification, alienation, and standpoint. The basis of Lukács's theory of class consciousness as elaborated in *History and Class-Consciousness* is the idea of reification (and its consequence, alienation). By reification, Lukács meant the process by which capitalism turns workers into dehumanized objects and commodities, thus alienating them from the work and its products. Lukács describes reification as something of a paradox because workers are collectively objectified in such a way as to prompt their subjective awakening because they see themselves as agents, or subjects, in society while being treated like objects without agency.

The conceptualization of the worker as "subject-object" gets at how the very process of reification generates a potentially agentive working class standpoint. Being forced to recognize oneself as an object reveals the basic motor of capitalism itself: the commodity relation.[58] Another way of putting this would be to say working class experience in capitalism is founded on the oxymoron of "free labor" (subject-object). That contradiction produces openings for conversation and education about the character of the capitalist system itself. In this way, alienation is both the consequence of objectification and a resource for consciousness of it. Localized complaint and limited spontaneous struggles against the terms of labor (i.e., strikes) are basic expressions of a working class standpoint. When, during crisis or struggle, dominant rationales for society break down, there is a battle for consciousness. Lukács explains that during such battles, more abstract, political mediation must take place with working class standpoint as only a beginning.

Standpoint Theory

Following Lukács, feminist theorist Nancy Hartsock identifies the most important aspect of standpoint theory for rhetoricians: Although standpoint is inherent in the antagonistic social relation, "the vision available to the oppressed group must be struggled for and represents an achievement" accomplished in the (rhetorical) processes of education and organization.[59]

Thus, key to both Hartsock's and Lukács's formulations is the idea that a revolutionary standpoint is not an automatic possession of the worker or woman (or woman worker); it must be rhetorically achieved in the domains of organization, education, and struggle in order to serve its "historically liberatory role."[60]

Lukács argues that organizations of the most forward-thinking workers (political parties) functioned to introduce elements of conscious control into what had been spontaneous and limited protests on the part of workers. Hartsock's feminist standpoint theory draws similar conclusions. In feminism, this process of emergent and theoretical mediation took the form of consciousness-raising[61] that grounded feminist theory not in women's essence, but in women's experience of existing social relations. By extension, we could regard labor, socialist, and other social movement organizations as performing the task of rhetorical mediation of the consciousness of the exploited and oppressed.[62]

I have posited that truth is a function of standpoint or perspective in a system of power. If that is so, then we don't expect truth claims to represent an objective, universal reality. Different groups have divergent interests. As standpoint theory explains, underdogs have a better view of the big picture of society from the bottom up. What a critic would seek in a truth claim is not correspondence to a universally experienced reality. Instead, we might ask whether a claim or set of claims represents the *interests* of the group being asked to believe it. In work I coauthored with Kathleen Feyh, we propose that one possible resource is the term *fidelity*, defined as the perspectival resonance of a message (in narrative or other form) with the shared experiences and interests of those whose identities are called into being by the discourse.[63]

Walter Fisher argued for both fidelity and coherence—the capacity of a narrative to hang together sensibly on its own terms—as standards for evaluating claims of belief. However, for my purposes, coherence is less useful since it assumes that a narrative without reference to reality outside itself could still be judged as an adequate communicative act. My uncle who claims he has no need for engaging other points of view because his opinion makes sense in itself would be operating according to a coherence standard, which is ultimately relativist. I am not arguing that the Left should "reach" across a values divide and operate only on the terms of an opponent's own narrative system. Fidelity, on the other hand, asks the critic or audience member to evaluate a claim against not some simple empirical fact or presumed universal truth but with regard to the collective interests of the people being asked to accept that claim—to their standpoint.

Synthesizing the concepts of fidelity and standpoint, then, fidelity is a condition under which the construct of truth claims aligns with the class standpoint of its addressees. Michael McGee and John Lyne, writing of the rhetoric of inquiry, explain this approach:

> Obviously, there is the need to sort and evaluate conflicting testimony on the matter at issue . . . but more significantly, there is the need to negotiate competing claims proceeding from two different domains of human rationality. Ordinary people who make up juries and the voting polity "narrativize" or "dramatize" exigent situations. That is, *they look for stories that put alleged facts into a narrative sequence that can be judged more or less probably* as an account of what happened or what might happen. . . . [The argument] is an attempt to make wise and prudent choices from among competing truth claims. . . . The object of rhetoric of inquiry is to *test knowledge claims proceeding from these two domains of reason against the moral and material requirements* of exigent circumstances to determine what should be treated as fact.[64]

In other words, we may employ a fidelity test based on the interests and needs of people vying for their truths to become belief. Identifying fidelity is complicated, but its major merit is that it does not presume that we have access to an objective reality without need for rhetorical mediation. In other words, it is not so simple that people whose beliefs run counter to their interests are suffering simply from "false consciousness." The case studies in this book will employ the fidelity standard.

CONCLUSION: MEDIATION, STANDPOINT, FIDELITY

This book has the practical goal of understanding how progressives can help their truth claims become common sense and depends upon a theoretical position that their truth claims are more faithful to the realities of the groups they represent than contrary discourses. In other words, I am interested not just in a politics of truth but also in the possibility of truth in politics. To get at this problem and to enable a normative critique of better and worse (or more or less faithful) truths circulating in politics, theory is necessary.

To this end, in this chapter I have summarized the dispute in philosophy and rhetoric between advocates of realism and advocates of relativism. In contemporary theory and criticism, the challenges to realism as an Enlightenment foundationalism have been deep and compelling. In response to these challenges, I have attempted to use two bodies of work to posit a nuanced "rhetorical realism" that does not participate in the naïve commitments of foundationalism to an objectively discoverable and universal Truth. This position occupies the space, in philosopher Richard Bernstein's words, "between objectivism and relativism,"[65] that is, between foundationalism and anti-foundationalism, realism and relativism, absolutism and subjectivism.[66] I agree with Bernstein when he argues that between relativism and realism, there is a field of practical political judgment and action that requires communication that admits multiple perspectives. This dispute is not incidental to the larger project of enabling progressive forces to win others to the project of social change.

The first body of work in constructing my position comes from scholars of the rhetoric of science. They have described very carefully how rhetoric mediates our understanding of scientific knowledge. Second, Marxist thought builds on the idea of mediation, noting that knowledge is perspectival and that, therefore, mediators—unions, parties, and so on—also express divergent perspectives. The idea of fidelity helps us to envision a way to evaluate whether the knowledge that is circulating as common sense is in the interest of particular groups—the oppressed and exploited.

While attempting to represent the oppressed and exploited, Left-wing scholars and activists sometimes assume that there is a clear, uncomplicated truth to put up against deception and mystification. Truth is supposed to counter power. But what if we realize that we live in a society of contending, perspectival truths, all vying for power? Truth is then not the opposite of or counter to power. Rather, we need to put some power behind our truths. Because of a tendency to wield facts like hammers, parts of the Left have avoided the subtler and more persuasive ways of bringing awareness to exploitation and oppression. The Right, however, has had no problem in bringing to bear an entire arsenal of rhetorical strategies, including what I call "the big five": affect, embodiment, narrative, myth, and spectacle. I now turn to an exploration of these in the next chapter. Can ordinary people use these forms to "speak truth to power"?

CHAPTER 2

Toward a Spectacular Struggle, or, on the Power of the Big Five

RECENTLY I opened up the *New York Times* and found under the heading of "Most Popular" an article titled, "That Whale You Just Clicked On? It's Doomed."[1] The article recounts the work of wildlife photographer Paul Nicklen, who posts gorgeous photos of very cute animals as "clickbait." These images often go viral. When readers open the image, they also find text:

> A newborn harp seal hides behind a piece of sea ice and seeks shelter during a blizzard. Harp seals give birth to their pups on the sea ice in late February or early March. With human induced climate change and the loss of sea ice, harp seals are losing their birthing grounds. This photograph was taken a year ago. In 2007, more than 70% of the pups died due to poor ice conditions. In 2010, almost none survived. As I type this, baby harp seals are struggling to survive yet another terrible ice year near the Magdalen Islands. If we want to save baby harp seals, then we need to alter our carbon emitting ways. I start to see hope when two great leaders like @justinpjtrudeau and @barackobama discuss solutions to this global crisis that affects us all. Please follow us on @sea_legacy as we continue to share images that highlight the most important issue our race has ever faced.

Nicklen describes his method: "I hang a cute animal picture out there like bait and reel them in." Article author Amanda Hess comments,

I'm hooked. Intellectually, I understand that climate change is one of the most important issues facing our planet. But practically, I ignore it. The problem feels too big, and the science too boring. I've never found a convenient time to watch "An Inconvenient Truth." I haven't paged through a copy of *National Geographic* in my adult life. I'm part of the problem.

But now, a crew of wildlife photographers and conservationists has found a way to reach me through one of social media's shallowest pleasures: ogling marine mammals on Instagram.

"Climate change is so huge, so uncomfortable, and so overwhelming, it's hard to talk about it," Mr. Nicklen said. "And often the best scientists are the worst communicators." Hess makes my argument here: namely, that conventional tools for conveying information about complex and urgent social and scientific issues (like *An Inconvenient Truth*) do not easily reach even the most literate consumers of information. Cute mammals appeal to our emotions. Our evolutionarily attuned affection toward infant mammals[2] drives our connection with such issues. Nicklen understands his role as a rhetorical mediator of scientific information.

In the previous chapter, I concluded that we should see rhetoric as a mediating force between *episteme,* or ground-level, experiential knowledge, and *doxa,* or commonly held belief. The key question for those who seek recognition of their interests and struggles in public life is how to use rhetoric to make that shift, to articulate their experience in ways that make common sense.

Antonio Gramsci regarded politics and culture as sites of struggle for whose interests and ideas will take the leading role in society. He called this process the struggle for hegemony. Hegemony refers, in military terms, to a balance of power dominated by one set of interests. This state of affairs is always subject to challenge and even revolution, during which a rising group's forces seize hegemony. For Gramsci, hegemony also has a cultural dimension. He argued that popular culture and political discourse are places where ordinary people can contend for representation. They accomplish this task by undertaking collective education and consciousness-raising, and then by circulating their stories and realities in cultural products.

This process is most effective in the context of broader social struggle, when challenges to legal and political rule accompany and produce shifts in cultures and identities. For example, the U.S. movements at the end of the 1960s, including the women's liberation and civil rights movements, shifted the terms of the national conversations about race and gender. Television programs like *The Mary Tyler Moore* show represented single career women for the first time, and minorities and the poor, including the trash hauler and his son in *Sanford and Son,* gained positive images as well. The production of those narratives and their popularization depended upon and fueled the movements for social change that opened the way for new common sense to emerge.

Massive shifts in popular consciousness cannot happen through rhetorical skill alone. However, I am arguing in this chapter that the Left can and should consider employing the massively persuasive strategies embraced by conservatives. I call these the "big five," and they are narrative, myth, affect, embodiment, and spectacle. It's not as though all progressives have shunned these techniques. As I noted in the introduction, music, art, film, sport, drama, and many other forms have been crucial to building solidarity and inspiration on the Left.

However, many cultural critics share the attitude of critic Chris Hedges, whose work I generally appreciate very much. However, in his book *Empire of Illusion,* he condemns what he calls the "triumph of spectacle" and advocates a critical literacy as an antidote. He gives as an example professional wrestling, with its "stylized rituals" that are "public expressions of pain and a fervent longing for revenge."[3] His argument is that these constructed battles take the reality of economic hardships of the working class and translate them into a mythic illusion. Working people, he writes, are asking to be fooled, in wrestling, in reality television, in the movies, and in the "cult of the self," a "perverted ethic" behind Wall Street's looting of the economy. Summarizing the critique, Hedges writes,

Hour after hour, day after day, week after week, we are bombarded with the cant and spectacle pumped out over the airwaves or over computer screens by highly paid pundits, corporate advertisers, talk-show hosts, and gossip-fueled entertainment networks. And a culture dominated by images and slogans seduces those who are functionally literate but who make the choice not to read. There have been other historical periods with the high rates of illiteracy and vast propaganda campaigns. But not since the Soviet and fascist dictatorships and perhaps the brutal authoritarian control of the Catholic Church in the Middle Ages, has the content of information been as skillfully and ruthlessly controlled and manipulated. Propaganda has become a substitute for ideas and ideology. Knowledge is confused with how we are made to feel. Commercial brands are mistaken for expressions of individuality. And in this precipitous decline of values and literacy, among those who cannot read and those who have given up reading, fertile ground for a new totalitarianism is being seeded. The culture of illusion thrives by robbing us of the intellectual and linguistic tools to separate illusion from the truth.[4]

He goes on to condemn public mythology and defends the idea of factual reality, while admitting: "Reality is complicated. Reality is boring. . . . The ability
to amplify lies, to repeat them and have surrogates repeat them in endless
loops of news cycles, gives lies and mythical narratives the aura of uncontested
truth . . . and all complex thought, ambiguity, and self-criticism vanish."[5]

Chris Hedges lives in the reality-based community. And he is right that the
elites who run the economy, the nation, and the nation's wars deploy mythology, narrative, spectacle, and emotion to convince ordinary people that life is
as it should be. The fact that they use these mechanisms, however, is not the
core of the problem. If we were talking about the use of poster art in the revolutionary movements of 1960s France or the singing of anthems and hymns in
the civil rights movement, Hedges might not have the same level of disdain for
emotion and spectacle. If faced with the dramatic pitting of employee against
boss in farmworkers' field theater, Hedges would likely not bemoan the workers' lack of literacy. If we were talking about vast protest marches led by carriers of huge antiglobalization puppets in the late 1990s, he might not demand
that the activists employ other, more literate, modes of address. No. I think
the issue is not about these universal rhetorical tools. The problem is whose
agenda they are serving.

Hedges's critique is also fundamentally elitist: Look at all of these dupes
of mindless popular culture who allow themselves to be fooled by drama
and entertainment instead of reading the news and going to their city council meetings. Look at these idiots who would rather watch wrestling or *Big
Brother* than engage with an admittedly boring reality.

What if, as cultural studies scholars argue, we saw popular culture as one
terrain for critical expression alongside enjoyment? What if the Left could
command not only facts but also the imagination? As I have hinted, of course,
the Left has not always avoided drama, emotion, spectacle, and the like. But
in the era of truthiness, it is easy to condemn all popular discourse as illusion
and attempt to counter it with facts of a particular kind, those one can find in
books and journals and newspapers, which are ostensibly superior to anything
that could be fun, awe-inspiring, sublime, beautiful, distracting—or cute. Far
be it from anything that masses of people might enjoy at the end of the day
or on a holiday.

Sport is an interesting domain in this regard. While many scholars in the
culture of critical discourse dismiss football and other commercial sports as
only so much bread and circuses, sporting events have frequently been sites of
protest and struggle. From the four Olympic golds won by black athlete Jesse
Owens in track and field in the 1936 Nazi-led Olympics in Berlin, to the Black
Power salute given by Tommie Smith and John Carlos on the podium in 1968,

to Billie Jean King's victory against Bobby Riggs in the "Battle of the Sexes" tennis match in 1973, to Muhammad Ali's antiwar and black nationalist politics, to the decision in 2016 by San Francisco 49ers quarterback Colin Kaepernick to sit through the national anthem to support Black Lives Matter—sport has provided platforms for considered and powerful protest.[6]

More broadly culture work, from the vernacular (local, bottom-up) expressions of communities and movements to mass commercial sporting or reality television events, builds identity, consciousness, confidence, and persuasive skill on the part of ordinary people to advocate for ourselves. We use culture to solidify movements and express our goals through art and music. Under the right historical conditions, those expressions move from local knowledge to take hold in the public's imagination. The Right knows how to do this work in the interest of elites, and Hedges is right in arguing that *their* spectacles do not comport with the interests of working people, women, the poor, and otherwise oppressed people. My point is that the form of the message is not the main problem. It's about the people using those forms and to what and whose ends. I will spend the remainder of this chapter describing those rhetorical forms and how they work, with examples from conservative and progressive discourse. I begin with affect and emotion.

AFFECT AND EMOTION

It was Enlightenment philosopher René Descartes who famously asserted the superiority of rational thought over feelings and the mind over the body: I think, therefore I am. Feminists and many others have noted how that formulation privileges elite men who could afford to ignore the brute realities of physical existence and the need for reproductive and household labor. Cartesianism has been part and parcel of justifying the oppression of women and slaves as remote from the workings of the abstract mind. Descartes was also speaking for a new class of citizens who, in progressive fashion, wanted to rule the world through reason rather than the mystified and arbitrary divine right of kings. However, the appeal to reason in Enlightenment thought was an ideal MO for the rule of mercantile capitalists who also asserted the rationality of the free market and the objectivity of their own interests. In other words, reason was very handy in making the new rule seem more democratic while excluding those mired in the muck of labor and household work from governance. As we saw with Kant, and later Habermas, the idea that people should set aside their particular interests and deliberate over an allegedly universal common good does not tend to benefit those excluded from the common *goods*.

The reign of reason also circumscribed the bounds of appropriateness in public life. Anyone contesting the prevailing state of affairs and the rules of inclusion automatically appeared to be unreasonable, sectarian, and over-wrought. And while there's nothing wrong with a well-reasoned debate, expecting the toiling masses to feel no outrage at their exploitation is itself a form of oppression. The merchants, industrialists, monopolists, and bankers only pretended not to need or experience feelings, in any case. Competition, which drives the economy, thrives on greed and desire. And when it comes time for territorial or economic conquest, instilling patriotic fervor is very useful. When the state needs the nation to pull behind such an effort, popu-lism captures the passions of the populace.

These appeals work because human beings are embodied, feeling crea-tures, whose drives to defend our life, safety, and future are powerful moti-vators. Neurobiologists and psychoanalytic scholars alike have observed that people experience intense, preconscious physiological states of arousal, pain, pleasure, anticipation, and many other feelings. These states of intensity con-stitute what theorists call *affect*, which is a category describing one's inchoate feelings before they are given the names of emotions. Emotions are mediated affects. In other words, society tells us what each state means: Butterflies in the stomach must mean love, sweaty palms mean anxiety, an adrenaline rush means fear or excitement. Sluggishness and the inability to go to work trans-late as depression. Collectively we name our experiences in order to make sense of them. As Sarah Ahmed explains, affect is what lies at the intersection of the somatic—or bodily—and the social.[7]

However, in the precognitive realm of feeling, the intense absence of sense or meaning, according to some theorists, makes people vulnerable to appeals that make sense of (and exploit) those feelings. Ernesto Laclau has explained how *populism*, or a mode of appeal that wins people to an impassioned col-lective project, taps into a desire for coherence and explanation and tethers people to a goal or demands based on pre- or irrational motivations.[8] On the Right, we can see how, in the wake of the September 11, 2001, terrorist attacks, political leaders were able to turn fear and abjection into a will to war. In the case of the presidential campaign of Donald Trump, we can see how his per-sona and rhetoric (even if somewhat incoherent) tap into the economic anxi-eties of Americans and connect them to the promise to "make America great again." It is a promise that feels good to many people.

Yet populism is not inherently conservative in itself. On the Left, we have seen it at work in calls for labor solidarity in song and protest. We hear it in the rhetoric of someone like Bernie Sanders, who tapped the affect of workers and youth to connect to a project of critique and reform in the 2016 presidential race (despite throwing his lot eventually behind a pro-corporate Democratic Party). The fact that affect and emotional appeal do not work through reasoned, propositional argument does not make them malign. There are versions of populism that exhibit fidelity to the interests of "the people" they invoke, and others that win people to causes contrary to their own interests, for example racism and the scapegoating of immigrants. Affective appeals also tap the experience of feelings in the body, much like in a revival meeting when the sick and injured come forward to be healed by the laying on of hands.

EMBODIMENT

Closely connected to affect, embodiment simply refers to the power of a message when it asks audience members to experience a communicative act or interaction in their bodies. It also refers to how bodies are sites of regulation and discipline with regard to race, class, gender, and sexuality. To learn something "in the body" is to incorporate it into the self, making our habits and feelings seem natural and common-sensical.

Bodies in sports and in war are groomed for antagonism against others whose bodies are made to appear enemy or alien. When children can ride on dinosaurs in the Creation Museum, it is made more believable that humans and dinosaurs lived alongside one another. When one sings or recites a pledge or an anthem with others, bathed in collective sound and song, one ties the body to the cause, making commitment more visceral. When one marches in formation, it is easy to realize how one belongs to one collective as opposed to another.[9] The training and entrainment of bodies is a culturally and politically infused thing. Debra Hawhee notes that the imbricated training of mind and body in ancient Greece was aimed at producing citizens of the proper character and virtuosity for antagonistic political practice.[10] When training is thorough, doing what one is expected to do becomes a matter of "muscle memory," automatic and a matter of course.

As with affect, embodiment does not "belong" exclusively to either the Right or the Left. Protest movements have long relied upon the capacity of disobedient bodies to disrupt labor, traffic, commerce, and the flow of business as usual to instantiate new habits of congregating and behaving. Nonviolent civil disobedience during the civil rights movement asked participants to feel and know both resistance and oppression in their bodies; even as a student could sit in at a lunch counter and violate the reality structure most powerfully, a mob or the police could inflict trauma on that student's body. As organizers well knew, both experiences firm up an activist's commitment based on the bodily proof of both injustice and power to challenge it. Standing to sing the national anthem is a powerful expression of common cause, but so is refusing to stand or to kneel, or choosing to raise a fist in the air. What we know in our bodies and what we learn through their actions become powerfully sedimented in experience. It is because we can identify with other beings in this process that we are also able to see ourselves in the stories our society tells about our life in common.

NARRATIVE AND MYTH

Rhetorical scholar Walter Fisher famously proposed the "narrative paradigm" to describe human communication. He argued that reasoned debate is not the native mode of social engagement among humans. Instead, he argued, we tell stories to one another that win mutual identification, values, and directions for action. When a story broadly tells a collective tale about origin, purpose, and destiny as set against villains and obstacles, it is a mythic narrative. Narratives are compelling because of their capacity to invite others to identify with characters in the story, despise villains, get caught up in the drama, and end up sharing the narrative's conclusions about shared values and knowledge. For this reason, Fisher proposed a set of standards for evaluating narrative that do not depend upon empiricism or rationalism. Stories, even mythic ones (like religious narratives and *Star Wars*), tell truths that are of a different order, truths about belonging, social order, and shared commitments.

Fisher has been charged with being somewhat sanguine about the workings of narrative. Following the cautions of theorist Kenneth Burke, critics like William Lewis point out that good stories can be compelling in dangerous ways as well as pro-social ways. In a speech delivered to the (Communist) American Writers' Congress in 1935, Burke advocated that the Left embrace the mythic power of appeals to "the people," rather than "the workers" or the "proletariat." His speech was not well received. However, rhetoricians to this day laud Burke's wisdom in recognizing the positive impact of mythic discourse.[11]

In the same speech, however, Burke noted that we must be able to tell the difference between a "good" myth and a "bad" myth. In other words, how do we know whether an invocation of common purpose serves or betrays the interests of those invited to join in? The Communists of his day argued that language specifying the working class in appeals to the cause were more appropriate because they did not imply that workers and employers, and all others in a given society, shared the same interests. Instead, employers and workers have an antagonistic relationship, but would all be swept up together in the category of "the people." The Congress was suspicious of emotional and universalizing discourse.

It is possible that both parties were both wrong: Burke was wrong about the suitability of the language of "the people" in describing workers specifically, and the AWC was wrong in rejecting the tool of myth altogether. So, how are we to tell a good myth from a bad one? Walter Fisher supplied a vocabulary for evaluating the ethics or politics of a narrative. He argued that a good story exhibits both coherence—it hangs together and is sensible within itself—and fidelity—it represents the experience of the people invited to identify with the narrative. The coherence standard is troubling because it cannot account for the power of a disruptive or fractured story to challenge received wisdom and to ask readers to *dis-identify* with prevailing norms and values. In some cases, an incoherent narrative captures someone's experiential truths more faithfully. The fidelity standard is very useful in asking critics to judge whether the story being told represents not hard "facts," but rather the experiences and interests of those asked to identify with the story. Such judgments require a political frame and are always made from the perspective of the critic, who may or may not be part of the group being invoked.

The example that comes to mind is Beyoncé's hit song and video in 2016, "Formation."[12] The song and video feature a broken narrative that seems to be by turns about black female empowerment, Southern culture, black heritage, sexual relationships, police violence, and New Orleans history, emphasizing the devastation wrought by Hurricane Katrina. In the video, Beyoncé sings and dances with other black women in a Southern plantation home in antebellum period dress, making an ironic comment on U.S. history. This comment is amplified in her valuing of "authentic" or "natural" black hair and nose shape: "I like my baby heir with baby hair and afros / I like my negro nose with Jackson Five nostrils / Earned all this money but they never take the country out me / I got hot sauce in my bag, swag." The women dance "in formation"; Beyoncé seems to be calling on black women to line up military-style to do battle against racism and to assert their own power, as they "slay." Beyoncé embraces her success in the market ("I go hard, get what's mine, I'm a star," and "Best revenge is your paper [money]," and "You might just be a Black Bill Gates in the making"). But she also honors poor blacks in New Orleans with imagery of people in that city and audio samples from both Messy Mya and Big Friedia, both queer, black vernacular musicians in the New Orleans scene. Her insistence that no one can take the country out of her constructs her belonging in that community. As one of my earlier communication professors at Penn State taught us, "information" can be thought of as "in formation." He was cautioning us undergraduates to beware of how what we were taught as truth calls us to march in concert with dominant norms. Well before I encountered Foucault, my mind was blown.[13] However, here I make the obverse case: namely, that actual information can organize insurgent bodies to welcome collective protest "in formation."

In a controversial move, the video version ends with an image of Beyoncé wearing a Givenchy dress. (In perhaps a moment of critical excess, the name "Givenchy" is printed in red all over the dress.) She is lying on top of a sinking police car. This image was read as a direct reference to both a critique of the devastation of Hurricane Katrina and an indictment of police for violence against black people. In a subsequent performance of the song at the Super Bowl 2016 halftime show, Beyoncé and her dancers marched in (sexualized) costumes reminiscent of the uniform of the 1960s group the Black Panther Party for Self-Defense. Both of these moments generated widespread controversy and conversation. In interviews, she made explicit her commitment to movements against police brutality.

The song, video, and halftime performance could not pass a narrative coherence test. It is work plentiful with visual and lyrical allusions and disjunctures. But how might a critic go about assessing the song's fidelity to its multiple audiences? One of those audiences includes working class and poor blacks in New Orleans. Beyoncé exhibits solidarity with those groups while also calling attention to her exceptional status as a wealthy, powerful celebrity. Another audience consists of black women, to whom she seems to direct an empowering message to transcend the legacy of slavery and, collectively, "slay." A mass popular audience without political or identity stakes can find a narrative foothold on the brief sexual digression and the sound and spectacle of the performance itself.

The publics into which "Formation" inserted itself provide some clues as to how faithful Beyoncé's audiences found the text. Newspapers and magazine articles have directly connected her work to multiple police murders, including those of Alton Sterling and Philando Castile. *Rolling Stone* noted,

> Beyoncé has become one of the most vocal public figures with regards to police brutality, racism and violence against the black community. Her "Formation" video—where she posed atop a sinking police car in New Orleans—and Super Bowl performance—where she donned a Black Panther-inspired outfit—led to the Miami Police Union threatening to boycott her tour opener in Florida citing her "anti-police message."[14]

Audiences who are pro-police reacted negatively to this work. Black audiences who identify with feminist and antiracist projects enjoined a vigorous conversation that is explicitly about the fidelity of the video and song to black communities, particularly their resonance with the experience and interests of black women. Scholar Zandria Robinson argued that the song operated within an oppositional narrative of critical blackness. Shantrelle Lewis described how she found the Super Bowl performance to be "a national moment of seemingly audacious Black pride."[15] Even so, Lewis explained, Beyoncé used the city and its people as props in scenes that trigger traumatic returns to the trauma of Katrina and its racist aftermath.

Lewis points directly to the fidelity problem in her article: "What does it mean to speak for a marginalized community who has not asked for your pronouncements? From an outsider's perspective, it would seem as if Beyoncé, by returning to the devastation of Katrina, is centering New Orleans, but she is not. She's rather exacerbating a trauma." Lewis's argument is that Beyoncé cannot "speak for" the communities referenced in the songs and videos in a faithful way. In other words, public controversy about the performances centers on the enactments and failures of fidelity. This is the question that critical audiences attempt to answer. It is a question that rhetorical critics should also ask, even if, as in this case, the answers are neither simple nor fixed. One way to assess the fidelity of a narrative like this one is to listen to representatives from affected communities.

In contrast, Hedges's Left-wing critique cannot fathom the complex political work accomplished by even commercially produced narratives. He might also object to how Beyoncé turns a political critique into a spectacle. His criticism would miss the incredible resource spectacle can provide to political rhetoric.

SPECTACLE AND CELEBRITY

Postmodern philosopher Guy Debord diagnosed post-1968 capitalist society as the society of the spectacle, by which he meant "the production and consumption of images, commodities, and staged political events."[16] A spectacle is a special form of rhetorical mediation that involves a striking, often ritualistic, visual or performative display. Reducing complex messages to dramatic contrasts (hence becoming mythic in character), spectacles capture audience attention in a big way. I have already addressed numerous spectacles in this chapter, from cute animal photos to the Super Bowl halftime to a music video. Spectacles are also designed to induce awe and the feeling of an encounter with a phenomenon that is larger than life; they arouse excitement and other emotions.

The image is at the core of spectacle, and the literature on the rhetoric of photography and other visual forms can help us understand how images work as arguments, organize perception, and produce metonymic images as representatives of social problems. In addition to mobilizing affect, images locate viewers inside a particular point of view; many photographic images warrant policy and state action.[17] For example, I have argued elsewhere that images of Afghan women after 9/11 warranted U.S. invasions of Afghanistan and Iraq.[18] As Susan Sontag notes, part of the power of a realistic photograph lies in its ability to convince viewers that it represents a transparent reality. What we see in a photograph, we are tempted to take to be true.[19]

Spectacle is to the image as myth is to narrative: the same strategy but made majestic. The classic work addressing how politics uses spectacle is Murray Edelman's influential book *Constructing the Political Spectacle*. Even back in 1988, Edelman recognized the signs of a post-fact era (which indicates, perhaps, that what we are panicking about now is not new): To say that citizens who are informed about politics are better at promoting their own interests is to take for granted "a world of facts that have a determinable meaning and a world of people who react rationally to the facts they know. In politics, neither premise is tenable, a conclusion that history continually reaffirms and that observers of the political scene are tempted to ignore."[20] Political acts create publics and construct situations to which citizens should attend. Politics is marked by the instability of "referents of politically significant signs that constitute political and social history" and the attraction of minimizing ambiguity and uncertainty.[21] Edelman's line tends toward relativism: For him, moral certainty is a core danger leading to genocide, persecution, and so on, and some of history's worst atrocities can be rationalized. At the same time, he insists on identifying a symbol's material basis, not in certain facts but in the contexts of "privilege, disadvantage, frustration, aspiration, hope, and fear in which it is experienced."[22]

All political discourse shapes meanings in strategic ways to produce quiescence, arousal, support, or opposition in the service of particular ideologies and courses of action. In other words, spectacles are powerful and interested, that is to say, motivated by particular interests in particular material contexts. Edelman's argument resonates with my own: namely, that truth is perspectival and that we should be less concerned with the hard facticity of an appeal than its social and political motivations and consequences.

Edelman's book goes on to explore how some issues become social problems deserving of political attention when others—for example, poverty, unemployment, and discrimination—are constructed in ways that put their urgency into the background. The designation of "non-problems," beneficial problems, and ambiguous problems cultivates differential responses to them. Rationalizing the persistence of a problem is a powerful strategy. Likewise, political leaders and designated enemies are constructs who become signs of success or failure and whose personae are designed to evoke psychological adherence. Moreover, commercial news, driven by the profit motive, presents political news in spectacular dramatic form.

Celebrity is a special kind of spectacle, one in which the body and voice of a highly visible, famous person take on a representative role in culture. Celebrities stand in for identities, beliefs, and values; their voices can give extra weight to political truth claims. They are talented and interesting, and these qualities give their judgment credibility in some circumstances.[23] For example, on January 8, 2016, actress Meryl Streep accepted a Golden Globe award with a speech lambasting the values that Trump's presidency would entail: hatred, discrimination, and curtailed civil liberties. Her speech went viral on every social media platform at the moment of her address; audiences around the world linked to her words as representing them, with the amplified credibility of a famously talented and credible person. Celebrity is fraught because celebrities often represent elites and their interests and also because they may lack subject-area expertise.

Spectacles are perspectival. In other words, the creation of meaning is strategically guided by "the incentive to preserve privileges or to end inequalities" through the "definition of means, ends, costs, benefits, and rationality."[24] Political claims cannot be definitively verified in a situation of multiple perspectives. Rhetorician Wendy Hesford's book *Spectacular Rhetorics* examines some of the most insidious deployments of spectacle—even among global human rights activists and organizations—to warrant scapegoating, war, exploitation, rape, and other violations.[25] But while Edelman's critique of dominant ideology is incisive, he also urges the use of language and other symbols to subvert dominant meanings that sustain inequality.

Importantly, Edelman does not recommend that resistance take the form of an impossible, objective, fact-based response to spectacle. Left scholar Douglas Kellner agrees. While he laments the takeover of all social and political life by media spectacles and the culture of celebrity, he recognizes how political battles must, in the society of the spectacle,[26] "be fought out on the terrain of media spectacle." He writes, "A democratic politics of the future must invent a progressive spectacle politics that will further the goals of democracy, justice, human rights, environmental protection, and a progressive agenda."[27]

WHAT ABOUT HUMOR?

Humor is a special case. It is one vehicle of mass address that liberals and progressives have embraced, for example in the satire of Stephen Colbert; the comedy news programs of John Stewart, Trevor Noah, and John Oliver; and *Saturday Night Live*'s sketches mocking politicians and their foibles. Comedy can be an accessible form of political critique. At the same time, however, comedy assumes an "in crowd" of people who already agree with the posture of the comedian and often takes an elitist, "mocking" tone toward conservatives. This is especially true of irony and satire. As I and others have argued, satire is often taken literally by audiences who are not already "in the know" about the political critique being made; irony produces a kind of distance from the issue being critiqued such that the "getting" of the joke stands in for other kinds of action. Humor can provide a sense of catharsis for people seeking expression of their critical feelings and thoughts alongside pleasure in being surprised by something incongruous or ridiculous.[28]

I enjoy memes that capture my anger and criticism in such a way that diffuses negative feeling and emphasizes my sense of common cause with others who are circulating the same bit of humor. My favorite example of this is the meme "Pepper Spray Cop." In 2011, police shut down an Occupy demonstration at the University of California Davis. During the confrontation, one officer deliberately and brutally sprayed each protester in the face, and sympathizers with the students were horrified and momentarily stunned. It was difficult to know how to respond. Then, someone posted an image of the cop photoshopped into an image of the Statue of Liberty, so that he was spraying the face of this icon of free expression. After that somewhat sobering instance, the memes gathered humor and also sharpness as the cop appeared in famous paintings; on the cover of Pink Floyd's *Dark Side of the Moon* album; spraying Mount Rushmore, Harry Potter, SpongeBob, babies, and cute Internet cats; and so on.[29] One particularly powerful instance was the insertion of the cop figure into Kim Phuc's photo of a girl fleeing naked from a Napalm attack during the Vietnam War. The surprising visual analogy comes from its being positioned in the place of U.S. troops. The metaphor works in two directions: The military, by comparison, takes on the connotation of casual brutality; the cop then picks up the identity of a military condemned in the photo for its brutal aggression. For viewers who accept the critique of U.S. imperialism and of police brutality ahead of time, this juxtaposition makes cathartic sense. The meme circulated on social media among people who shared the critique and who used the meme to connect the critique to others in their circle. Outsiders, without the meaning frames enabling interpretation, may have found the image to be hateful or unintelligible. This broader inaccessibility, along with elitism, distancing effects, and comic juxtaposition (which doesn't always have to be lighthearted) is not included among my list of more earnest major strategies used by the Right while being held under suspicion by the Left.

TWO PROBLEMS BY WAY OF CONCLUSION

Here I have defined five tremendous rhetorical resources that the capitalist Right has historically embraced to bolster its regime. Opponents of the status quo cannot afford to dismiss these tools. To do so is elitist and self-defeating. Rather than holding political discourse today to a "just the facts" standard or lamenting ostensible citizen illiteracy, critics can employ the fidelity standard to assess the motivation and class belonging of discourse. Whose show is it? Whose story is told? Is the telling in the service of existing rule or counter-hegemonic struggle? These are not simple questions, but they can inform the practice, in Edelman's terms, of a progressive political critique based on the material contexts of political rhetoric. I return to Gramsci's insight that culture is important ground for staging political contestation.

However, for Gramsci struggle cannot be a matter of sophisticated rhetorical messaging alone. There are two reasons behind this caution. First, even the most effective, affective, emotionally resonant, and dramatic expression of the situation of the oppressed cannot sweep away the material power relations (the ownership and control of society's resources, the monopolization of political power by elites, the profitability of misogyny, the utility to capitalism and imperialism of racist scapegoating) that are the source of oppression. The knowledge we mobilize must, at the end of day, be useful in mobilizing *us*, in body and in our capacity to disrupt the economy, physical space, and business as usual. Second, the production of new, counter-spectacular political meanings cannot happen in a vacuum.

One of the ancient rhetorician Aristotle's most powerful concepts is that of the *enthymeme*: a form of reasoning that does not rely on hard fact and syllogistic reasoning but rather depends upon resting appeals on established common ground between persuader and audience. When a movement's goals involve violating the reality structure both at the level of economic and state power and on the terrain of culture and politics, that movement's messages may be unintelligible, so foreign as to not make sense, much less common sense. When we witness shifts in gender roles and race relations, expanding rights for marginalized groups, employer reforms in wages and benefits—it is usually in the context of a groundswell of actual, physical protest, the most powerful enactments of which involve labor strikes (because they interrupt the profitability of business). Antagonistic action and new political expressions occur simultaneously, each affecting the other.

We need affect, embodiment, myth, narrative, and spectacle. We need embodied struggle motivated by outrage, taking embodied forms, and productive of new narratives. We need spectacular struggle.

CHAPTER 3

Pants on Fire!

On the Rhetoric of Fact-Checking in U.S. Political Culture

IN 2015, the Center for Medical Progress (CMP), a conservative antiabortion organization, and its director, David Daleiden, published online a series of videos taken at abortion clinics in California, Florida, and Texas. The videos purported that the clinics were engaged in fetal tissue harvesting for profit in league with medical tissue procurement companies. In the first three days after the videos were posted, 1.5 million people viewed them; the ultimate viewership reached into the tens of millions. After professional review, a study cited in the *New York Times* concluded that the videos had been altered and manipulated and therefore should not be taken as depicting the "reality" of abortion clinics and their handling of fetal tissue.[1] Representatives of national abortion-rights organizations announced the exposure of the hoax across U.S. news media.

During this controversy, then–presidential contender conservative Carly Fiorina expressed her horror at witnessing what she saw in the video: "a fully formed fetus on the table, its heart beating, its legs kicking while someone says we have to keep it alive to harvest its brain."[2] The response of liberals and progressives was to mock Fiorina as either a melodramatic liar or someone confused between the CMP video and another video showing a miscarriage, or stillbirth.

The debunkers declared the matter resolved. However, it is possible that Fiorina did see something gruesome and troubling and became confused. That confusion should not be mistaken for ignorance or stupidity or mere political maneuvering. And in fact, one of the dozen videos published online shows a late-term fetus whose leg either kicks or twitches. The problem is that this image came from outside the context of Daleiden's investigation and was not an example of an abortion performed at the clinics his operatives were recording. But Fiorina *did* see a kicking leg.

Beyond that detail, close examination of all of the video footage originally published, regardless of editing or manipulation, reveals that it tells a powerful story accompanied by riveting images of fetal remains. It is a story that powerfully employs narrative, myth, affect, embodiment, and spectacle—all of the "big five." It is a story that attempts to establish that workers at Planned Parenthood and other clinics are engaged in a fetal-tissue-selling scheme, that the tissues involved came from fetuses at late stages of development, and that clinic staff exhibit callous disregard toward the fetuses whose parts they are harvesting.

For viewers without significant background and contextual knowledge, that story could stand as a powerful indictment, not primarily of the selling of fetal tissue, but of the practice of abortion more generally. The videos were difficult even for me, a staunch and knowledgeable advocate of abortion rights, to watch. In addition to the inserted video of a fetus "kicking," there is graphic footage of actual clinic staff sorting a fetal leg out of a tray of unidentified material. It is not kicking, but it is gruesome, and it is clearly a leg. I am not claiming that every event and person represented in the videos is accurate. What I am suggesting is that the footage is compelling in a way that exceeds the capacity of fact-checking to disarm it.

In terms of the "big five" strategies, the videos employ affect and emotion through the display of grotesque images of fetuses designed to provoke outrage and pity; they also construct a mythic narrative in which abortion providers are monstrous villains.

IN RESPONSE, the rush to nitpick and file lawsuits has not been effective in making the acceptance of women's right to choose abortion a matter of common sense. I will return to this example at the end of the chapter to discuss how another method might enable a more productive critique and engagement with opponents of abortion rights. Unlike Daleiden, abortion rights advocates refused the "big five" and stuck to appeals to bare facts. While this strategy was effective at documenting Daleiden's knowing manipulation of interviews and images, which in turn supported successful lawsuits against Daleiden and his organization, it did little to undo the powerful effects of the "big five" in mediating information through interpretive frames.

This example and any number of others reveal that journalistic fact-checking as currently practiced is an inadequate tool for evaluating political accountability to reality. Another word for fact-checking is *debunking*. Rhetorical scholar Kenneth Burke charges fact-checking with narrowness of focus, hyper-thoroughness, and naïve empiricism:

> The typical debunker is involved in a strategy of this sort: He discerns an evil. He wants to eradicate this evil. And he wants to do a thorough job of it. Hence, he becomes *too thorough* in an avalanche of arguments, a snowing under, a purely quantitative mode of propaganda.[3]

Fact-checkers operate in this debunking mode. In this chapter, I use the rhetorical concept of *stasis* to understand how fact-checking responses to truth claims literally "miss their mark." I develop two examples demonstrating this critical method. Then, relying on the work of Erving Goffman and Kenneth Burke, I recommend and develop the idea of "frame-checking" as an alternative mode of critique. Finally, I return to the abortion video controversy to think through what a more fitting rhetorical response might be to counter its impact.

THE EXPLOSION OF FACT-CHECKING

There has been an explosion of efforts to "fact-check" political rhetoric, starting with those of the *Tampa Bay Times*'s PolitiFact project and the fact-checking blog of Glenn Kessler at the *Washington Post*.[4] The American Press Institute has documented this surge:

> Though precise figures are hard to come by, the available evidence tells a fairly dramatic story about the growth of fact-checking. One count early this year found 29 branded fact-checking ventures in the US, all but five of which were established since 2010. . . . Though dedicated, full-time fact-checkers remain relatively rare, almost every major national newsroom has embraced the genre in some way. The list of outlets that engage in some form of fact-checking includes elite standard-bearers like the *New York Times*, the *Washington Post*, the *Associated Press*, and *National Public Radio* as well as *USA Today*, the three major broadcast networks, CNN, Fox, and MSNBC. In

addition, scores of smaller news outlets at the state and local level offer fact-checks during elections or around major political events like the State of the Union address.[5]

One indicator of this effort's inflated status is that a Google search of the term fact-checking in August 2017 returns more than 7 million results.

As noted in the introduction, the widespread outcry against the perjurious commander in chief and the alleged crisis of truth constitutes what Stuart Hall and his team, quoting cultural scholar Stan Cohen, called a "moral panic": a situation in which "a condition, episode, person or group of persons emerges to become defined as a threat to societal values and interests."[6] Editors, scholars, politicians, clergy, and other experts diagnose a condition or problem and thus position themselves as the credible proposers of remedies—all located within a bounded set of political, economic, and cultural expectations. Discourses surrounding the objects of a moral panic are always ideological. They take a situation and mediate its interpretation and uptake in ways that are always imbricated with power.

If we regard this rush to facticity as itself ideological, we see that the embrace of mainstream journalism and the implicit support for Trump's major opponents, along with Hillary Clinton and the Democratic Party, are consequential. Audiences are asked to accept what we once knew were partial and interested accounts of reality as given fact. The corporate news media, once targets of ideology critique for their framing practices, become authoritative in a way that belies that critique. The cry of "fake news!" implies that we had some faith in the news before this historical moment as conveying "truth." Readers have taken thirstily to pro-corporate, traditional news sources as if those sources were now fountains of undiluted, clear political truths rather than ideological gatekeepers. Furthermore, obsession with facts ignores how economic hardship and anxiety generate popular desire for narratives explaining social crisis at the levels of values and action, refusing to generate compelling narratives in response.

Meanwhile, journalists who perform fact-checking investigate a politician's claim and rate it on some sort of "truth-o-meter" scale from "true" or "mostly-true" to "pants on fire!" (referring to the children's rhyme, "Liar, liar, pants on fire!"). While "fake news" is hardly a new phenomenon, reporters have argued that Trump's presidency out shadows all that came before it in outright mendacity. In response, fact-checkers have chronicled the president's daily lies in minute detail.[7]

These ostensibly noble efforts face a number of challenges, including rampant bipartisan political manipulation of truths, the apparent inattention paid by consumers of political information to questions of fact, the demonstrated power of elites to determine what information circulates as truth in mass media environments, and the critical limits of efforts attempting to document myriad falsehoods without taking on the values frames and political perspectives that set the conditions for the productions of "truths." As Mark Andrejevic has argued, we operate in an era of information overload. While audiences have access to vast amounts information and an array of contested narratives, the multiplication of accounts of reality can make the adjudication of evidence extremely complicated, if not overwhelming. Paradoxically, the swirl of information and misinformation in the "post-truth" era serves prevailing interests even as perspectives available online multiply.[8] In short, "telling the truth"—and telling truth from lies—is not a simple task, as both truth and falsehood are complex and multidimensional.

THE COMPLEXITY OF FALSEHOOD

As Marxist theorist Raymond Geuss argues, falsehood is not only a matter of empirical misrepresentation. As I noted in the introduction, a rhetorical perspective acknowledges that all truth claims are *mediated,* or in other words, filtered through the perception, interpretation, and explanation of people with varying power and perspectives. Any account of falsehood needs to account for the relationship between truth claims and power. While, as Geuss argues, there is indeed a category of *epistemic* falsehood that refers to simple lies, he notes that ideology—or the pattern of commonsense ideas that frame and inform ideas and behavior—can also be false in a *functional* way, in which plausibly true ideas can function nonetheless in the service of oppressive power. He also posits a category called *genetic falsehood,* in which persuaders' motives are suspect as warranting intentional mystification.[9]

For example, in the abortion video controversy, the claim that the videographers witnessed and filmed a fetus still alive after an abortion is demonstrably false in the epistemic sense. In the functional sense, the implicit claim as to the cavalier treatment of fetal remains by clinic staff is plausible but still used in such a way as to bolster antiabortion interests. The interrogation of Daleiden's motives (which go beyond revealing the truth) would lead to the charge of genetic falsehood: Whatever may be accurate or inaccurate about the video, the fact that its creator has an obscure agenda discredits it as false in the genetic sense.

Geuss argues most controversially that critics of ideology could legitimately fault a claim on the basis of who is making it—a category of falsehood that he calls "genetic falsehood." Geuss is basically arguing that what we in rhetorical studies often discredit as the "genetic fallacy"—the idea that the motivation of an arguer can discredit an otherwise reasonable claim—is not a fallacy in every case.

I do not want to have myself or my argument mistaken as relativist. I argue in chapter 1 that truth is perspectival, not subjective, such that a discourse may be evaluated by fidelity to the interests of its audiences, not correspondence with something we can access immediately as a fact. My argument asks readers to think more broadly about falsehood in terms of political power, such that the perspective of the oppressed compels a different account of reality than that of the oppressor. To a large extent, the differences between the two are more on the levels of naming, definition, and evaluation rather than bare description. As I note in the introduction, what appears to a conservative as perversion is the condition of freedom for a transgender person. What appears to be the smooth operation of free enterprise to the employer can be experienced as alienation and exploitation by the employee. A manager attempting to mediate the worker's experience to induce cooperation need not deny the work process, pay, or conditions, but her claims should be suspect on the basis of their motivation. The framing of experience motivated by the employer's interests is genetically false to the interests of the workers.

Like Geuss, Jon Elster describes the complexity of what we might think of as truth. His work attempts to understand how ideology—invested patterns of ideas that explain and justify society as it is—establishes belief. In his schema, there are three overlapping forms of ideological production: the interest-based dissemination of distorted ideas (genetic falsehood), the failure of imagination that happens when people are convinced to favor the existing social system, and the psychological comfort of palliative discourses such as religion and patriotism.[10] In our case, Planned Parenthood identified the videos as deliberate, interest-based, and therefore distorted. However, even if Daleiden were earnest in his attempts to represent activities of abortion clinicians, viewers inclined against abortion might find the affirmation palliative, or comforting. For most viewers, the videos limit our frame of reference and impair our capacity to imagine a broader debate, say, about women's rights and reproduction.

Faced with this complexity, fact-checkers miss the opportunity to interrogate these various kinds of falsehood, because they (the fact-checkers) are resolutely committed to debunking at the epistemic level. I learned about this commitment in 2014 when I attended a retreat held by the American Press Institute about the value of and prospects for the fact-checking enterprise. During our discussions, I raised this problem: Fact-checking misses the forests for the trees. Does it matter as much whether Barack Obama ever held a gun (a challenge posed by conservatives, in response to which handlers produced an obligatory photograph of the president with a rifle) as having a broader debate about gun violence and the role of the nation-state in controlling access to weapons? Does the question of whether General Motors moved thirty thousand or seventy-five thousand jobs to Asia matter as much as having a public conversation about globalization and the exploitative flow of labor? In response to my concerns, other participants at the workshop nodded in agreement. However, the merits of the enterprise overall went unquestioned. Resorting to a narrow empirical baseline, these fact-checkers miss the point: It's not about what's in the box but who gets to decide its boundaries and exclusions, and who gets to shape facts for public sense-making.

A QUANTITATIVE MODE OF PROPAGANDA: AN EXAMPLE

Two recent examples of fact-checking journalism reveal the tendency of fact-checking to "miss the point." The first is about the critical report by the inspector general (IG) on presidential candidate Hillary Clinton's use of personal phones for emails in her role as secretary of state.[11] In the article (clocking in at more than 3,400 words), the factcheck.org writer takes each subcategory of the report's main claim that Clinton was wrong to use her personal email for official business. In the fact-checking process, it examines at great length Clinton's claims that her use of personal email was "allowed by the State Department," "fully complied" with department regulations, and was the "same thing" as what had been done by her predecessors.

Quoting the IG report and numerous officials in incredible detail, the factcheck.org article concludes that although Clinton had not signed an agreement restricting her "sharing of work-related documents," her personal system was not "approved," and Clinton found evidence of security breaches and did not report it. The checker could not confirm that Clinton's predecessors had used personal email. In conclusion: Clinton made a mistake and admitted it.

An update at the bottom of the article corrects a quotation from a campaign spokesperson: "Fallon said the Clinton campaign agrees with the IG finding that 'her practice of copying aides on her emails did not end up producing a full record since State's IT systems didn't save everything.' But that doesn't mean she didn't take steps to comply."

Like all formal fact-checking attempts, this article relies on the empiricist assumption that it is possible to measure public statements against an absolutely certain reality and therefore it would be possible to produce discourse that corresponded with that reality. This assumption, however, is belied by how the process of confirmation and refutation relies upon *other actors'* (the IG report, campaign staffers) *statements* or representations of reality. In other words, every attempt to get at the facts of the matter necessarily relies upon mediation and interpretation.

The article also demonstrates the trait of *over-thoroughness*. As Burke put it, one is buried in an "avalanche of arguments." The column takes up minutiae on the questions of whether Clinton used her personal email account, whether such use was sanctioned, whether it was formally prohibited, whether there was a lapse in security, whether she was telling the truth about her email use, whether she lied or simply made a mistake, and how serious that mistake was.

The most significant limitation of this instance of fact-checking, however, and of the practice in general, is *narrowness of focus*. If one were to ask a potential and undecided voter what concerned her about the Clinton email scandal, she might well respond: "Is she trustworthy?" The public probably does not want Clinton to be let off the hook in a series of minute technicalities. Rather, the salient questions are, did she imperil national security? Did she lie intentionally? Can I trust her to be an ethical commander in chief?

ALTERNATIVE CRITICAL APPROACHES

The Stasis System

The fact-checker does not help such voters to answer such actual and vitally important questions. This failure happens because the fact-checking enterprise operates at a very low level of deliberation, or *stasis,* a concept developed by the ancient Greek scholar of rhetoric Hermagoras.[12] Through continual engagement with the rhetorical practices of the Greek *polis,* he observed that politicians often argued past each other when each participant was operating on a different part of the question at hand. Hermagoras developed what is now called the "*stasis* (plural *staseis*) system." A *stasis* is a basic or central issue of dispute, originally defined in legal or forensic terms. At any of these "stopping points," an advocate could craft a disagreement with opposing counsel. In any case, it would be crucial to discover where the heart of the disagreement lies. In Hermagoras's scheme, there are four *staseis*:

> Question of fact or conjecture: Does it exist? Did it happen? Who did it?
> Question of definition: How can the act or event be defined?

Question of quality: What is the character of the act: right or wrong, good or
bad? What characteristics might make us evaluate it differently?
Question of jurisdiction: Who has authority over this action? What should
be the direction of action?[13]

The enterprise of fact-checking limits its attention to the *staseis* of definition and conjecture, missing bigger questions of value and direction of action
entirely. In the case of the Clinton email example, there is ambiguity over what
counts as a lie: Does it have to be intentional? Can a person be "mistaken"
without having lied?

Fact-checking performs at the *stasis* of conjecture in only a limited, micro-
attentive way, producing an overly thorough account of almost nothing. It is
also forensic, or legalistic, in character, focusing on what someone may have
said or done, therefore emphasizing the blameworthiness of political rhetors
on the most minute of questions. The article concludes without being able to
determine Clinton's truthfulness.

Here is another example from the same site: Did presidential candidate
Donald Trump adopt a false identity and voice in a telephone transaction in
1991? After experts compared the call-in question to other instances of his
speech, they declared, yes, it is he. But here's the interesting part of the story:

We don't take any position on Trump's use of an alias, but the fact is that he
denied using one while being interviewed by *People* magazine in 1991 even
though there is evidence that it was indeed him.[14]

Here is a direct, explicit refusal to move up the *stasis* chain to a question of
quality: "We don't take any position on Trump's use of an alias." But of course,
readers will want to know whether Trump was right or wrong, playful or
deceitful in the 1991 conversation. How can we know? What weight should
we give to a moment in 1991 when deciding who will lead our country? Is it
right or wrong to adopt a false persona? Does the answer depend on who is
performing it and in what context?

More recently, *New York Times* columnist Timothy Egan calls Trump the
"Lord of the Lies" and advocates "an instant fact-check on statements made
by Presidential candidates onstage."[15] He adds,

And while doing such a thing is unlikely to ensure that the debates would be
substantive, it could at least guarantee a reality foundation at a time when
fact-free speech is the language of the political class.

Here Egan acknowledges the central problem with fact-checking: It is unlikely to guarantee anything about substance. In addition, he acknowledges that in spite of continual fact-checking, Trump, a member of the political class, has escaped major consequences for lying. In other words, Egan makes a case against his own argument. Fact-checking has not worked in Trump's case (or in any case of the "political class's" immunity from accountability), and it does not get at questions of substance. I resonate with Egan's outrage and wish for greater accountability.

However, in this and in many other cases, reporters, trapped in the epistemic and reliant on an empiricist worldview, miss an opportunity to educate the public, enable conversation about what matters, and play a role not of bureaucratic tic recorder but of guide to democracy.

Frame-Checking

If we want to critique political discourse as potentially false in some way or damaging to the practice of politics, and the checking of facts does not make an adequate intervention into critique, what resources do we have as citizens and critics to assess the character of political truth claims? As an alternative to fact-checking, I propose *frame-checking*.

Kenneth Burke, whose essay on the limits of debunking was helpful earlier in this chapter, makes productive contributions to the idea of evaluating rhetorical frames. In *Philosophy of Literary Form*, he defines frames as strategies for handling public content that persevere to the point of having universal relevance. A frame is a habit of interpretation that evolves in typical, recurrent situations.[16] Media critic Todd Gitlin called our attention to how news media frame protest events in trivializing and misleading ways in their selection of images, sound, voice-over, editing, and other techniques.[17] Political communication researcher Jim A. Kuypers published work advancing "framing analysis" as a rhetorical perspective in 1997. Kuypers argues that frames are powerful rhetorical entities that "induce us to filter our perceptions of the world in particular ways, essentially making some aspects of our multi-dimensional reality more noticeable than other aspects. They operate by making some information more salient than other information."[18]

Thus, research in communication studies has identified frames as the strategies for handling social truths through filtering for salience and emphasis. Frames mediate our perception and evaluation of reality. In his fundamental work *Frame Analysis,* sociologist Erving Goffman writes that instead of asking what reality is, the critic ought to ask, "Under what circumstances do we think things are real?" and "Under what conditions is the feeling of reality generated?"[19] Frame analysis can get at these higher-order questions by observing how discourses selectively direct attention, involve audiences intimately with the matter at hand, and construct coherent and noncontradictory schemes of making sense of the world. He notes that there are several different worlds of truths, including science, philosophy, myth, and the supernatural. In this context, frames are central to the production of meaning, belonging, and consent to rule because they offer perspectives that organize experience. Goffman thus defines frames as "schemata of interpretation" or "principles of organization which govern events—at least social ones—and our involvement in them."[20]

Shanto Iyengar and Robert Entman have conducted extensive and important social-scientific research on news framing that establishes its effectiveness. Entman defines frames as techniques, both conscious and unconscious, that involve "*selection* and *salience*":

> To frame is to select some aspects of a perceived reality and make them more salient in a communicating text, in such a way as to promote a particular problem definition, causal interpretation, moral evaluation, and/or treatment recommendation for the item described.[21]

As Scheufele and Iyengar explain, framing is not so much about what is communicated as it is about "*how* a given piece of information is being presented (or framed) in public discourse."[22]

Frames are socially produced and relatively stable mechanisms of organizing public interpretation of truth claims in political culture. Frames delimit perspective. When there are competing frames, there is a struggle for control over the shaping of experience. The influence of a particular frame is determined by the capacity of a group to control technologies of mediation. Frames vary depending on perspective and experience. However, the frames of powerful elites circulate more generally and more successfully than those of subordinates. As Marx aptly noted, "The ruling ideas of any given epoch are the ideas of the ruling class."[23] To the oppressed and exploited, the perspective of ruling class frames is *false* because it does not resonate with their lived experience or actual interests in liberation. In times of quiescence, dominant frames—for example, the casting of the poor as criminal—may go unquestioned. In times of questioning or crisis, however, the opportunity is ripe for those who interpret experience in a different way, one that exhibits greater fidelity to the perspective of marginalized groups.

For this reason, the critique of framing is potentially a powerful antidote to unquestioned domination justified by untruths at various *staseis*. To discover the frames operating in a given instance, citizens and critics must attend to two features of them. First, identify the *stasis* at which a controversy is playing out and notice how the selection of *stasis* is strategic and instrumental in framing that controversy. Second, the critic should call attention to what the frame around the discourse "contains" and directs our attention to and what it leaves out, silences, backgrounds, or omits. Narratives are often the sites where one can notice which perspectives are selected and which are deflected. Following Goffman, we must notice how discourses selectively direct attention, involve audiences intimately with the matter at hand, and construct coherent and noncontradictory schemes of making sense of the world.

We ask, what is allowed to "count" inside the frame as reality, and what are the text's strategies of "realizing"—creating the feeling of—reality? Social frameworks aim at persuasion and attempt to "key in" participants, or win them to a certain interpretation of experience. Keying is what happens when groups share frameworks of interpretation about action that they are engaged in. I believe that such frameworks can be ideological, that is to say, rendered as invisible naturalized common sense associated with a dominant group's interests. However, the process of framing is not permanently stable. Transformation in perception occurs when people mis-key or rekey the frames governing a situation. Such instances can occur in disputes over the existence, definition, and quality of objects and events.[24]

In order to name operating frames, it helps to understand them tropologically: They work through metaphor and metonymy. A frame asks us to see one thing—say, a fetus—as something else, or something more complex, say, a person. Or it asks us to define abortion as the murderous treatment of unborn life by practitioners, without reference to adult women, who are left out of the frame. We can also identify more general frames such as the scandal frame, which reduces the activities in question to a crime or moral outrage deserving of attention and condemnation.

Observing these elements of political truth making can then lead to insights about *invention,* or about creating a counter-discourse that meets the prevailing frames at the same *staseis* and employs narrative and other strategies to shift the perspectives from which truth is being told. It is possible to deliberately "mis-key" the meaning of abortion. Let us return to the case of the "baby-selling" videos to put these principles into operation.

FRAME-CHECKING THE ABORTION VIDEO CONTROVERSY

The following discussion is based on my viewing and analysis of all of the videos as they were initially published online by the Center for Medical Progress. There is a total of twelve videos, each ranging between nine and thirteen minutes long.[25] Four of the videos were compiled to make the finished series "Human Capital."[26] These videos contain excerpted sections from the other recordings, which consist of extended interviews with Planned Parenthood staff, leadership, and clinicians along with lengthy footage of pathology lab visits by the undercover investigators, who are posing as potential procurers of fetal tissue. Much of the footage was taken at a national conference of abortion providers and over meals with Planned Parenthood officials and procurement company representatives.

The "Human Capital" series is organized and framed by a lengthy interview with Holly O'Donnell, a phlebotomist and former procurement employee for StemExpress, a for-profit tissue procurement and selling corporation. O'Donnell recounts her harrowing experiences as she discovered that she was expected to coordinate with clinic staff to arrange for the delivery of certain intact parts, convince patients to consent to tissue donation, and to witness and take part in fetal dissection, including, allegedly, the extraction of a brain from a fetus's head.

In addition, the video series features a compilation of footage of interviews between CMP staff and clinic personnel both in clinics and at restaurants and conventions, footage of visits to clinics, footage of clinic staff sorting through fetal tissue, and testimony of trauma having to do with working with fetal tissue. The frame is one of realism, in which a sense of reality is conveyed by the tactic of amateur secret recording, the use of natural sound in ordinary spaces, the interview format, and the use of images. As Susan Sontag once noted, the most persuasive effect of a photograph is the idea that it is true.[27] Viewers of seemingly realistic images are discouraged, by their very realism, from noticing active framing on the part of the producers. The inclusion of black-and-white footage in some of the videos and the form of an undercover documentary lend the account additional realism.

Beyond the overall framing of itself as a representation of an unmediated reality and the framing of the transactions in fetal tissue as a scandal, the videos offer a number of other frames that define the character, or quality, of the events represented. These frames include the provider as profiteer, provider as monster, and fetus as child. In addition, the videos frame abortion as a process without women. It becomes a relationship between provider and fetus. In detailing each frame, I will use primarily examples from the "Human Capital" series, with occasional reference to the other videos.

Provider as Profiteer

In the videos, abortion providers and leaders of the Planned Parenthood Federation of America (PPFA) are represented as willing to bend or break the law prohibiting the sale for profit of fetal tissue in order to profit themselves and their local clinics. The interviewers persistently ask about particular body parts (neural tissue, liver, heart) and push for an agreement to provide their false company with profitable fetal parts, including the brain. The interviewers focus heavily on procuring "thymus," a crucial immune system organ, located in the chest, where T-cells mature. Fetal thymus transplantation is still experimental, and tissues are needed for research. There is evidence that fetal thymuses are less susceptible than other sources to rejection by a host. Hence, access to fetal thymus tissue is potentially lucrative. It is possible that the interviewers' obsessive questions about the thymus tissue were designed to prompt conversation about value and profit about harvesting later-term remains. While clinic staff acknowledged that they could find thymus tissue, none reacted with excitement or mentioned potential profitability.

However, these medical directors, research directors, and clinicians appear to admit without compunction the financial benefits that would accrue if Planned Parenthood chapters could openly provide fetal tissue for a fee. For example, Planned Parenthood Federation of America's senior director of medical services, Deborah Nucatola, describes over lunch how Planned Parenthood sells the body parts of aborted fetuses and admits that late-term abortions provide more intact pieces.

At the national conference, doctors discuss relationships they have with the procurement company Advanced Bioscience Resources (ABR); images of ABR's and StemExpress's "fees for service" menu appear in the video. Samples from fetuses of sixteen weeks or longer gestation command a higher fee. Some Planned Parenthood officials and doctors discuss how they alter their surgical methods in order to preserve the intactness of such fetuses. Those methods include a two-day dilation process to expand the cervical opening before the procedure, and turning fetuses into breech (feet-first) position so that the head emerges last, at the largest point of dilation.

As the *New York Times* explained, there is nothing illegal about either these activities or donating tissue, with patient consent, to medical researchers. Investigations upheld Planned Parenthood's claims that any fees charged were to cover only the costs of securing, storing, and transporting tissue, and that, in fact, Planned Parenthood likely took losses in these exchanges.[28] At the same time, interviewees carelessly implied that they were interested in making a profit. Nucatola explains that chapters just "want to break even" in tissue donation, but "if they can do a little better than break even and do so in a way that is reasonable," she would be happy. In an office setting, the director of research for Planned Parenthood Gulf Coast describes fetal parts as "all just a matter of line items."

Elsewhere in the footage, Dr. Mary Gatter, president of Planned Parenthood's Medical Directors Council haggles with the fake procurement agents and jokes about the potential profitability of fetal tissue sales, saying, "I want a Lamborghini." What is likely an attempt at humor can be interpreted as an admission of mercenary motives. Another clinician discusses the "need to get our stories straight," warning against selling fetal tissue in an "anti" (abortion) state: "We don't want to get called on selling fetal parts across states." In response to a proposal to purchase from the fake research company (the interviewers), a worker says, "We need to see what we can get out of it."

The national director of the Consortium of Abortion Providers for PPFA engages in a long conversation at the convention with a local provider who wants to openly receive fees for supplying fetal tissue because, in her view, they are doing a service for which they should be paid. She is frustrated with the prohibitions of the law. After urging the provider to be careful because of the possibility of negative publicity backlash, the director states, "I think it's a great idea, but do it right." Several national and local officials discuss why there is and will be no national policy regarding fees for fetal tissue because of the need for plausible denial of accountability.

Melissa Farrell, medical director at the Gulf Coast chapter, discusses the provision of fetal tissue as a "diversification of [Planned Parenthood's] revenue stream with intact fetal cadavers as 'line items.'" She discusses how clinicians can retrieve an intact brain from a second-trimester fetus if they "get creative." Another doctor calls Planned Parenthood "a volume institution" and states that there are no clear regulations of the process of tissue donation and remuneration. She warns against making donations public: "Imagine the New York Times headlines. The headlines would be a disaster." She admits that "saying it's used for research gives us cover."

In fact, however, the New York Times reported the ways in which this footage was selectively edited to make the providers' comments seem as self-incriminating as possible. Even so, it is incredible that the clinicians and directors interviewed would be so naïve and forthcoming, not to mention that they would harbor such attitudes in the first place. In addition to appearing to be profit hungry and oblivious to the law, they are framed so as to seem as callous about abortion as possible.

To establish this frame, the videos construct a powerfully effective narrative that tells a story of the provider as profiteer. This characterization of clinic personnel becomes mythic in nature as additional footage is organized to turn providers into monstrous figures.

Provider as Monster

Deepening potential viewer discomfort, video footage shot inside the clinic shows nurses and doctors fishing through trays of fetal remains to show the investigators different kinds of tissue: lungs, other organs, and yes, that tiny leg. More than establishing a black market in baby parts, the images and interviews frame providers as casual and callous about what appear to be parts of babies, the remains of abortion procedures. One explains how "less crunchy" extraction methods are helpful in getting whole specimens. Another explains how arranging for a breech (feet-first) presentation helps the head to "come out whole" because "the big head can't come out unless there's significant dilation." When dealing with a later-term fetus, "Usually you can see the whole brain come out." A doctor discusses the "induction of fetal demise" at twenty-one weeks. Nucatola explains these processes while enjoying a salad and a glass of wine.

O'Donnell describes how difficult it was to secure tissue from a particular doctor who performed abortions "viciously fast." She describes StemExpress employees coldly pressuring patients in distress—"girls throwing up"—to give their consent for donation. Interspersing these segments of interview is a significant framing technique. Right after O'Donnell states, "I'm not going to tell a girl to kill a baby just so I can get money," the scene cuts to the Nucatola interview in which she is describing how she tailored cases to tissue procurement needs: "For example, I had eight cases yesterday, and I knew exactly what we needed," which were cases of seventeen-weeks' gestation or above. "I knew which cases were more likely to give what was needed."

A particularly disturbing scene is from the interview with O'Donnell, who describes being asked to manually cut through a fetus's face to reveal the brain. (We do not see the act performed, nor is there any corroborating evidence that such an event occurred.) At another point, clinicians laugh about "sending baby heads in the mail." But most powerful in establishing the provider-as-monster frame are the images: nurses digging in bags of mush or raking through trays to find particular parts to show the interviewers as if it's all just in a day's work. Of course, it is part of the day's work, and sections left on the editing room floor might have contained context, for example, that aborting a twenty-one-week-old fetus would be done only under the most dire and necessary circumstances, or that dark humor is common in such settings.

However, the conversations and images are unfortunately, as framed, damning. The doctors, nurses, and directors appear monstrously callous.

Readers will recall that a mythic narrative is one that pits value systems against each other in a grand tale of good versus evil. When the providers are framed as monsters, the narrative about their activities becomes mythic, establishing a claim at the *stasis* of value that would have been effectively countered by a parallel value claim representing antiabortion activists as villains. The abortion videos cast a mythic narrative of good versus evil and life versus death in rendering providers as monstrous opportunists.

Fetus as Child

Both of the frames described above depend on the most important and powerful frame of all: the fetus as child. This frame has affective appeal at its foundation. The fact that this frame is a longtime staple of antiabortion discourse does not inure the viewer against the graphic images in the footage, designed to provoke pity, grief, and disgust. The series features images of technicians handling trays of fetal remains and identifying parts: feet, neural tissue, legs, eyeballs, all backlit in clear glass trays (which O'Donnell calls "pie pans") on the counter.

The fourth and fifth episodes, only pieces of which were used in the "Human Capital" series, center their attention on pathology lab footage. In episode 4, the CMP interviewers, posing as procurement specialists, ask a group of doctors and nurses if they can see what was collected that day: "I just want to see one leg." Although reluctant, a nurse does pull out some tissue from a twelve-week fetus: "Here's a heart. Here's a foot." The doctor calls the fetus "war-torn." The technician fishes out a leg. In episode 5 (in footage not included in "Human Capital"), practitioners offer up a later-term case, what they call a "fresh specimen," declaring, "It's another boy!" The gendering of the remains encourages viewers to see the fetus as a fully formed child, as the phrase "It's a boy!" would generally only be uttered upon the delivery of a live infant. Staff members then proceed to identify pieces as lungs, intestines, placenta, leg, arm, and hand.

One particularly controversial moment does show what is meant to be an intact, late-term fetus, which appears in the first episode. It turns out that, on close examination, this image is not from the clinic in the video but has rather been imported from elsewhere, the Grantham Collection for Bioethical Reform. Another image of a stillborn child cradled in his father's hands was also imported opportunistically. These substitutions are the clearest instance of manipulation in the videos. This is a long-standing strategy of antiabortion discourse: to substitute all late-term fetal images for what is surely a wide range of fetal development—from the unformed in early weeks to the later-term remains. Celeste Condit describes this maneuver as metonymic—substitution of one dimension for the entirety of a complex phenomenon.[29] The strategy is key to establishing the frame, fetus as child. It is not explained that any late-term abortions were performed under severe circumstances (risk to life and health of the mother, severe deformity, unviability) and as the result of hard choices. This choice of image plus the focus on identifiable, if tiny, anatomical parts frames the aborted fetuses as well-developed baby-like entities. Such viewers as Carly Fiorina, primed to respond emotionally to the killing of "innocent life," become deeply invested in the broader narratives that the videos construct.

FACT-CHECKERS' RESPONSES

Ignoring the power and complexity of the rhetorical work of the videos, fact-checkers investigated the videos and their claims and concluded that Planned Parenthood did not profit and did not break any laws. Therefore, the videos' claims were declared to be "false." Abortion rights organizations claimed victory and filed a lawsuit against Daleiden and his organization, which resulted in indictments. However, the fact-checkers failed to respond to the questions of value raised in the video. Even at the *staseis* of conjecture and definition their response was off the mark: "We are not *selling* baby parts." However, regardless of profit or legality, the clinics are performing abortions and supplying fetal parts to researchers. Factcheck.org focused even more microscopically on whether the $30 to $100 fee Nucatola mentions as the cost per sample would constitute a profit for Planned Parenthood. (The answer is no.)[30] It goes into detail on the content of a 1993 law that delimits the conditions for legally supplying fetal parts for a fee and describes how it is legal if fees do not exceed procedural costs and do not result in a profit for the supplier.

The realistic imagery of the documentary, however, encourages viewers to consider fetuses as babies and abortion as gruesome and murderous. Whether Planned Parenthood engaged in the altruistic donation of tissue for medical treatments and research or sold baby parts for profit is almost beside the point.

As the *Atlantic* pointed out,

> Even if there's nothing illegal, it's easy to see how the video is a coup for the anti-abortion movement. The pro-choice and pro-life movements tend to talk about abortion in very different terms. Those who support abortion

couch their argument in terms of women's bodily autonomy, or in terms of a right to privacy. Abortion opponents sometimes use similar rights language, speaking of the rights of the unborn. Yet they also often use graphic images of aborted fetuses, for example, to highlight the visceral reality of abortion. There's some debate about this practice among pro-life campaigners, but pro-choice activists acknowledge that abortion isn't pretty and that there's an easy disgust factor to it. (There's a reason that although a majority of Americans favor legal abortion, a plurality also say it's morally wrong.)[31]

The insight that advocates and opponents of abortion "tend to talk about abortion in very different terms" points directly to the failure of the pro-choice community to address the question at the same *stasis* at which their opponents are operating.

Rhetorical scholar Celeste Condit, along with a number of other critics, has established the weakness of the abortion rights argument: It is abstract and legalistic. It does not have recourse to powerful, visceral images. Its only main narrative is the story of women seeking illegal and unsafe abortions in which images of adult women make them appear to be victims only of their own choices. A fetus rendered as a baby can only be read as an innocent victim—of the woman, doctor, and procedure. Abortion isn't pretty. Neither is childbirth or war.

But abortion advocates ignored the power of the image and responded abstractly and legally, claiming that the videos did not achieve their goal, which, ostensibly, was to discover a black market in fetal body parts. However, as the *Atlantic* noted, the videos achieved a different goal: to cultivate public disgust about the abortion procedure and distrust of abortion providers as uncaring and callous.

An article in the *New York Times* noted,

> Abortion opponents hope the videos will provoke people to consider the humanity of the unborn, much like discussing ultrasounds can—albeit in a much more jarring and graphic way. Ms. Conway, the Republican pollster, calls this a "shock the conscience, warm the heart" approach.[32]

This coverage points to the frames at work in the videos. They frame the unborn as persons, they frame abortion as an issue of emotional response rather than political reason, and they frame abortion providers as heartless murderers. The entire project occurs within a "scandal" frame that defines the activities of Planned Parenthood as shocking and morally questionable.

Moreover, the videos strategically cultivate the emotion of viewers, embodying the act of witnessing wrongdoing, showing the remains as spectacle, telling a narrative of, if not corruption, callousness. All of these strategies work to discredit abortion advocates and weaken public resolve on the question of a woman's right to choose. Although the *Washington Post* argued that the videos would likely have no impact on the stable public U.S. consensus that abortion should be legal in some circumstances,[33] it failed to note the successful, progressive implementation of restrictive antiabortion laws in numerous states, which have resulted in the closing of large numbers of clinics. The efforts of the political action committee American Legislative Exchange Council (ALEC) have generated widespread but unscientific concern over fetal pain and viability.[34] A report by Emily Crockett notes that the rate of attacks on abortion providers increased after the videos' release.[35]

ALTERNATIVE FRAMING STRATEGIES

In this context, what might a fitting response to the CMP videos have been? I have suggested that the technocratic and legalistic crowing of the abortion rights leaders is feeble in response to the frames operating in the videos. The response operates at the wrong *stasis,* conjecture rather than quality; it fails to engage the story and images of abortion opponents. It does not address the scandal frame set up by Daleiden. It does not work to reframe abortion and the work of its providers in the historical context of women's liberation from the reproductive role, a freedom women seek whether or not abortion is legal. The rhetoric of abortion providers also avoids the higher-level question of women's rights to control their reproduction, a question that could frame a response in a way designed to understand the broader truths evoked by the scandal.

We can envision a better response. Imagine pro-choice organizations responding immediately with another video, set in a provocative scandal frame that exposes Daleiden and his outfit, but also and more importantly counters the antiabortion videos at the *stasis* of quality by interviewing women who have undergone the procedure and their reasons for doing so. To counter provider-as-profiteer and provider-as-monster frames, the videographers could interview staff about the conditions of their work that could make performing abortions routine and the disposal of remains a necessary activity. Workers could describe their fear of being picketed, harassed, or worse because of the necessary work they do. They could explain the miserable contexts of later-term abortions, only rarely entered into by choice, and the small consolation of contributing tissue for research. The frame of fetal personhood is the most crucial to confront. Instead of late-term fetuses, the central images of persons in the pro-choice response would be of women. Music and sound could be used to draw out emotions in sympathy with the women and appreciation of the staff as not heartless murderers, but as heroes. Thus the response would embrace affect, embodiment, myth, and narrative to meet the CMP's "personhood" frame with an alternative definition of personhood and an emphasis on the humanity of providers and patients.

An additional dimension would reframe the provision of fetal tissue as miraculous and lifesaving rather than as a commodity. Footage could feature recipients of donations and researchers discussing the necessity of fetal tissues to medical progress and patient life. Women who had an abortion could discuss how good they feel about making this kind of contribution. Such mis- or rekeying would, unlike fact-checking, pull back to expose more of the context and scene of abortion, the patients and practitioners of it, and the supplying of fetal tissue for research.

To some critics, this effort might seem naïve, mawkish, and manipulative. There may be other modalities, for example using irony and parody so as to sabotage and disrupt rather than rekey the videos' frames. Burke would advocate such creative deconstruction through incongruity.[36] In Goffman's terms, it would be more radical to "disorganize the world," that is, to render dominant worldviews unstable, rather than to respond measure by measure to how the frames are already working.[37]

However, a deconstructive response might run the risks of mocking or marginalizing a point of view and narrative frame shared by hundreds of thousands of U.S. residents; it is likely only to appeal to those looking to denigrate the Right. In addition, it is risky because, as a great deal of research has shown, many audiences have trouble telling satire from earnest representation—not because they are stupid, but because frames that seem absurd to one group can make sense to another. I am an advocate of critical disruption; *invention,* however, requires a less elitist and more strategic approach.

It was difficult for me to examine these videos from my perspective as a longtime (and ongoing) supporter of abortion rights. One of my arguments in this book is that progressives and the Left should adopt a standpoint of greater humility when engaging conservative discourses, to recognize the strength of their strategies and to criticize our own defensive habits of response. The rush to fact-checking is a comfort when we do not want to engage our opponents on matters of value and substance, when we do not want to risk the security of our own points of view. In the political arena, patience and generosity are not always the appropriate moves, but in scholarship and criticism we can and should take the risk of engagement.

CONCLUSION: FRAME-CHECKING AS PERSPECTIVE AND METHOD

In the introduction to this book, I discussed the problem of power in the constitution of what counts as truth in our society. As rhetorician Ronald Walter Greene has noted, governance today is less about deception than it is about having control over what is "in the true."[38] In other words, to control the rhetorical framing of belief is to control "realization," the capacity to determine what appears in a given situation as truth. This framing process will always trump simple debunking efforts.

At the same time, I am arguing in this book that we cannot do without accountability standards completely. Rhetorical theorists have long concerned themselves with the relationship between rhetoric, or the strategic craft of public, symbolic influence widely understood, and knowledge. Robert L. Scott notably announced that "rhetoric is epistemic," by which he meant that the rhetorical enterprise, understanding the transmission of knowledge, always involves interpretation and strategy (and hence, is not a matter of simple transmission).[39] Falling short of Greene's claim that what we consider to be truth can only be what is "in the true," Scott's position resonates with my project of understanding how divergent social groups' knowledge becomes, through rhetorical practice, common sense.

Without the capacity to assess some fidelity between what is in the true and what people struggling to present their truths experience, critique is impossible. However, acknowledging the contingency, complexity, and necessary mediation of belief does not necessitate refraining from evaluation of the truth claims of competing interests in society. My analysis of fact-checking controversies demonstrates how frame-checking is an alternative method of capturing how contending truth claims may be taken on at various *staseis* from conjecture through policy, with especial emphasis on *quality* or value. Goffman advocates the method of "re-keying" or shifting the register of analysis of an interaction or controversy. The *stasis* system is one tool for critical "re-keying."

In addition, I have argued that we may recognize the rhetorical strategies of such conservative discourses as antiabortion videos—narrative and imagistic realism, affective appeal, embodiment, and spectacle—without condemning them and thereby limiting ourselves to nitpicking and debunking. This awareness then leads to the possibility of rethinking *invention*—the crafting of persuasive frames for alternative truths more faithful to women's experience (as well as those of other oppressed groups) that can meet the discourse of quality on one side with a careful rhetoric of quality on the other.

Fact-checking is a process that denies its own rhetoricity. That is to say, the practice itself is a rhetorical frame. Its practitioners believe that most falsehoods are of the first, most simple type, and that in correcting errors they are providing the public with "correct" facts. This assumption and the public's acceptance of it are profoundly ideological: The implicit claims are that redressing power imbalance is a matter of fact-finding and that watchdog journalism can hold politicians accountable by comparing their claims to discernible facts. However, the investigation of facts rarely moves toward awareness of how knowledge functions in the service of power or how the bigger issue might be a lack of imagination with regard to what can be known and done. The *fact* of fact-checking actually prevents the expansion of critical thinking by implying there is nothing beyond "just the facts." Fact-checking is palliative, on Elster's terms. It is comforting to think that there are meaningful checks on the truthfulness of politicians. In this way, fact-checking is itself an example of ideological control. It is well intentioned, but in a very real sense, it lies.

I have argued that fact-checking is an ideological distraction that prevents ordinary people from assessing the claims that guide perception and action—from understanding "truth" as something more complex than "facts." To say that fact-checking "lies" is to note how it operates as a set of claims not in the interests of ordinary people trying to interpret and explain the world. For this reason, I give fact-checking a "Pants on Fire!"

CHAPTER 4

Framing Whistleblowers—Secret Agents and Queer Failure

A 2013 news story from National Public Radio (NPR) attempted to make sense of U.S. Army whistleblower Chelsea (formerly Bradley) Manning and her release of more than 700,000 classified documents to WikiLeaks: "Bradley Manning Had Long Been Plagued by Mental Health Issues."[1] The NPR story relies on biographer Steve Fishman's 2011 essay, "Bradley Manning's Army of One."[2] The story begins with host/anchor Melissa Block asking Fishman to provide background to the Manning case. Fishman responds,

> He grew up, in many ways, on his own: child of a divorced family, kind of kicked out of one home, departed another, then kicked out a second time from the first home, a kid who lived in his car, lonely. He was a gay man who had trouble growing up in Oklahoma being accepted, and then really a series of events leading to the Army where he didn't find a home either. He's 5'2" tall, 105 pounds, and wasn't really ever accepted by the warrior contingent he found himself among.

In just a few sentences, this statement frames Manning as a troubled, queer, feminine person whose personal difficulties, not moral outrage or political goals, motivated her disclosures. She is depicted as an outsider to masculine military culture and traditional familial norms. While NPR and many other media outlets leveraged this frame in their coverage, they do not condemn outright Manning's actions. The "troubled queer" frame, to the contrary, seems to exonerate her from prosecution, at least symbolically. Being positioned as a queer whistleblower discredits her actions while excusing them, but in terms that further invalidate Manning and her voice.

In contrast, Edward Snowden, who, in 2013, released thousands of documents exposing the National Security Agency for its widespread bulk collection of the private communications of U.S. citizens and those abroad, was treated more seriously, although he continues to live in exile to escape prosecution. His leaks provoked a public domestic and international outcry, and his story became one of international intrigue and heroism.

Both agents sought to disclose disturbing truths about the power and actions of the U.S. state; they were both motivated to speak truth to power. However, they met with entirely different consequences. What explains these differences in treatment and outcome?

One part of the answer lies in how each character was mediated and motivated by strategies among the "big five," especially those of narrative, myth, affect, and embodiment. While Snowden's story is cast in the mythic narrative of the masculine agent, Manning's queer body denies her access to those dominant and accrediting frames. The mobilization of affect on her behalf was double-edged: The more she became a pitiable prisoner of the state and oppressive gender roles, the less agentive she appeared to be.

In addition, I argue that differences in journalistic mediation and framing were key to determining Snowden's success and Manning's failure. Manning more or less dumped her hundreds of thousands of facts with WikiLeaks without making meaning or order of them (without directly engaging the "big five"), whereas Snowden sought the mediation of reporters Glenn Greenwald and Laura Poitras, who revealed the information about NSA leaks to a mass audience after a process of interpretation and framing of the facts that Snowden brought to the table. Edward Snowden was cast in the role of a mythic hero against the tyrannical state, while Manning did not have recourse to a narrative in which she could enact this masculine agentive role.

Moreover, in Manning's case, the truths about the U.S. war in Afghanistan emerged alongside her personal disclosure of a shifting gender identity. As Bradley Manning became Chelsea Manning, personal and political disclosures became intermixed. Without the adequate provision of political meaning frames for the released documents, her evolving gender identity became their frame; in other words, the act of whistleblowing was framed as a function of queer disorder. The troubled embodiment of gender scripts posed a rhetorical problem for Chelsea Manning.

Paradoxically, that frame did not make an exculpatory difference when it came to trial and sentencing. President Obama commuted Chelsea Manning's sentence and thankfully, after seven years, she is free. However, the time she served in prison was torturous, and even foreshortened, it was unprecedented for a whistleblower. Snowden's character, on the other hand, was cast as that of a smart, professional, white, heterosexual man (with a girlfriend! as coverage obsessively reminded us), deploying what I have come to call the "straight, normal, middle-class white guy" frame. Greenwald and his colleagues also depicted Snowden as a savvy secret agent pitted against an overweening surveillance state, unjustly sentenced to exile. The difference in framing is ideological and points to the price of successful mediation: complicity with broader norms of intelligibility regarding race, class, gender, and sexuality. The price of refusing (or being unable) to fit those categories is unsuccessful mediation and its consequences: oppression, stigmatization, and incarceration.

I proceed in this chapter by drawing out the key frames that capture the differences between the mediation of the disclosures of these two figures. First, the framing of Manning and Snowden differentially exhibit a "public/private" frame, in which Manning's queerness dislocated the political import of her revelations into the realm of personal experience. For Snowden, in contrast, the revelation of details about his private life affirmed his credibility as an agent speaking truth to power, thus locating the conversation about NSA spying in a political rather than personal domain. While Snowden discussed his worry that attention on himself as a person would distract from the impact of the news about NSA spying, the dramatic coverage of his life on the run, chronicled in a book by Glenn Greenwald, drew in readers and provoked engagement with the political matters at hand.

Second, the coverage of these figures and their tribulations diverge in an agent/victim frame. Whereas Snowden is represented as a spy-like fugitive dodging capture to reveal U.S. violations of citizens' civil rights, Manning is consistently portrayed, even in coverage favorable to her, as a victim of her upbringing and merciless captors. A frame related to the agent/victim pairing is that of the criminal/traitor. Although both terms connote wrongdoing, descriptions of Snowden as a traitor enabled a defense of him as a patriot. When Manning is painted as a criminal, the opposite term is *innocent,* which does not carry the agentive meaning of *patriot.* While one can defend Snowden as a fugitive hero, Manning is trapped in a frame that renders her vulnerable in any case: either as someone rightly facing punishment or as someone victimized by the military court and her jailers.

The agent/victim frame is also closely connected to the hero/traitor frame, in which Snowden is cast, as in most coverage, as a hero, whereas Manning was successfully prosecuted as a traitor to both the state and to gender norms. As I noted above, a divergently gendered framing of Manning and Snowden contributed to their reception. In contrast to the careful construction of Snowden as a "straight, normal white guy" across news coverage of his exploits, Manning's queerness is figured in coverage as always having tainted her childhood. Queerness is an essence in this narrative, one that taints her revelations and renders them as personally motivated. In addition, the emergence of a new gender identity for Chelsea Manning occurs alongside the disclosures of U.S. wrongdoing in the wars in Iraq and Afghanistan.

The queerness "sticks" to the political revelations, impairing their credibility with audiences ignorant of or closed off to the experience of transgender persons. The image of Manning as distorted implies that her knowledge and motives are also warped. These differences in coverage reveal the operation of a "queer/normal" frame. I turn now to a discussion of my selection of texts for analysis before detailing the framing work done by them.

NEWS NARRATIVES AND MEDIA FRAMING

I base my argument here on the analysis of books, films, and articles that have a biographical dimension; in other words, beyond relaying basic information, they tell a story about the sources of that information: Manning and Snowden. In addition to book-length biographies and documentary and fictionalized dramatic films featuring each whistleblower, I gathered relevant news articles by searching major newspapers for stories featuring narrative coverage in addition to a provision of basic information. My main sources are the *New York Times, Washington Post,* and *Guardian.* The *Post* and the *Guardian* are selected because they were the original outlets for Manning's and Snowden's revelations, respectively.

After gathering these stories, I examined them closely to discover frames operating in the narratives. As I have argued in other work, biographical narratives invite reader identification with protagonists whose lives resonate with readers and viewers. Biographical narratives are also profoundly ideological insofar as they feature characters whose fate is governed by dominant values.[3] When Manning is convicted and imprisoned, her queerness is associated with criminality and punishment. When Snowden hides out in a Hong Kong hotel room to share his knowledge with reporters, his revelations are characterized as clandestine truths shared under conditions of duress and danger. Thus, frames do not only make meaning of information; they also serve as forms of social and political discipline, reinforcing dominant ideas about war, national security, and masculinity.

The book-length works that narrate Manning's experiences include *The United States vs. Pvt. Chelsea Manning*, a graphic (cartoon) telling of the courtroom proceedings during which Manning was convicted, by Clark Stoeckley; *The Passion of Bradley Manning: The Story Behind the Wikileaks Whistleblower*, by Chase Madar; *Private: Bradley Manning, WikiLeaks, and the Biggest Exposure of Official Secrets in American History*, by Denver Nicks; and *Truth and Consequences: The U. S. vs. Private Manning*, by Kevin Gosztola. In addition to the books, the Manning story appeared in documentary form twice on PBS's *Nightline*: "The Private Life of Bradley Manning" and "Wikisecrets" (both in 2011).

Snowden's efforts have garnered wider circulation in the book *No Place to Hide: Edward Snowden, the NSA, and the U. S. Surveillance State*, by Glenn Greenwald (2014); *The Snowden Operation: Inside the West's Greatest Intelligence Disaster*, by Edward Lucas (2014); *The Snowden Files*, by Luke Harding (2014), who, like Glenn Greenwald, writes for the *Guardian*; and *Dark Mirror: Snowden and the American Surveillance State*, by Barton Gellman (forthcoming in 2017). In addition, there is a Snowden reader containing a "Complete, Concise Guide" to Edward Snowden; *Snowden*, by Ted Rall (2015); and a book by Snowden himself, *Everything You Know about the Constitution Is Wrong* (2013). In addition, the documentary film by Laura Poitras, *Citizenfour*, and the dramatized feature film *Snowden*, by Oliver Stone (2016), (which bears the subtitle *The Only Safe Place Is on the Run*) circulated Snowden's story widely with mass audiences.[4]

The titles suggest the differences in framing that I will unpack below. *The Passion of Bradley Manning* both ties his persona to that of a Christlike martyr and invokes the erotic resonance of the word *passion*, signaling an emphasis on Manning's gender identity and sexual orientation. To call another book *Private* likewise locates Manning's story in private rather than political life, with the pun on her former Army rank. The books and films about Snowden, in contrast, feature a political emphasis on the U.S. surveillance state, intelligence, and the Constitution. The narratives feature Snowden "on the run." The blurb for the book *Snowden* reads, "*Snowden* is a portrait of a brave young man standing up to the most powerful government in the world."

In addition to books and movies, I gathered and examined the framing strategies of hundreds of news articles largely from the *Guardian*, but also from the *Washington Post* and the *New York Times*, focusing on stories that included a narrative about the characters of Snowden and Manning.

THE IMPORTANCE OF MEDIATION AND
MEDIA(TION) FRAMES

Readers will recall the particular definition of *mediation* I laid out in the introduction to this book: Mediation does not only refer to the technologies of *mass* mediation of information. It refers to any process of interpretation or alteration that happens *between* some baseline knowledge and its public uptake. For example, when a teacher, community organizer, expert, friend, family member, or reporter interprets or explains some feature of reality—a scientific observation, personal experience, the workings of a machine, and so on—she is engaged in the process of mediation. In a society dominated by commercial mass media and social media, this process often cultivates normative and oppressive ideas. However, the importance of naming mediation as a more general process is that no idea, image, or "fact" can be transmitted unchanged through media technology to audiences. The mere existence of the technology is not what makes mediation important. It is the interpretive work of human beings that does the mediating of experience so that it can become understood in common sense.

Thus, when Todd Gitlin in his important work *The Whole World Is Watching* defines media frames, he is not talking about the fact that we receive information about movements for social change from technologies like television, film, radio, and now computer-based media. A media frame is a set of principles of selection, omission, and emphasis that shape an audience's perception of events. Reporters, Gitlin observed, engage in such habits as covering over protesters' own voices with their own in voice-over, undercounting participants in public demonstrations, focusing on the most extreme or discreditable representatives of any group or movement, and so on.[5] But it is not the media technologies (of television, magazine, or newspaper) that are making those choices. The people describing events are making the rhetorical or persuasive choices that end up shaping audience perception, whether they are conscious of this process or not. Knowledge and experience cannot be transmitted from one setting or one person's experience to another's without this process of mediation, in which someone is making choices about what to emphasize, include, or omit.

For this reason, I would rather call what Gitlin names "media frames," "mediation frames," to emphasize the rhetorical agency that intervenes between raw experience and the meanings we attribute to it. With regard to Snowden and Manning, how reporters and filmmakers made decisions to emphasize either the public or the private dimensions of their contributions, their status either as agents or as victims, and their traits as either "normal" or "queer" made a great deal of difference in how their "facts" were received.

Reporters often commented on their own processes of mediation in the context of debates and conflicts over which news outlet did a responsible job of covering the leaks. For example, a *Guardian* headline noted, "Edward Snowden's Leaks Cause Editorial Split at the Washington Post."[6] The *Post's* editorial board wanted to constrain the release of information in case it might harm intelligence operations vital to U.S. interests. In another example, all of the books about Snowden's exploits focus heavily on the drama of his contacting *Guardian* reporter Glenn Greenwald and documentary filmmaker Laura Poitras with obsessive detail about secret meetings, the sharing of encryption software, and the rules of engagement. Snowden and the reporters negotiated over when, how, and what kind of information would be published.[7] Greenwald, in both articles and in his book about the experience, often criticizes other outlets and editors for their lack of courage and failure to embrace the watchdog role of the press. Snowden said that he thought the mainstream media could not be trusted.[8]

Greenwald's book-length account of the Snowden leaks, *No Place to Hide*, features a telling conversation in this regard. Greenwald notes that it was important for Snowden to publish the documents "journalistically,"

> working with the media and writing articles that provided the context for the materials, rather than just publishing them in bulk. That approach, he believed, would provide more legal protection, and, more important, would allow the public to process the revelations in a more orderly and rational way. "If I wanted the documents just put on the Internet en masse, I could have done that myself," he said. "I want you to make sure these stories are done, one by one, so that people can understand what they should know."[9]

In an interview in Greenwald's introductory article in the *Guardian*, Snowden said that "he admires both Ellsberg and Manning, but argues that there is one important distinction between himself and the army private." The article quotes Snowden: "I carefully evaluated every single document I disclosed to ensure that each was legitimately in the public interest." "He purposely chose, he said, to give the documents to journalists whose judgment he trusted about what should be public and what should remain concealed."[10]

Snowden and others expressed criticism of Manning for releasing facts "en masse" without journalistic mediation that would help people understand "what they should know" to WikiLeaks. Snowden tweeted that WikiLeaks's "hostility to even modest curation" was misguided.[11] *Curation,* here, is another word for *mediation.* However, Manning did attempt to get the attention of major news publishers but was not taken seriously. The reasons for that neglect will be addressed later in this chapter. Now I turn to an examination of how journalists mediated the information provided by Snowden, packaged alongside a narrative of his character and adventures that made the information more compelling and credible.

FRAMING EDWARD SNOWDEN

Public and Private

Coverage of Edward Snowden throughout his disclosures and life on the run focuses on his public, political persona and his political actions. He is frequently quoted as saying, "I don't want this to be about me," modestly deflecting attention from his character. At the same time, he knows that for the sake of effective mediation, he must identify himself and become part of the story. In *No Place to Hide,* Snowden comments, "I want to spark a worldwide debate about privacy, Internet freedom, and the dangers of state surveillance. . . . I want to identify myself as the person behind these disclosures. I believe I have an obligation to explain why I'm doing this and what I hope to achieve."[12] This contradiction appears elsewhere, indicating both sophistication with regard to the rhetoric of self-presentation and awareness of conventional media framing that makes news all about the personalities of individuals. For example, Greenwald notes in his book,

> Snowden's only fear about outing himself was that he would distract from the substance of his revelations. "I know the media personalizes everything, and the government will want to make me the story, to attack the messenger," he said. His plan was to identify himself early on, and then disappear from view to allow the focus to remain fixed on the NSA and its spying activities.[13]

Largely, mainstream coverage did not pry into Snowden's private life or attempt to explain his actions as functions of a dysfunctional personal life. There is some attention paid to his girlfriend, a feature of the discourse that I will explain below, and his father, who visited him in Russia. He expressed concern that his family and friends could be targeted, saying in one interview, "My family does not know what is happening. . . . My primary fear is that they will come after my family, my friends, my partner. Anyone I have a relationship with. I'll have to live with that for the rest of my life."[14] However, these revelations are few, as the majority of the news coverage focuses on the content of the leaks and the principle of the protection of privacy, both concerns in the public interest.[15]

A key moment in deliberations about whether to return to the United States was the question of whether Snowden would have recourse to a "public interest defense," in which he could justify the release of confidential government information during any legal proceeding.[16] In addition to focusing on this question, coverage across the mainstream media noted Snowden's public role, as nominee for Glasgow University Rector[17] and as *Guardian* person of the year.[18] He won a human rights award in Sweden. He received numerous offers of asylum from what Bolivia's and other governments called "the empire," and a movement developed in his defense. From exile, and amid ongoing calls for extradition, he has continued to comment on the politics of surveillance and related legislation in the United States and Europe. His revelations sparked inquiry across the globe about the U.S. spying efforts. He was honored with both a bust in a Brooklyn park and a hologram.[19]

In 2016, alongside the release of Oliver Stone's film *Snowden*, politicians including Bernie Sanders, whistleblowers including Daniel Ellsberg, celebrities including Susan Sarandon, and activists leading the Black Lives Matter movement wrote publicly in support of his being pardoned, saying, "Edward Snowden did this country a great service. Let him come home."[20] Malkia Cyril, the executive director of the Center for Media Justice, explained the impact of Snowden's revelations to the Black Lives Matter movement in terms of the constant state surveillance of black Americans and the role model for telling the truth.[21] In all of these stories, Snowden's personal life is out of sight as reporters and others focused on how his public acts have been consequential.

What little we do find out across the board about his personal life can be summed up as follows: A sickly child born in North Carolina whose parents eventually divorced, Snowden did not finish high school but instead completed his GED. He grew up mostly in the shadow of NSA headquarters in the DC-Maryland suburbs. He had an attractive girlfriend who was a pole dancer. After a failed attempt to enter the armed services, he then took up a number of increasingly high-level positions in the NSA and CIA, working undercover overseas and in the United States. As a contractor for the NSA in Hawaii, he began collecting documents exposing the extensive domestic and foreign U.S. surveillance apparatus. He disappeared to Hong Kong, where he met with *Guardian* journalists to deliver the documents and have them curated for the public. With the aid of the WikiLeaks organization, he fled Hong Kong, escaping extradition to the United States. Since then, he has been living in exile in Russia.[22]

On the whole, the *Guardian* carefully crafted a persona for Snowden as intriguing, enigmatic, and courageous. In this mythic narrative, these traits are connected without fail to his political motives and actions while giving readers a personal hook into his story. Importantly, Snowden's actions matched his persona insofar as his purpose, as framed, was to expose the unwarranted public encroachment into the private lives and communications of the U.S. people and foreign leaders. In other words, he is positioned as the protector of privacy and the denier of political access to his and others' personal worlds—the ultimate heroic role of a public figure. In spy literature, heroes often appear without a backstory or stable personal life, which ironically makes them more compelling as objects of identification; casting Snowden in this role both backgrounded his personal life *and* made for an exciting narrative with an identifiable hero. The narrative of international intrigue is closely tied to how Snowden is represented as a competent political agent.

Agent/Victim

In these narratives of intrigue, Snowden is continually active, "on the run," "on the move," busy with work on his computer, reading, or writing. Coverage frequently allows him to provide narrative for his actions in his own words, in the first person: "I did this; I did that." Most importantly, he explains his decision to disclose NSA secrets and the actions he took as self-consciously and rationally motivated. As he and reporters tell it, he was completely in control of what was leaked, to whom it was leaked, and how and when news of his actions appeared in public.

Ted Rall's graphic account *Snowden* lionizes the public contributions made by Snowden: "Thanks to a young man named Edward Snowden, we know that the U.S. government spent hundreds of billions of our tax dollars to build the most sophisticated, wide-ranging, and intrusive surveillance apparatus ever conceived . . . to watch us."[23] Later, Rall adds, "What Snowden saw at the CIA alarmed him. If Americans learned the truth, they'd protest. But they didn't know."[24]

Rall and others craft and amplify a persona for Snowden of leader and noble public servant: "Snowden thought, 'Someone's got to tell the truth.'"[25] "Disgusted, Snowden took matters into his own hands."[26] "We know these things because Edward Snowden told us."[27] "Snowden is unique: In an organization that selects for unthinking conformists, he searched for the truth and followed it to an ideological awakening. Only Snowden could blow the whistle on the NSA."[28]

With slightly more subtlety, *Guardian* accounts also underscore Snowden's uniquely courageous leadership. The publication's introduction to "Snowden: The Whistleblower Behind the NSA Leaks" stated, "Snowden will go down in history as one of America's most consequential whistleblowers."[29] In the piece, Snowden comments, "You can't wait around for someone else to act. I had been looking for leaders, but realized that leadership is about being the first to act."[30] Highlighting Snowden's persona as courageous, the article quotes him as saying, "I'm not afraid because this is a choice I've made." While Snowden may face persecution and prosecution, the emphasis is on his capacity to choose—to have agency in determining his fate.

The clearest indicator of agency is when one's actions are consequential. Although major reform of the U.S. surveillance apparatus has not occurred, widespread coverage highlighted the extent to which Snowden's revelations did catalyze some reforms and generate widespread public unease. In the United States, a federal appeals court determined that the NSA bulk collection programs were illegal, and the collection authority expired in 2015.[31] European, Asian, and Latin American leaders raised questions and criticisms after discovering that the United States had used its bulk collections methods on their governments and populations. The intervention by reporters—their efforts at mediation—was active in selecting which pieces of news to report, which items to emphasize, and which details to leave in the background.

One piece of information troubling this agentive narrative, clearly, is that Snowden has been condemned to exile lest he face the kind of prosecution that put Manning in prison on a thirty-five-year sentence. Two framing strategies counter this potential contradiction. The first is to report that Snowden is not languishing. For example, the *Guardian* reported in May 2016 on a conversation in which Snowden claimed, "I'm actually more fulfilled now, more connected now, and more effective now in my work."[32] The second countervailing thematic note is the interpretation of exile as a piece of a dramatic narrative in which Snowden is an enigmatic but supremely competent spy.

Our Man in Moscow: The Most Wanted Man in the World

Ironically, reporters establishing the secret agent narrative frequently begin by telling readers how much Edward Snowden is *not* like a spy. The point of this framing, however, is to say, "You won't believe it, but he's a spy"—or enough like a spy to capture public imagination. Another irony in this characterization is that Snowden's stated purpose is to discredit spying. For these reasons, coverage invoking the spy drama must also assuage any anxiety that Snowden is like the leaders of the agencies he indicts. For example, in one of the first articles introducing Snowden to the world, the *Guardian*'s editorial board writes,

> Edward Snowden is a very modern spy—neither gun-blazingly dashing nor cat-strokingly sinister. He is young, tech-savvy, quietly articulate, and intensely interested in human rights. His work did not involve high speed car chases or elaborate gadgets, just a desk and a computer. Using these simple tools he could spy on anyone, anywhere. . . . He has stepped out of the shadows and revealed himself to be the source of the *Guardian*'s string of recent disclosures.[33]

He is, the article goes on to say, "the most wanted man in the world."

With that mythic fanfare, readers are introduced to the shy, geeky kid who is able to take down the world's most powerful security establishment. Dozens of times in the press, Snowden's activities are called "exploits," "trials," or a "saga," which is another word for *myth*. Details selected for inclusion enhance a sense of drama. Snowden first contacted Greenwald using the code names "Verax" (*truth*) and "Cincinnatus," after a conservative Roman statesman who epitomized manliness and civic virtue.[34] Greenwald and his team in both articles and in the book *No Place to Hide* tell readers that they met Snowden in a room in the hotel where there was nothing besides a bench and a large statue of an alligator. The detail is cinematic in its visual clarity and its very strangeness. Snowden would approach holding a Rubik's Cube—simultaneously geeky and pretentious, with the added connotation of intelligence. They were to exchange passcodes before proceeding to a room where people's phones were placed in the freezer and where Snowden used the computer only under a hood that prevented ostensible cameras from seeing his passwords. Snowden placed rolled towels under the door in case of eavesdroppers. Everybody jumped and Snowden made a nervous joke when the fire alarm in the hotel went off unexpectedly.

For the sake of clarifying the importance of framing, I could rewrite the sequence like this: We met Ed in the hotel lobby. He was holding a Rubik's Cube. That's pretentious, I thought. We went up to his room, where he took precautions to avoid any efforts to listen in. It was annoying when that fire alarm went off.

Now, it is likely "true" that Snowden did plan the details like the alligator, the freezer, the hood, the passcode, and so on—which shows that he was effective at *self*-framing. But writers and filmmakers have choices as to which details to include and emphasize. In this case, details that enhance drama and the sense that Snowden is special and especially significant are key to the frame.

Furthermore, additional details of this kind abound to catch readers up in the drama and repeatedly establish Snowden's security credentials. Here are a few examples: "He was very concerned that we would be followed by local intelligence agents. Assuming he had some deep involvement with US spying agencies and knew what he was talking about, I deferred to his judgment." "Snowden said that they should pick him up and bring him to a safe place. It was, he said, 'time to enter the part of the plan where I ask the world for protection and justice. But I need to get out of the hotel without being recognized. . . . I'm in the process of taking steps to change my appearance.'"[35] This story builds suspense and involves readers in wondering whether he will pull off his escape. The narrative takes on mythic dimensions in casting Snowden as a heroic agent confronting a villainous state. Critics of Snowden had trouble in reversing the hero/villain poles of the argument despite attempts to persuade the public that Snowden was a traitor.

On the second day after the revelations broke, an article in the *Guardian* under Ewen MacAskill's byline appeared: "Edward Snowden: NSA Whistleblower, Fugitive, Hero . . . Or Traitor?"[36] The piece is full of passages like this one:

> As he pulled a small black suitcase and carried a selection of laptop bags over his shoulders, no one would have paid much attention to Ed Snowden as he arrived at Hong Kong International Airport just over three weeks ago. But Snowden was not your average tourist or businessman. In all, he was carrying four computers which enabled him to gain access to some of the US government's most highly-classified secrets. Today, just over three weeks later, he is the world's most famous spy, whistleblower and fugitive, responsible for the biggest intelligence breach in recent US history. . . . It is thought he is now in a safe house.

Here the pattern is apparent: He doesn't look like a spy, but he is one, a fugitive no less, staying in a "safe house," a concept Americans would know about from the spy film genre, plugging Snowden's story into the espionage frame more securely.

Describing events as a "saga" of a wanted fugitive who is seeking safety underground, even basic coverage explaining what had happened takes on a tone of hushed reverence and daring.[37] An Associated Press article gives a blow-by-blow account of his movements in the urgent present tense:

May 20: Edward Snowden, 29, arrives in Hong Kong, just after taking leave from his National Security Agency contracting firm Booz Allen Hamilton.... June 9: Snowden, who claims to have worked at the National Security Agency and the CIA, allows himself to be identified as the source of disclosures about the secret U.S. surveillance programs.... June 24: Snowden has a seat booked on an Aeroflot flight bound for Cuba, but is not seen on board.[38]

In the phrases Snowden "claims," "allows himself," and "is not seen," he is an invisible agent who successfully disguises his identity and route. The passage, which is essentially a chronology, implies that there is duplicity at work: Snowden makes claims, which means we don't know whether they are true; he *allows* himself to be named, but this act is remarkable; he makes double plans to confuse his would-be captors.

An article in the *Christian Science Monitor* sums it up neatly:

If the Edward Snowden saga didn't feel enough like a spy flick yet, Senate Intelligence Committee Chairwoman Dianne Feinstein pushed it over the edge when she told CBS's *Face the Nation* that "the chase is on."

The author of this article quotes a professor of sociology: "The story is extremely Hollywood-esque. News is character driven.... Snowden is a very compelling character from a storytelling perspective."[39] Thus, not only does this author invoke the spy thriller narrative, he also comments self-reflexively on the fact that he—and everyone else—is doing so: "Snowden is a compelling character." But the passage implies that it is Snowden himself who is compelling. My argument is that regardless of whether he has any inherent compelling qualities, it is the *framing* that makes it so.

Rall's graphic-novel account similarly plays up the spy thriller motif. He doesn't write that Snowden departed the hotel in a taxi. Instead, he writes, "He got into a taxi and vanished."[40] "During his stay in Kowloon he had been half-expecting a knock on the door at any moment—a raid in which he would be dragged away. He explained: 'I could be rendered by the CIA. I could have people come after me—or any of their third-party partners.'"[41]

Luke Harding likewise ramps up the drama: "Now that Snowden's identity was out, he had just become the most hunted man on the planet. The chase was already on."[42] And more:

The lawyers were soon sucked into Snowden's cloak-and-dagger world. Albert Ho describes a rendezvous. He got into a car one night at an agreed spot and found Snowden inside, wearing a hat and sunglasses. Snowden didn't speak, the lawyer told the *Washington Post*. When they arrived at the home where Snowden was staying he whispered that everyone had to hide their phones in the refrigerator."[43]

Later, the article proclaims, "Snowden had escaped the net and was en route to Moscow. The bastard had got away!"[44]

Critics of Snowden's actions play right into this narrative frame. For example, detractor John Bolton argues that his actions had grave political implications, especially with regard to China, whose government, because of Snowden, could assume a stance of moral equivalence with the United States.[45] Bolton engages in the wishful thinking that Snowden's sympathizers could not "control the story line" or the Snowden "legend" indefinitely. The irony is that his own account of how serious Snowden's crimes were serves only to buttress the legend.

Lucas's *Snowden Operation* likewise enforces the spy narrative by arguing that Snowden is tied to Russian interests. In the chapter "Our Man in Hawaii," Lucas attempts to reveal how improbable Snowden's story is:

> After incomplete formal education, he enlisted in the US Army but left after a few months—having broken his legs in an accident, *he says*. After joining the NSA as a security guard, he moved to Geneva to work for the CIA there, under the cover of an attaché at the American mission to the UN. This is a remarkably successful trajectory. Nobody has yet explained whether he displayed previously hidden talents, had served somewhere else to good effect, or benefited from powerful sponsors.[46]

Elsewhere he adds,

> Snowden's life in Moscow is shrouded with secrecy. He has a job, but nobody knows where. Barring a brief, staged meeting with journalists and activists at the Moscow airport, he sees only his supporters. He has not given a proper press conference or opened himself up to any form of scrutiny. . . . Nobody knows where he lives. None of this inspires confidence in the idea that he is a free agent. It supports the theory that he is a Russian one.[47]

Bolton probably has not reflected on the fact that, in the context of a spy thriller, the *more* improbable a person's credentials and capabilities are, the *more* credible they are. The legend of Snowden as "impossibly" successful does little to challenge the prevailing story; it only puts a reverse valence on it by evaluating the mystery man as a traitor rather than as a hero. Luke Harding, although sympathetic to Snowden and his aims, writes, "It appeared the mystery interlocutor was an experienced spy. Perhaps one with a flair for the dramatic."[48]

Greenwald eventually responds explicitly to the detractors' claims, quoting Snowden: "He predicted he would be portrayed not as a whistleblower but a spy. 'I think they are going to say I have committed grave crimes, I have violated the Espionage Act. They are going to say I have aided our enemies in making them aware of these systems. But this argument can be made against anyone who reveals information that points out mass surveillance systems,' he said."[49]

A year later, *Guardian* reporters Alan Rusbridger and Ewen MacAskill (in an article actually called "I, Spy: He Doesn't Drink, He's Reading Dostoevsky, and, No, He Doesn't Wear a Disguise") ask him directly if he was a spy for Russia. Snowden says, "If you were running for office, you'd be in trouble."[50] This wry nonanswer leaves the question hanging.

There is one moment of mediation in the popular media that challenges Snowden's omnipotence. In an episode of the comedy show *Last Week Tonight*, host and comedian John Oliver conducts "person-on-the-street" interviews showing that many ordinary people had no idea who Edward Snowden was; those who had heard the name thought he had wrongly leaked dangerous information to WikiLeaks, confusing him with Manning. When Oliver shows this footage to Snowden, Snowden appears to be disappointed. The segment proceeds by exploring whether U.S. citizens would be more disturbed if they knew that the NSA could gather pictures of their genitalia, or "dick pics." The people on the street universally express outrage that the government could see "their junk." Snowden confirms that the government could collect citizens' sex texts, but wryly comments that he hadn't thought to frame the revelations in terms of dick pics.

Oliver's segment affords two insights about mediation. The first is that the curation and publication of the leaked information in major news outlets could reach policy-making elites and other members of an intelligentsia class, but that humor, particularly satire, might offer another vehicle for translating complex information to a mass audience. Second, it is helpful to contextualize information about the dangers of surveillance in concrete terms of citizens' personal lives rather than principled abstractions about the defense of privacy.

However, most of the coverage of Snowden's leaks and his process of disclosing them does not spoil the spy-agent narrative. In choosing to live in exile, Snowden appears as an intelligent and careful agent of his own destiny, in distinct contrast to the persona of Chelsea Manning, covered as a victim of torture and solitary imprisonment, a suicide risk, and a person needing to be saved.

The victim persona, as Amanda Davis and I have argued previously, is paradoxical. Assuming the victim stance provides a person the moral high ground, her actions, if in question, can be explained by the context of victimage.[51] However, the persona of victim is not in general credible unless supplemented with a rhetoric of agency and power. With regard to Snowden, the facts of his exile and fear of prosecution are matched with his capacity to cope with and triumph over them. Despite his distance from the United States, his voice reaches thousands of Americans in virtual public lectures, popular books, and major motion pictures.

Finally, Snowden's personal agency is rendered as that of a hero rather than a traitor. The enigmatic, dynamic persona prevents the interrogation of any private insecurities or motives, or even any weaknesses. While President Obama labeled him a traitor, that label has not uniformly influenced general public. U.S. public opinion polls showed mixed reception.[52] A US News and World Report Poll in 2015 showed that even if Snowden faced disparagement at home, leaders and citizens in other countries favored him strongly.[53]

The Straight, "Normal," White-Guy Frame

Closely related to the image of Snowden as a man of international intrigue is the framing of him as a heterosexual, masculine (despite his small stature), white, professional, and rational person. The exception to the tendency to avoid Snowden's personal life is reporters' obsession with his girlfriend, Lindsay. In Oliver Stone's film, she plays a necessary romantic foil for the drama in fictionalized accounts of her disapproval of his embrace of the life of an international spy. That conflict and the representation of her as a beautiful, sexy yoga instructor and pole dancer provide the sexist, but obligatory, sources of appeal for mass audiences. It is important that the most widely known text of Edward Snowden, this film, exaggerates his heterosexual credentials, confirmed in countless repetitions elsewhere of the information he has a girlfriend. His girlfriend got to join him in Russia, the Guardian reported. Another whole story is about her describing how she feels lost at sea, writing a blog called "Adventures of a world-travelling, pole-dancing super hero."[54]

A critic of the film Snowden comments, "Why are we watching Lindsay teaching a class in strip aerobics?"[55] Indeed. But the answer, of course, is that Lindsay's sex appeal is part of the framing device establishing Snowden's normalcy and even manliness. In addition, the near-pornographic imagery grabs the attention of a particular set of viewers.

It's not just at the cinema that this device is working. In one of the first articles from the Guardian, the authors write, "Some details emerged on Monday about Snowden's girlfriend, with whom he shared, 'a very comfortable life' in Hawaii. . . . The TV show Inside Edition identified her as a dancer based in Hawaii. . . . For the public, Snowden's relationship with her may turn out to be one of the more intriguing questions about his backstory. It is not known how long they were together or how they met. . . . The couple lived in a blue house with a neat lawn."⁵⁶ In addition to mentioning the "intriguing" relationship between Snowden and his girlfriend, the passage frames their lives as "normal," complete with a tidy house, a signal of a normal familial life. While he is represented as within U.S. mental health norms, he is also represented as extraordinary and compelling. These characteristics buttress his perceived masculinity, and by extension, credible political agency and voice.

These credentials are significant in the other news coverage but in more subtle ways. The key dimensions of his masculinity are courage and control, traits that appear together across coverage of his experience. For example, a TV interview conducted by NBC's Brian Adams repeats the myth that Snowden was "the most wanted man in the world"; his actions are "cloaked in secrecy" and he is "wanted for espionage."⁵⁷ However, in a subtler way, Snowden's character is revealed as capable, controlled, articulate, and, therefore, masculine. Williams comments, "He came *armed* with talking points" (emphasis added). He introduced himself as "Ed." He was very calm, Williams noted. While claiming he was not a spy, he answers questions about his work experience by amplifying his role in international espionage: "I was trained as a spy, worked undercover overseas pretending to work in false jobs with a fake name." He worked for not only the NSA, but the CIA and the Defense Training Academy. He points out that coverage to date had downplayed his spy credentials, while simultaneously denying spying.

He is also humble, however, in recounting his failed stint in basic special forces training. Although he wants to return to the United States, he feels that it is not appropriate for him to advise the president regarding a pardon. "I wouldn't presume," he comments. Throughout the interview, he focuses on his revelations that the NSA and other agencies can listen in on any person in the world without her knowledge using everyday technology like cell phones. "Chilling," Williams observes. And perhaps the word describes Snowden's persona: "chill" and in control.

The *Guardian* also stressed how "normal" and "authentic" Snowden appeared to be. These labels can only be understood in terms of characterizations of Manning as queer and perhaps motivated by distorted motives. "Normal" is masculine; "authentic" is trustworthy.⁵⁸ In the article introducing Snowden, Greenwald writes,

Asked by reporters to establish his authenticity to ensure he is not some fantasist, he laid bare, without hesitation, his personal details, from his social security number to his CIA ID and his expired diplomatic passport. There is no shiftiness. Ask him about anything in his personal life and he will answer. He is quiet, smart, easy-going, and self-effacing. A master on computers, he seemed happiest when talking about the technical side of surveillance. . . . But he showed intense passion when talking about the value of privacy. . . . His manner was calm and relaxed.

This passage establishes Snowden's earnestness and control: Ask him and he will answer. He is a *master*—note the masculine language here—at computers, in control, if geeky. He is controlled: "calm and relaxed."

Other sources emphasize Snowden's courage, which is also framed as masculine. For example, Peter Bradshaw in the *Guardian* uses very gendered language in describing Poitras's *Citizenfour*: "This documentary is about that very remarkable man," who has "considerable courage," who "risked his neck," and who is unemotional under pressure.[59]

He is the subject of a comic book and a computer game, *Snowden Saga: Escape from Den of Iniquity*.[60]

On June 16, 2013, the *New York Times* described Snowden's actions as reflecting "his own considerable ambition, disguised by his early drifting." He is accomplished, having studied Mandarin and martial arts. That last detail about martial arts makes the sentence mean: He is a geeky scholar who can take you down. The same article describes how he spent his formative years in the "rebellious technogeek counterculture" and has an "anti-authoritarian spirit." The article stresses his preoccupation with politics, his competence, courage, composure, and reasonableness. Putting the final touch on these characterizations is where the article describes Snowden's growing unease and determination to act. Significantly, for the analysis of masculine frames, it quotes him as saying, "I got hardened."[61] A similar portrayal emerges from the *Christian Science Monitor* review of the documentary *Citizenfour*: "Instead of an aging, shadowy operative, we have instead a scrawny 29-year-old who resembles nothing so much as a computer science grad student" who "seems eerily normal and composed," with an account of NSA spying backed up by "extensive corroborating footage."[62]

On an interesting note, in studying the reviews of films, we are examining framings of framings that repeat, amplify, and/or recirculate the guiding narratives of the films. The *New York Times* review of *Snowden* describes "Edward" as a rational, ethical creature—"'responsibility' is one of his favorite words—and the movie takes pains to be reasonable." The author does not write, "This film portrays Snowden as a paragon of responsibility." The review picks up the narrative as if it were original to the news story. And again, the article stresses the heterosexual relationship: "The relationship between Lindsay and Edward is the key to the film [and to the whole story], since it establishes what is at stake for the hero as he faces the conflicting demands of love and duty. It also affirms that he is a nice, normal, humble guy."[63] In this single passage, Snowden's heterosexual credentials are tied to his rationality and ethics. He is responsible—in other words, a "stand-up guy." It is this set of characteristics that makes Snowden, in contrast to Manning, "normal," code for recognizably masculine. In sum, rather than the decisions of a person driven by personal troubles, Snowden's actions appear as the careful political disclosures of a person whose agency rivals that of international spies, complete with an enigmatic personal life and the savvy negotiation of a life of rebellion against authority.

The framing of Chelsea Manning, whose military disclosures might have been more damning of U.S. foreign policy than Snowden's exposure of the NSA, is a funhouse mirror opposite of the representation in journalistic and popular media of Snowden, with few exceptions. As Marc Tracy put it in the *New Republic,*

> To anyone who knows the first thing about Manning and who read Glenn Greenwald's profile of Snowden yesterday, the differences between the two young men are as obvious as the resonances. Manning had been, according to all accounts, deeply unhappy (among other reasons, he was a gay man in the Don't Ask, Don't Tell military) and shy, and had suffered significant setbacks in his career; Snowden appears eloquent and poised, and had been living with his girlfriend making $200,000 a year while doing, according to him, not all that much work as an NSA contractor at Booz Allen Hamilton. Manning leaked to a guerilla outfit run by a pretty obvious megalomaniac, Julian Assange; Snowden leaked to a Constitutional lawyer turned award-winning journalist at *The Guardian,* which, for all its right-wing critics, is an esteemed, nearly 200-year-old newspaper, as well as to *The Washington Post's* Barton Gellman, who has won two Pulitzer Prizes.
>
> Most conspicuously, Manning appears not to have discriminated in deciding what to leak, and chose an outlet that was unlikely to discriminate, either. By contrast, Snowden claims he deliberately *didn't* leak everything he could have gotten his hands on, and even explicitly contrasted this restraint with Manning.[64]

This passage captures nearly every frame that shaped public opinion of Manning: In contrast to Snowden, she is mentally troubled, unsuccessful, impulsive, and irresponsible. She also did not fit the frame of heroic masculinity.

FRAMING CHELSEA MANNING

The Public Private

If Edward Snowden appeared in the press and in fiction film as the hero without a country, a rational, political, and "normal" man protecting the people's privacy, Chelsea Manning was the warped version of a government whistleblower: defined by her private struggles, suffering physically and mentally, victimized and abused, and, above all else, *queer*. As a number of queer theorists have argued, to be queer is to trouble the categories of public and private; political struggle has centered on winning the private rights (such as sexual freedom and marriage) of LGBTQ* persons, or on forming intimate enclaves of survival and cultural expression. Queering public life opens up the visibility of personal, intimate matters of sex, gender, and transformation. When the queer subject intentionally deploys this process, it can be a source of strength and affirmation. However, when the broader society at large pries open the personal history and spotlights the struggles of a queer person, the effect is disciplining. For Manning, there could never have been a public, political persona; she did not possess the prerogative to declare her personal life out of bounds for public scrutiny.

The story of her leaks is intensely personalized across most of the journalistic coverage, books, and documentaries. Unlike the portrayal of Snowden as a superhero in narratives emphasizing reason, control, and intelligence, Manning's actions were commemorated in an opera: the vehicle for drama and emotion. Composer Ted Hearne said, "It's a portrait of somebody in great emotional turmoil."[65]

There is disturbingly little attention to the leaked documents themselves, although the *New York Times* and *Guardian* attempted to publish some of the most concerning tidbits in the war logs. The most widely circulated piece of information was the video that came to be known as "Collateral Murder," which shows soldiers in an Apache helicopter strafing civilians and journalists, including a child, with apparent abandon and disregard for civilian life. It is important to understand how the personalization of Manning's character and actions in the media diminished the impact of these and other revelations.

Those who tell the Manning story most frequently begin with her discovery of her homosexuality and then of her emerging gender identity. Her conversation with the man who ultimately would betray her, hacker Adrian Lamo, was undertaken by anonymous text, in which Manning shared plentiful details of her life and bragged about her access to confidential documents about the wars in Afghanistan and Iraq. From the start, the two narratives—the emergent queer identity and the revelation of state secrets—proceeded together, destabilizing any boundary between public and private.

This dual disclosure enabled media producers to engage in what I have elsewhere theorized as *therapeutic rhetoric*, or the transforming of social problems that are most properly understood as political, collective, and structural into personal problems.[66] While the Manning narratives evoked an emotional response, they did so in a depoliticizing way. Therapeutic framing explains crisis or disruption in terms of the personal psychopathology of individuals. Chelsea Manning's treatment in the press is a textbook case.

Most narratives begin her story in a family that started out more or less idyllic but that was thrown into crisis by substance abuse and divorce. Manning appears as a "precocious" and bright youth with delusions of superiority and grandeur in the telling. Joining the army as a way toward an education, Manning found herself at odds with the hypermasculine military culture and acted out violently against other soldiers, including a lesbian sergeant. The narrative describes how she retreated into the computer, hacking massive databases of war logs. When she opens up to Lamo, her desire to leak information is understood to be a function of her psychological troubles. That she decided to use WikiLeaks and Julian Assange as vehicles meant her association with "perversion"—enacted in Assange's history of alleged sexual assaults—was further cemented.

The *New York Times* introduced the public to Manning as follows:

> He spent part of his childhood with his father in the arid plains of central Oklahoma, where classmates made fun of him for being a geek. He spent another part with his mother in a small, remote corner of southwest Wales, where classmates made fun of him for being gay.[67]

The article goes on to discuss how his "desperation for acceptance—or delusions of grandeur—may have led him to disclose the largest trove of government secrets since the Pentagon Papers." Interviews with neighbors and schoolmates reveal that he was strange and thought to be gay. He was bullied. He often became uncontrollably angry. As the *Washington Post* similarly noted, Manning was "odd," "unstable," and "troubled."[68]

Another aspect of this explanation of her as troubled and out of control psychologically was the accusation that she disclosed information in a reckless and uncontrolled way. Although she has asserted that she did attempt to sift information in order to protect any vulnerable soldiers, diplomats, or spies—and despite the fact that no one has been harmed by the disclosures—the controlling narrative portrayed her as out of control along the various axes of her life and actions. In this way, her victim status did her no good in the public eye, because it generated the idea that someone out of control personally cannot take public action in a measured or rational way.

Agent/Victim

Across the news coverage, there is some acknowledgment that Manning's goals were to share information, educate the public, and inspire action. She is repeatedly quoted as saying to Adrian Lamo, the chat partner who eventually disclosed her actions, "It's important that the information gets out. If it gets out, it might actually change something." She especially wanted U.S. citizens to see the "Collateral Murder" video.[69] In an opinion essay published by the *Guardian*, Manning herself wrote from behind bars,

> When I chose to disclose classified information in 2010, I did so out of a love for my country and sense of duty to others. . . . The concerns that motivated me have not been resolved. As Iraq erupts in civil war and America again contemplates intervention, that unfinished business should give new urgency to the question of how the United States military controlled the media coverage of its long involvement there and in Afghanistan.[70]

The essay goes on to describe the contrast between media reports of a successful Iraqi election and Manning's military experience and knowledge of how corrupt those elections were. She mounts an extensive critique of the embedded reporter program as a form of control over reporting. She expresses the opening up of information to the public as her motive. In a later column, she advises the United States on how to engage ISIS more effectively through neglect rather than airstrikes.

Further engaging the public, Manning joined Twitter from behind bars. Moreover, she wrote a bill to protest journalists and curtail the use of the Espionage Act.[71] In a contrasting move to earlier reporting, Edward Snowden sent birthday greetings to Manning in 2014, with a message congratulating her for inspiring the public.[72] Across the publications I have examined, there is partial recognition that her actions had consequences and that she had acted as a political agent. The *New York Times* published the Iraq and Afghanistan war logs, breaking them down into revelations about private contracting, the effects of the "surge" in Iraq, civilian deaths, abuse of prisoners, the little-known role of Iran's military, and so on.[73]

There are other accounts featuring Manning's political agency. A story in the *Washington Post* took stock of her leaks, quoting experts who affirm the public service performed by the "Collateral Murder" video.[74] An earlier *Post* story calls Manning "a baby-faced tech savant," but also begins with her statement of motive: "He just wanted people to 'see the truth,' to prompt 'worldwide discussion, debates, and reforms' over foreign policy."[75] Arguing that Manning's actions were in the *public* interest, the *Post* also argued that the government should give Manning a plea deal.[76] This sort of reporting on her political voice and public agency provides a counter-frame to the dominant ones positioning Manning as disturbed. The video "Collateral Murder" has been viewed millions of times.

Even so, the most common answer to the question, "What motivated Manning?" is that the soldier was "troubled." When a person's actions are posited as effects of mental disturbance or an unhealthy scene, her capacity for self-conscious agency is minimized. Manning was denied the right to make a "public interest," whistleblower defense, a tactic that depoliticized her disclosures. The most sympathetic coverage of Manning portrays her as a perpetual victim whose gender identity is misunderstood, whose various personal crises led to alienation in the military and the broader society, and whose imprisonment and mistreatment further imperiled her well-being.

In a 2016 interview with Amnesty International, Manning stated, "I am always afraid. I am still afraid of the power of government. A government can arrest you. It can imprison you. It can put out information about you that won't get questioned by the public. . . . It is very terrifying to face the government alone."[77]

In 2011, the *Guardian* called her pretrial confinement "cruel and unusual." The article documents the following abuses:

> Manning is made to stand naked outside his cell this morning, and apparently on all future mornings. This is the culmination of a punitive regime which has gone on for 10 months under which, although untried and unconvicted, he is not allowed to sleep or exercise in his cell during the day, is denied any personal possessions, and is barred from conversing with the guards. Every five minutes he is required to answer that he is fit, and, if he turns his face away while asleep, he is immediately forcibly woken up. In an

Orwellian trick, this is dubbed "prevention of injury" for his own protection. When Manning finally protested, sarcastically, that he could no doubt injure himself with the boxer shorts which are all that he is left with at night, the boxer shorts, too, were taken away.[78]

Later, a psychiatrist would testify in court that this mistreatment had damaging effects during Manning's court-martial. The United Nations torture chief ruled the treatment cruel and inhuman.

Note how this description evokes pity for Manning for this humiliation. At the same time, Manning is framed as absolutely abject, as far removed from being an agent of her own destiny as one can be. The pattern is widespread. A *Guardian* article protests her solitary confinement: "For more than seven months, Manning has been held in 23-hour-a-day solitary confinement at a Marine brig in Quantico, Virginia, denied sunlight, exercise, possessions, and all but the most limited contact with family and friends. The conditions of his detention are being described as torture." The same article details how prisoners on suicide watch are stripped of clothing, bed, blanket, and toilet. The title of this article is "Lonely Battle Against Solitary Confinement," emphasizing both Manning's victimization and the brutal privation and privatization of her confinement.[79] After her suicide attempt, she was denied contact with lawyers and friends.

Manning herself revealed her ordeal in a letter to her lawyers: "I was stripped of all clothing with the exception of my underwear. . . . I became upset. Out of frustration, I clenched my hair with my fingers and yelled: 'Why are you doing this to me? Why am I being punished? I have done nothing wrong.'" Manning recounts having to stand, naked, at parade rest, with legs apart and hands behind the back, as the supervisor and guards stared.[80] That Manning got the word of her mistreatment to her legal team was an act of agency. After protests of her treatment at Quantico, Manning was moved to Leavenworth, in Kansas, where she would have access to recreation and sociability. Yet the feminization of Manning's imprisoned body, alongside her account of pulling her hair and yelling, frames her as feminine and histrionic rather than capable and rational. There is no political agent in the scene of humiliation even when the point of the coverage is to support Manning.

For writers and citizens who did not support her actions, her sexuality and gender identity were aligned with treason, much as homosexuality was during the Cold War.[81] Gender treason and political treason merged together in the narrative frames over the course of her jailing, trial, and imprisonment on a sentence of thirty-five years. The queering of her image and voice enabled politicians and anti-queer citizens to so distance themselves from her as to warrant the longest sentence ever served by a whistleblower.

The dimensions of queer identity that framed Manning as pathological include being childlike or juvenile, emotional to an extreme degree (histrionic), small and ill-equipped for masculine military life, and otherwise out of control. For example, from Denver Nicks's *Private*, we get a narrative of "kid with ego complex meets other guy with ego complex who manipulates kid."[82] It describes Manning as anxious, politically conscious, pro-capitalism, pro-military; a person with intellectual confidence but a juvenile and overinflated sense of ego; a person who was fundamentally unstable. Nicks attributes Manning's decision to leak state secrets to her emotional distress:

> His initial interest in leaking came at a time when he was under significant pressure as an all-source intelligence analyst in Iraq but before the repeated episodes of profound emotional and psychological breakdown that began in mid-December and continued until his arrest. Incidents extending back to the spring of 2009 at Fort Drum, and farther back into his adolescence and childhood, revealed a person prone to manic outbursts. But the total psychological unraveling that began to manifest itself in December 2009 occurred in tandem with, not directly prior to, the leaking. This timeline would become essential many months later as the public sought to understand not just what Manning had done, but why he had done it.[83]

And likewise, Nicks writes, "His friends wonder whether his desperation for acceptance—or delusions of grandeur—may have led him to disclose the largest trove of government secrets since the Pentagon Papers."[84] Elsewhere Nicks attributes "emotional turmoil" to Manning, who was "tormented, abandoned, and heartbroken."[85] Manning engaged in "bizarre behavior," including an episode where she was found with a knife and talked about how he had no personality.

> All artifice of stability in Brad's life disintegrated. The brigade psychiatrist diagnosed him with an "occupational problem and adjustment disorder with mixed disturbance of emotions and conduct," and recommended he be discharged. Command had the bolt removed from his rile and demoted him. Manning tells a superior officer that his gender confusion was making life difficult.[86]

In these passages, Manning's gender complexity is tied directly to pathology. To the extent that affect is mobilized in defense of her actions, the result is the denial of her agency.

In this way, Manning's defenders employed the frame of queer pathology in order to defend Manning against charges of espionage. They also exposed the misery of Manning's treatment in prison in order to galvanize public outrage. Indeed, protesters mobilized and marched on the military base chanting, "Free Bradley Manning!" Protesters decried the threat of indefinite solitary confinement, noting that she was punished for having a copy of the issue of *Vanity Fair* featuring transgender celebrity Kaitlyn Jenner and an unauthorized tube of toothpaste.[87]

In 2016, Chelsea Manning attempted suicide in prison, one of several such attempts. That action prompted public outcry against her confinement. But the act of passive resistance also prompted repression in the form of solitary confinement, which only makes the suicide risk greater. Coverage of this action garnered sympathy and outrage on behalf of Manning. But calling on this frame had double-edged consequences for Manning's defense. On the one hand, as the *New York Times* reported, her attorney David Coombs "elicited testimony that depicted his client as a smaller, sadder figure—a damaged and confused young man whose decision-making capacity when he decided to leak the files was impaired by extraordinary stress." The defense "sought to portray Manning in human terms, from a difficult childhood." He called an army captain and psychologist who testified, "His abnormal personality traits became more prominent—he was acting out his grandiose ideation." She had fetal alcohol syndrome and was underweight, for good measure.[88]

The defense crafted this victim persona in order to exculpate Manning. It is a sympathetic portrait designed to mitigate Manning's fate. At the same time, however, it underscores Manning's *queerness*, which discredits her claims to the special circumstances of emotional disturbance. And it buries the documents Manning discovered and all of their implications under the story of a small, sad person.

The *Guardian*, although largely supportive of Manning, published a report on a documentary film that allegedly showed that Manning was "mentally unfit" to serve in the military.

> The American soldier at the centre of the WikiLeaks revelations was so mentally fragile . . . that he wet himself, threw chairs around, shouted at commanding officers and was regularly brought in for psychiatric evaluation. . . . Despite several violent outbursts and a diagnosis of adjustment disorder, a condition that meant he was showing difficulty adjusting to military life, Manning was eventually sent to Iraq, where it is alleged he illegally downloaded thousands of sensitive military and diplomatic documents and passed them on to the whistleblowing website WikiLeaks.[89]

Note the implied causal chain: Mental fragility and adjustment disorder led directly to the stealing and leaking of state secrets. And this narrative is everywhere.[90] It influenced Democratic commentators, for example those on Salon.com, who noted, "It sounds like he has pretty serious emotional problems and turned out not to be a particularly effective whistleblower." Another pundit commented that Manning was "a guy seeking anarchy as a salve for his own, personal, psychological torment."[91]

Hero and Traitor, or Leaking from the Wrong Places

Greenwald and the *Guardian* lauded Manning as a hero whose goal was to spark public debate.[92] Greenwald rebuts the idea that Manning was communicating with enemies of the United States, denouncing both the government's original intention of trying Manning under the Espionage Act and the implications for reporting and journalism if all leaks rose to the standard of espionage.[93] The *Guardian* also ran a series of columns explaining how Manning was a hero, not a traitor. Others, of course, condemned Manning for endangering diplomats and others.

These charges rested on accusations of irresponsible leaking:

> The *Post* and many others in print and broadcast journalism sift and check information and take care not to reveal sources and methods or to endanger lives in bringing secrets to light. Wikileaks and Pfc. Manning showed less care. They spilled classified government data into the open, in some cases endangering individuals who were identified in diplomatic cables. Pfc. Manning had taken an oath to protect secrets, which he broke. No system of secrecy can function if people ignore the rules with impunity; it is reasonable that Pfc. Manning be punished in some way for breaking those rules.[94]

Contrary to this account, Manning has claimed that she first tried to give her information to the *Washington Post* and the *New York Times,* but was not taken seriously.[95] After the fact of the leaks to WikiLeaks, the *Times* and other journalists tried to present digests and chronologies, but the mass of information was overwhelming and complex. Manning's decision to send the trove of documents to WikiLeaks associated her with Julian Assange, who was universally portrayed as a creepy, sinister outlaw. Manning was guilty by association.

There is a connotative connection between Manning's culpability in disclosing both state and personal secrets. Their connection could be summed up in the charge that she was "leaking in the wrong places." The sexual pun is intentional: Manning as a gay man engaged in the exchange of bodily fluids with partners of the wrong gender; Manning as a trans woman is, according to heterosexist and transphobic logics, presumed to leak both *to* and *from* the wrong places; Manning as a whistleblower leaked to a queer and pathological outlet with a queer and pathological figurehead. These layers of queering frame Manning's personal life and political goals as hopelessly imbricated and inextricable from one another. The normative gender script of heroic masculinity was a narrative to which Manning had no recourse.

CONCLUSION: MANNING'S QUEER FAILURE

In contrast to Edward Snowden's framing in the news media as a straight, normal, rational man in control of himself and his actions, Manning's inescapable strangeness in the coverage and therefore in the public imagination meant that she did not have access to the same resources of mediation available to Snowden. Not only, as she explained, did the actual mass media disregard her initial attempt to interest reporters at the *New York Times* and *Guardian,* but rhetorical mediation—the process of framing—could not capture her as anything other than queer in the many senses of the word.

A *Times* article about her pre-court-martial notes that Manning "turns 25 on December 17 and looks much younger."[96] Another notes that Manning "barely looks old enough to drink," and is "a deeply troubled young man," "uncontrolled" and "erratic."[97] Most coverage of both the trial and court-martial emphasized Manning's small stature and juvenile appearance, making Manning the opposite of the commanding presence attributed to Snowden. Manning was small, irrational, and childlike. One witness is quoted as noticing Manning's "worrying behavior . . . screaming and . . . curled up in a fetal position."[98] At an absurd extreme, a biographical article in the *Guardian* at the end of Manning's court-martial described Manning, then still identifying as a man, as "the diminutive blond with a knack for computers who was 'very political and very clever,' but didn't quite fit in."[99]

Nicks's biography brings this insight together in the clearest way: Manning could not function in the "cauldron of hypermasculine army life. . . . He let loose a torrent of emotional unrest, blending his gender struggles with his morally conflicted feelings about the war in which he was now engaged. 'I feel like a monster.'"[100]

In this way, *queerness* reveals the limits of mediation in a homophobic and transphobic society where media are commercially controlled (and thus subject to the demands of popularity and advertiser interest). It is tempting to criticize Manning for not engaging in the careful self-scripting for major journalists that Snowden accomplished. She did fail to understand the importance of literal mediation. Dumping facts in a pile without interpretation, framing, or circulation does not move information into the commonsense imagination of publics. However, because of the constraints of gender ideology, or implicit, patterned, popular belief regarding gender and sexuality, Manning had no access to the script of the willful public hero.

For these reasons, the framing of Manning as queer cannot be separated from the workings of the other frames: As a queer person, she troubled the boundaries between public and private. She could not deny access to her personal life and her intimate choices. In a society where being queer is taken as a sign of psychopathology, her actions could not be understood as conscious political interventions with a rational purpose. In the wake of a process of dual disclosures, she appeared as a traitor both to the regime of gender and to the U.S. nation-state, conflated in the image of a strong masculine state.

There is an emerging literature in queer theory that encourages the acceptance of failure as a queer form of resistance. The inability to "fit" dominant scripts and narratives and the inevitable confounding of the organizing distinctions of modern life—public/private and masculine/feminine foremost among them—can be a productive resource if one's goal is to assert pride in difference and to operate in enclaves defined by difference and separation from the mainstream. For example, the queer rejection of the "normal" narratives of coming of age in a heterosexual context and marriage and family—the failure to progress—stands as a marker of defiance.

Manning does exhibit some agentive queerness, beginning with her simple announcement in 2013: "I am Chelsea Manning. I am a female." This announcement was received politically. The *Washington Post* commented, "It was a teachable moment, in public-statement form."[101] Asking that the public recognize her gender identity, Manning politicized what was private—a converse to how her queerness had been deployed to personalize the political. She also won the right to be confined under the name and gender identity of her choice and to receive hormone treatment, in addition making further demands of the military to allow her to grow her hair and wear cosmetics.

The military relented on the provision of hormone treatment only after Manning engaged in a five-day hunger strike, described in the *Guardian* as a political protest against solitary confinement, bullying, and denial of treatment for gender dysphoria.[102] Manning puts these demands in the context of struggles for transgender liberation.[103] And as a trans commentator in the *Post* notes, Manning has an opportunity to "help change the way Americans think about trans men and women."[104] The *Post* also, however, ran the news of Manning's gender identity under the perverse headline, "Manning Says He Will Live as a Woman."[105] The most prominent political intervention Manning made is to have been appointed to the honorary position of grand marshal of the San Francisco Pride Parade—and to be promptly uninvited. Greenwald made the political connections clear in a column where he lambasted the Pride organization for demonizing Manning as a criminal while welcoming corporate sponsors like AT&T and Bank of America.[106]

These are profound political moments. However, coverage framing Manning as abnormal—small, feminine, delusional, emotional, out-of-control, and traitorous in both gender identity and political decision—comes together to define her as fundamentally *queer*. Her confounding of popular meaning frames should be defended and protected, but it did not enable her to break open the scandals of the ongoing U.S. wars in the Middle East; it was disabling through no fault of her own.

For the purposes of my larger project in this book, the differential framing of Snowden and Manning points to the limits of truth telling in political culture. In the introduction I asked how rhetorical practices of inclusion and exclusion make certain truths into "common sense" while others languish. By themselves, facts have no political efficacy. To succeed in throwing information condemning the U.S. state of misdeeds over the transom from *episteme* to *doxa,* a rhetor must mediate that information using the "big five," in this case the resources of mythic narrative, to construct Snowden in the persona of a valiant hero combatting an ignominious state. It should be noted, however, that affect was a strategy of public discourse in Manning's case—but with the perverse result of discrediting her as a pitiful, ill victim. The "big five" don't always work in the favor of factions not already in power; existing narratives and frames may be sustained instead. The narratives that framed Manning as sympathetic also posited her actions as apolitical, and the narratives that framed Snowden as a hero bolstered dominant assumptions about masculinity and power.[107] When it comes to promoting the knowledge of the oppressed, Left rhetors should reflect on the conditions of possibility for the positive mediation of counter-knowledge. Otherwise, the champions of democracy and the knowledge it requires to thrive are lost.

CHAPTER 5

Cosmos and the Big Five Bang

IT TELLS a grand story about humanity's origins and destiny. It offers a number of moral lessons and commandments. Its spectacular techniques inspire wonder and awe. Its stories are parables pitting truth-bearing heroes against the willful ignorance of the powerful. Its tone is reverential. It calls the viewer to walk in its fantastic worlds. It offers the satisfaction of unity and belonging. It gestures toward the sublime.

Am I describing the rhetoric of religions, humanity's sources of origin stories and moral guidance?[1] Yes, in a sense—and no. I am bearing witness to the spectacular account of scientific discovery in the television program *Cosmos,* both its first incarnation narrated in 1980 by Carl Sagan and its 2014 update hosted by Neil deGrasse Tyson.[2] Both iterations of the program were responses to geopolitical exigencies: Sagan advised the use of technology for the advancement of science rather than for the terrifying nuclear arms race. Tyson employs his fiery pulpit to warn viewers about global warming and the choices we face if we are to save humanity. Both series, of thirteen episodes each, attempt to explain an impressive amount of scientific knowledge from the microcosmic to the, well, cosmic, and to present a history of advances in science from ancient civilizations to the present. These efforts are consequential.

Indeed, I recall watching Sagan's *Cosmos* religiously as an adolescent in the 1980s. It was a formative educational and televisual experience, one that

I share with many others in my generation. Along with *Roots* and the gruesome and horrifying televisual rendering of nuclear holocaust in *The Day After* (which I watched with my roommate during my first year at Penn State, both of us weeping openly), I can honestly credit *Cosmos* with instilling in me some of the seeds of critical consciousness and intellectual courage that guide me to this day.

Yet I doubt—although I can't say for sure—that the 2014 epic will have played such a role in the identities and values of the children and teens who have watched or will watch it now. Our media landscape is much more cluttered and distracting. I had very little to look at during the evenings besides network television. Now, rather than watching with others at the set broadcast time, most viewers will catch the program, if at all, on mobile and paid platforms, consuming bits of the narrative out of order on the uninspiring small screens of their telephones. As the *New York Times* noted, "If the new 'Cosmos' doesn't deliver quite the punch of the original, it's because it isn't 1980. Since then, of course, personal computers have put a vast array of knowledge in almost everyone's hands, and anyone with even a little curiosity about things scientific has been able to satisfy it easily."[3]

If the show does not leave a lasting impression on its audiences, changes in media use and new technologies will not have been the only barriers to its effectiveness. It is our historical moment of rising ultra-conservatism, popular skepticism regarding scientific knowledge, and a political environment that cultivates an inability to weigh competing truth claims that shape the program's reception. In contrast, Sagan's version appeared on the heels of two decades of progressivism and a wave of social movements that made challenging received wisdom a matter of course. Public fear of the possibility of mutually assured destruction found expression across popular culture. Sagan's claims and the trippy new cosmic knowledge he offered also, ironically, resonated with the "me" generation of the 1970s. The subtitle of his *Cosmos* was *A Personal Voyage*.

Tyson's program, produced and written by Tyson, Ann Druyan (who was married to Sagan), Brannon Braga, Mitchell Canold, and Steven Soter, bears the subtitle: *A Spacetime Odyssey*. Both series told stories on a grand scale, but the 2014 team signaled the collective character of their project more openly. In other ways, however, it pays direct homage to the first series. It has thirteen episodes following a circular narrative trajectory; it uses many of the same examples and even the same language as the first; it invokes Sagan in its imagery and stories; it features statements by Sagan in poetic voice-over at key moments (Tyson not possessing quite the same gravitas); and it borrows and repeats a sequence from the first series of simple line drawings representing the evolution of life from the pre-cellular to the human, set into motion by the animators. No flashy graphics could make that narrative any clearer. (And rather than leaving with the impression that humans are descended from a common ancestor shared with apes, which we are, I am struck by the fact that the key ancestor in our genetic past might have been—the shrew.) Both series feature both classical (strangely, the pre-Enlightenment baroque) and new music (in the original, trippy electronica by Greek composer Vangelis in the first series and a score by Alan Silvestri in the second) to amplify the drama of scientific discovery. Both feature reenactments of key moments in that history and the characters who drove scientific progress.

And, as my opening paragraph suggests, both—but especially the contemporary *Cosmos*—employ what I have called the big five rhetorical strategies that are commonplace on the Right but distrusted by many on the Left: narrative, myth, affect, embodiment, and spectacle. However, the program is riven through and through with a major contradiction in this regard: It does the rhetorical work of wonder and mystery while insisting at every turn that it is telling the truth and nothing but the truth as established by the scientific method. In other words, the show denies its own rhetoricity, that is, as a mediator of knowledge, while at the same time enacting it brilliantly. I therefore begin with the question of whether this apparent reluctance to come to terms with mediation is, as James Aune put it about Marxist thought, a "nuclear" contradiction (an apropos label in the present context).[4] Or might it be, possibly, the definition in practice of a rhetorical, realist text that obsessively references its own status as a construct while inviting viewers to identify with a project grounded in knowledges faithful to the interests of its publics?

In pursuit of an answer to this question, I examine in this chapter the thirteen episodes of the 2014 program with occasional reference to moments across the two series. First, I will illustrate how the series employs "the big five" and to what effect (as substantiated in both my viewing experience and others' reviews). Second, I explore signal moments when the show's narrative exhibits the "nuclear" contradiction inherent in self-consciously mediating information claimed to be "true." Making something of a turn, I discuss the role of works such as these in public education, where scientific controversies (particularly over evolution and climate change) work themselves out with the most serious consequences—in the battle for the hearts and minds of young people. It is in this context that assessing the rhetorical work of *Cosmos* can speak to its ethics and politics. Before launching into those arguments, however, I turn now to some background on the programs and their contexts.

ORDERING THE *COSMOS*

Cosmos: A Personal Voyage aired on the Public Broadcasting System in 1980. Its thirteen episodes represented the pinnacle of animation, graphics, and the integration of astronomical photography. *Cosmos: A Personal Voyage* has been seen by 500 million people in sixty countries; it won two Emmys and a Peabody award. It was the most watched series in the history of American public television until *The Civil War* in 1990.[5]

A thorough list and summary of the series' thirteen episodes (and of *Cosmos: A Spacetime Odyssey*) may be found on Wikipedia.[6] It should be noted here that the series begins and ends in a set of the ancient library of Alexandria, a premodern tribute to scientific knowledge that once contained, Sagan tells us, a million scrolls. In a nod to feminism, Sagan includes Hypatia among the scientists represented. In the final episode, he returns to the library, telling the story of its destruction by a suspicious mob. The capstone to this story is the murder of Hypatia (who was flayed alive by followers of Cyril), "the last scientist of Alexandria," for her allegiance to inquiry and reason. In this way, the series closes a circular arc with an inspiration and a warning. In between this opening and conclusion, audiences receive lessons in physics, astronomy, biology, mathematics, chemistry, geography, geology, the history of science, and cosmopolitan citizenship.

Neil deGrasse Tyson's *Cosmos* rounds a similar circle, beginning with the story of mystic Giordano Bruno, who was jailed, tortured, and eventually killed for insisting that God's cosmos was far larger than the church had recognized and that humans were not at its center. The last episode revisits this tale and also reenacts Sagan's visit to and lament over the library of Alexandria, with a similar but computer-generated set and verbatim use of Sagan's script.

The animation of *Cosmos: A Spacetime Odyssey* was directed by *Family Guy* creator and producer Seth MacFarlane, who, in addition to enjoying the fart jokes that were mainstays of his comedy, identifies himself as a serious science geek. His animation style, featuring flattened human figures and other objects, will be discussed in more detail below. In addition to these directors, the show featured state-of-the-art computer graphics. This program, airing both on Fox and on the National Geographic Channel, drew the biggest global audience ever for National Geographic.[7] According to *Variety*, 135 million people, 45 million in the United States, watched at least some part of the series. It garnered a weekly viewership of 3 million people.[8] It won Critics' Choice Awards for best reality series and best host.[9] However, the series lost viewers across its regular broadcasts.[10] There was some talk of a second season, but the show was not renewed.

The reception of the program was largely positive, with the predictable exception of fundamentalist Christians. Some critics identified ostensible historical and scientific errors in the program, for example, the claim that Venus's uninhabitability is the result of global warming like that faced by humans on Earth; the failure to indicate that the idea of the "multiverse" is at this point almost pure speculation; the commonplace but inaccurate inclusion of the sounds of spaceships and exploding phenomena, impossible in the vacuum of space; the overblown narrative about Bruno, who was not a scientist; and the metonymic reduction of the 13.8 billion-year-long "cosmic calendar" into one calendar year.[11]

Some Christians wished that scientists like Sagan and Tyson would acknowledge that many believers acknowledge the validity of evolution and the immensity and longevity of the universe. For example, the blog Patheos.com found the version of Christianity rebutted in the program to be a caricature or straw person, easy to defeat but unrepresentative of more complex views.[12]

Predictably, Christians committed to a literal reading of the Bible, especially the book of Genesis, responded defensively to the show. An Oklahoma station cut to a commercial just as Tyson was about to explain evolution. (They claimed that the interruption was an inadvertent error.[13]) Some Christian bloggers found the show infuriating in its claims, some of which, they argue, border on the supernatural: "theories of 'magical' Big Bang explosions that came from nothing" and the view that "human life started with endosymbiotic bacteria that evolved to a species that can contemplate the colonization of mars [sic]."[14] Jonathan Sarfati defended creationism against Cosmos on Creation.com, the website of Creation Ministries International (CMI), whose mission is "to support the effective proclamation of the Gospel by providing credible answers that affirm the reliability of the Bible, in particular its Genesis history."[15] Sarfati condemns the show's "dogmatic materialism," that is, the search for answers in the material world itself.[16] He rejects what he calls the theory of "goo-to-you" evolution, observing that Tyson acknowledges in the script that the story of life "sounds like something out of a fairy tale or myth." The website and others like it engage in a tactic common to Holocaust deniers called "false in one thing, false in all."[17] Noting the fallibility of Tyson's narrative in some particulars (for example, details of ancient history, manganese crystal growth rates, and biblical language), the authors encourage holistic distrust of the program's claims.

A prominent information source for young-earth creationists is Answers in Genesis, a site founded by celebrity creationist Ken Ham.[18] Its major strategy is to present arguments from scientists (for example, astronomer Danny Faulkner and biologist Elizabeth Mitchell) debunking theories of evolution and the age of the cosmos in detailed terms that make it seem that these writers have a secure grip on scientific and historical knowledge—they possess the veneer of pseudoscience, another tactic of Holocaust denial.[19] The writers on the site pay particular attention to the commonplaces of arguments for evolution: the dog (the same as wolves), the eye (God made it perfect), Tiktaalik (not a missing link between fish and amphibians), and the distant starlight "problem" (the answer to which involves a contorted explanation called Anisotropic Synchrony, to explain how light from distant galaxies can reach Earth within the literal biblical timescale).[20] In addition to elaborate reviews of Cosmos, the site offers a series of discussion guides to be used in educational settings, Questioning Cosmos.[21] This effort demonstrates the group's recognition that the key audience for scientific education consists of children and youth.

The influential Institute for Creation Research[22] put out a book, Guide to the Universe, in response to Cosmos. Its blurb reads, "From our radiant sun to the brilliance of distant galaxies, the vast universe reveals breathtaking beauty and majesty. Yet scientists tell conflicting accounts of its origins. Did God create it? Or did the universe just explode into existence?"[23] The publicity video affirms a six-day creation week and the idea of an Earth that is more than a "pale blue dot," "as Carl Sagan says." Direct responses to the Cosmos series malign the show's producers as debauched atheists.[24] Like Answers in Genesis, the center employs credentialed scientists who conduct research from a creationist standpoint that unsurprisingly supports the literal account of creation in Genesis.

Thus (Left) author Dan Arel at Alternet concluded happily that each of the thirteen episodes of the rebooted Cosmos "sent the religious right off the deep end."[25] What is most intriguing, though, about the Christian critique of Cosmos is that they rightly capture what might be perceived as a flaw in a text purporting to make a fact-based argument: namely, that Tyson and the show in general employ strategies of persuasion that expose their role as mediators. Critics note that Tyson "plays God" in scenes that resemble creation myths more than anything else. I will address the apparent contradiction below. However, I first will provide details regarding how the program does, indeed, employ the "big five" strategies common to conservative, and especially religious-conservative, discourse.

COSMOS AND THE BIG FIVE

The makers of *Cosmos* explicitly sought to reach broad and skeptical audiences by making use of the affordances of popular culture and visual effects. Ann Druyan, for example, explained to *Variety* how their efforts were designed to interest new audiences by including dazzling video effects and elements of popular culture such as animation featuring major actors' voices, including those of Richard Gere, Patrick Stewart, Marlee Matlin, and Kirsten Dunst.[26] Tyson told one interviewer that the show was designed to reach people "who know they don't like science. They've got no flame at all. So we're going to go in there and light it."[27] Reviewers at *The Atlantic* commented that the show engages in "scientific missionary work," while engaging in the "unapologetic looping of faith into science."[28] Indeed, the makers of *Cosmos* did make extensive use of every rhetorical tool available: narrative, myth, affect/emotion, embodiment, and spectacle.

Narrative

As rhetoric scholar Kevin McClure explains, the process of identification with a narrative is a poetic, aesthetic encounter with the symbolic dimension of a case rather than its propositional arguments.[29] With regard to young-earth creationism, McClure argues that we have to take seriously how the stories of Christianity are learned early in life from authorities and family; the narratives of Christianity shape the cultural landscape of Western culture and set into place a way of life. Thus, evolution-based science challenges the core identity of fundamentalist Christians and asks them to risk purgation from their communities and the loss of a grand scheme to the universe.[30] "Powerful forces of disidentification would be unleashed, requiring people to reconsider their social and spiritual identities."[31]

    Cosmos takes seriously the need to produce a coherent set of narratives that can win the identification of people raised in Christian communities. I have already mentioned the overall narrative arc of both series from past, to present, to future, and then back to the past. In addition to this pattern, each episode features internal narratives. Prominent among these is the representative anecdote, a term coined by rhetorical theorist Kenneth Burke to describe a "story or dramatic form which represents the motivational essence of the discourse."[32] Burke discovered in the rhetoric of biblical creation the anecdote of *action* as opposed to the scientific modality of describing nature as merely in *motion*, without agentive cause or motive.[33] In this sense, what the show

Cosmos does is to present science in terms of motion, which will fall short for anyone seeking an intentional maker, since it cannot identify the agents of causation, only the processes caused.

The representative anecdote can refer to a smaller narrative unit as well. In *Cosmos*, each episode is marked by the story of a perseverant and courageous scientific genius or visionary standing up against the attempts of ignorant and arbitrary authority to snuff out the light of new knowledge. This narrative represents the "motivational essence" of the entire program: It is a story corresponding to the program's exhortation to embrace the scientific method: to explore without fear and to question orthodoxies. Light-dark metaphors are used extensively in pitting the discoverers and explorers of light against the darkness of ignorance and power. These stories are animated in a flat and non-fluid style, a point to which I will return.

For example, in episode 1, "Standing Up in the Milky Way," Tyson recounts the biography of Giordano Bruno, an Italian mystic who envisioned a heliocentric and infinite cosmos; he stood up to the Inquisition, and the Inquisition, unfortunately, won. This story figures prominently in critiques, both secular and religious, of the program since there is a dispute as to whether Bruno's punished transgressions (which also involved magic and alchemy) had anything to do with his speculations on the cosmos. Moreover, Bruno was not a scientist but rather a visionary, making his story—rather than Kepler's or Copernicus's—an odd choice of initial overture. (However, both Kepler and Copernicus were devout Christians whose research was motivated to support and flesh out a vision of the cosmos as a product of divine creation; they were not specifically persecuted for their science. Galileo's embrace of "Copernicanism" was ruled as heresy by the Inquisition, and he was forced to recant his theory.)

The inquiry-repression anecdote appears in every episode, but a few of them are more significant for my purposes. In episode 3, "When Knowledge Conquers Fear," Tyson gives voice-over to the animated account of the foundational collaboration of Edmond Halley and Isaac Newton, a lonely student prone to mysticism, who challenged intellectual leaders in their observations of comets and the motions of the stars. William Herschel and his son receive the animators' attention in episode 4, "A Sky Full of Ghosts." Herschel explains to his son that he doesn't believe in spirits, but that in a way, some of the light we see from stars reaches us long after the stars themselves are dead. In a signal moment of historical and cultural inclusiveness, episode 5 ("Hiding in the Light") recounts stories of both the Chinese philosopher Mo-Tzu who invented the camera obscura, and the Arabic scientist Ibn al-Haytham, who theorized about the nature of light and advocated something like the scientific method. Not only did these figures pursue new ideas with courage, they suffered from the historical silencing of their contributions.

Women get similarly inclusive treatment in the series. Rather than focusing on Hypatia, as Sagan did, the producers of *Spacetime Odyssey* noted the historic work conducted by women at Harvard working for Edward Charles Pickering. These women, including Annie Jump Cannon, Henrietta Swan Leavitt, and Cecilia Payne, invented a stellar classification system and discovered a way to measure the distance to stars. Payne developed a method of determining the chemical composition of stars, running up against received knowledge and her advisor while writing the definitive textbook on the subject. After this story, Tyson states into the camera, "Have you heard of any of these women? No?" Wryly, he adds, "I wonder why," alluding to sexist exclusion of women's voices in the historical account of scientific discovery.

The anecdote in episode 7 ("The Clean Room") is of particular importance because of its modern underdog subject, Clair Patterson, who developed the science of dating objects based radioactive decay (in which decaying uranium turns to lead). While he was discovering the age of the Earth, Patterson also discovered the unnaturally widespread presence of lead in the air and soil of his time. He went up against the petroleum industry to prove that lead added to gasoline was poisoning the population.

In episode 10, "The Electric Boy," Michael Farraday rises from the slums to discover how magnetic fields made of waves and how electricity worked; he invented the generator and the motor in spite of failing health, thereby setting the basis for all modern electronic communication. The show quotes him: "Nothing is too wonderful to be true, if it be consistent with the laws of nature," he wrote.

In addition to stories of individuals confronting ignorance, this story also pits periods of time against each other as if they were persons. There were "public spheres of science" in Amsterdam during the Enlightenment and during the heyday of the coffeehouses across Europe, described by Tyson as oases of equality and laboratories of democracy. We see Huygens and Leeuwenhoek, complete with white curly wigs, playing the harpsichord and taking a walk at sunset to look through the telescope. Against these scenes—complete with scenes of salons as sites of music and debate—the authorities of mysticism, ignorance, and persecution rise in perpetual threat. Ionia and Amsterdam appear as models of cosmopolitanism.

Then there are the key narrative proofs of evolution, chosen because they are the *bêtes noires* (black beasts, literally) of creationism: the evolution of dogs and the evolution of the eye. The tale of dogs as a species distinct from wolves challenges creationists' theories that God made all of the animals as they presently exist at once, and that Noah could have rounded up all of the kinds of animals without gathering each specific type; wolves and dogs are said on this analysis to be of a "kind," and admitting to significant differences would undermine their case. Creationists also posit that the eye is so brilliant and complex a tool that it can't be explained by natural selection. Another key example for the theory of evolution is that of the tardigrade (episode 6), which looks like a mythical creature and is almost beyond belief: I never got a glimpse of anything like that in my biology classes no matter how many drops of water we put under the microscope. In fact, however, the tardigrade is an arthropod closely related to insects, and somewhat common. Its crucial characteristic is that it can survive extremes of climate, starvation, dehydration, immersion, and compression; it is extremely well adapted for survival, so much so that creationists believe that it could not have happened by evolutionary chance.

Sagan employed a similar device in the figure of the Heike (Samurai) crab, which appears to bear a human face on its back. What began as a random mutation became adaptive, as Japanese fishers would throw the anthropomorphic creatures back rather than harvesting them for food. For creationists, these remarkable examples are examples not of wondrous nature but of being overdesigned and finely tuned by a creator.

Part of the difficulty in explaining evolution is the vastness of its time scale. Four and a half billion years is what it has taken to get the eye in its current form, but it is difficult to imagine change over such an unfathomable period. In order for evolution to make sense, one must accept and come to terms with the idea of a universe that is 13.8 billion years old and an Earth clocking in at 4.5 billion. The story of life and the story of the stars must appear together to each give evidence for the other. Both *Cosmos* series understood that necessity. However, when you organize all human scientific knowledge so that it comes together in a coherent and elegant, if imperfect, explanatory system, you have the makings of myth.

Myth

Here I briefly revisit the definition of *myth* laid out in chapter 2, which puts forward a rhetorical conception of the term rather than its most common usage to refer to a story that is fanciful but erroneous or deceptive. Instead, a mythic narrative is one that tells the story of a people, its origins, and its destinies. A myth is an explanation of how and why things came to be the way they are. The function of a myth is to win a society to cohesion around a set of principles, identities, and directions forward.

Many if not most mythic narratives are metaphysical, positing a divine order that came into being by design. In pitching scientific knowledge, however, the makers of *Cosmos* also self-consciously embrace the conventions of mythos. The selection of the word *cosmos* itself not only refers in a commonsense way to the known universe and its objects. It more specifically in its etymology is positioned as the opposite of *chaos*: *Cosmos* is the emergence, through exploration and insight, of an ordered and comprehensible system. The description and theorization of such a system necessarily has a mythic character when rendered in narrative form (as opposed to mathematics). It locates humans in the broader order of things, for example, when Tyson gives viewers Earth's "cosmic address": Earth/Solar System/Milky Way Galaxy/Virgo Supercluster/Universe.

It is also not coincidental that the subtitle of the program calls itself an "Odyssey," which refers not to just any journey but to one of mythic proportions: The *Odyssey* by Homer depicted Odysseus's *epic* voyage; its wandering hero seeks a way home against natural and supernatural obstacles. He is in a world apart from ordinary people. So while *Cosmos: A Spacetime Odyssey's* aims include conveying scientific accounts of nature and positioning humanity as a very tiny figure on the cosmic scale, it also invites viewers to, as Tyson says, "Come with me" in an imaginary spaceship that travels the heavens, the Earth, and surveys all of its creatures.

The language of this invitation is often poetic. In the first episode of the 1980 series, Sagan famously intones, "The cosmos is all there is, all that there ever was, and all there will ever be." He describes feeling stirred by contemplation, experiencing a "tingling in the spine," and feeling as if falling "from a great height." And, "as if in a distant memory," "we are approaching the grandest of mysteries." The series explores the deepest past and calls humanity to its destiny: "The earth is tiny. We have the power to decide the fate of our planet and ourselves. Our future depends on how we understand the cosmos." Tyson concurs. Walking the "Hall of Extinction" in episode 9 ("The Lost Worlds of Earth"), Tyson comments about our looming climate disaster: "The future is written by us, right now."

In explaining evolution and biology, Tyson wonders at how there is one universal genetic code and organic chemistry for all life on Earth. "Life has billions of stories in a universal language. Where did that message come from? Nobody knows." Adding to the weight of this mystery, the narrative focuses on the most distinctive and beautifully adapted animals and plants. The hawk moth evolved a nearly foot-long proboscis to pollenate impossibly long orchids on Madagascar, for example. These are examples that my brilliant and Southern Baptist Aunt Mary would give me to make me wonder whether there could be, in fact, an intentional design at work. She once gave me a gorgeous coffee-table book of photographs documenting the repetition of patterns—like spirals—across planetary and cosmic nature. The same examples that captivate viewers to wonder also push against the envelope of credulity, especially if one forgets the 4.5-billion-year clock.

Just as with orders directed by deities, the order of the cosmos involves commandments. Various figures across the episode challenge systems of blind faith and urge viewers to employ the scientific method. Mo-Tzu, as noted above, told his students to engage in observation, openness to correction, and skepticism toward authority. Tyson himself makes this commandment as the season begins to come to a close in episode 12 ("The World Set Free"): "Challenge yourself. Follow the evidence no matter where it leads. Do not make judgments without evidence. Remember you could be wrong." Elsewhere in the same episode, he states,

> Science is a way to keep from fooling ourselves and each other. It has been misused. We can't afford to leave it to the powerful. It belongs to all of us. Its values undermine fanaticism and ignorance. We are uplifted by the scale and scope of the cosmos. We are inspired by what is actually real.

In the final episodes of both shows, viewers witness the triumphs of *Voyager* probes sending recordings of human experience beyond the solar system and returning the most distant images we have ever seen. *Voyager* sent for the first time an image of the whole Earth from a distance, very small and very beautiful. The 2014 series lets Sagan have some of the last words in voice-over:

> For every human being who ever was, that's home. All the joy and suffering, differences of religion, ideology, economics, from hunters and foragers to creators, cowards, kings, peasants, mothers, fathers, children, inventors, explorers, teachers, politicians, superstars, leaders, saints and sinners—all lived there on this mote of dust. The earth is a very small stage in the vast cosmic area. We've seen cruelty and war for control over a tiny fraction of a tiny dot. We suffer from delusions of self-importance. There is nowhere else to go.

Sagan adds, "We are star stuff contemplating the evolution of matter. We carry a legacy of cosmic evolution. We must come to know and love nature and become good strong links in the chain of life."

And so ends this epic: a holistic explanation of origins and destinies and a set of commandments for human behavior. We may be made of star stuff—but this is the compelling stuff of myth.

Affect, Emotion, Embodiment

As discussed in chapter 2, affect refers to a set of precognitive unnamed feelings that shape our experience and responses to the environment. When we identify and name these feelings, they become emotions. Affect and emotion are closely tied to embodiment, since both are experienced in the body. They are produced by visceral encounters rather than a set of propositional statements or arguments. Thus, images, sound, and movement are powerful catalysts of an audience's investment in a message.

The creationist Right understands how emotion is core to the experience of identification and learning. Education researchers Mark Bland and Elizabeth Morrison found in a study of religious students exposed to the science of evolution that the cognitive dissonance between faith and science generates the emotional response of anxiety.[34] Any advocate of evolution must take the importance of emotion in resistance to their claims very seriously. Sites of embodied identification are particularly powerful. In church, embodiment is exemplified in everyday practices like collective singing and other church rituals, and literally in the taking of communion, in which one becomes "consubstantial" with Christ. Music is key to both the power of worship and the power of identification in social movements, in which collectives "move together" in common cause.[35]

Proponents of creationism have created special cases of embodiment as well. For example, creation museums allow children to walk among dinosaurs; they create a narrative that visitors move through in a prescribed order. Kelly and Hoerl describe how the Creation Museum in Petersburg, Kentucky, physically enacts a sense of false controversy over the science of evolution. It stages scenes of controversy warranted by the credibility of the museum space. In other words, by virtue of being physically in a museum—in secular culture, a site of naturalized scientific knowledge—audiences are prompted to find the unsound evidence presented to be credible.[36]

John Lynch describes the same museum as an "embodied conversion narrative" that offers a "spatial sermon" to visitors.[37] Visitors enter the museum under the banner, "Prepare to Believe." The museum guides visitors' bodies through space:

> [The Creation Museum] is a rhetorical performance in concrete that uses one's movement through its space alongside the sequence of visual cues that one encounters, ranging from lighting and line of sight to the visual and verbal text of discrete exhibits, to produce its suasory force. As visitors walk

through the museum, they walk along the path of religious conversion from tension and doubt into awe and spiritual transformation of their identity.[38]

The process of movement enables the internalization of messages and the movement from opening scenes of dissonance and doubt, resolving the sense of crisis in movement from scenes of struggle and depravity into a Christian rebirth—literally, out of a dark tunnel into the light of the creation of the universe. Believing, in this sense, is doing.

Cosmos also understands embodiment as a rhetorical opportunity. Critics noted that the program is an "immersive experience" in a number of ways, beginning with its remarkable opening sequence. The segment occurs to the swelling sounds of original music by Alan Silvestri: beginning with a melody repeated by a lonely French horn, oboe, and flute; interrupted by a cymbal clash and swell of strings behind a repeating bell-like tone; followed by a huge swell of strings.[39]

To this music, images appear and merge into others, positioning viewers as if on a ride, first across Saturn's rings, which morph into a human eye. What we will come to know as the "spaceship of the imagination" crosses the eye as the eye becomes a spiral galaxy, which in turn becomes a spiral shell, held by a child on the seashore. Then the shell morphs back into an eye, which turns into the center of a ring nebula. The center/eye of the nebula becomes the second "o" in cosmos as the title appears.

In addition to capturing the movement and themes of the entire series—the story of the cosmos is the story of life on Earth and vice versa—the journey immerses the viewer in a sensorium of spectacular beauty, very satisfying in its establishment of order upon an enormous and complicated universe. (As noted above, the observation of patterns across the layers of the cosmos and the awe-filled sense that it is an ordered system also represent mythic appeals.) The device of the cosmic calendar, an illuminated set of squares that make up a floor, is likewise immersive as Tyson walks us through the 4.5-billion-year history of the Earth, at various points "entering" a moment—murky swamps, sweeping plains populated by dinosaurs, the interior of a cell, or of an atom, the atmosphere of the Earth and the sphere of the Earth as if viewed from elsewhere in the solar system. These investigations take place in the "spaceship of the imagination," a device also employed by Sagan. Sagan's ship was shaped like a dandelion seed; Tyson's is also seed-shaped, but sleek and black with a spherical, surround-sound viewing port. Horizontally, it looks like a sleek watercraft. Vertically it looks like a floating seed. (In both orientations, it bears an unfortunate resemblance to a coffin.)

When Tyson intones "come with me," the viewer takes a virtual position inside the ship and thereby in the experience of every star, nebula, moonscape, ring system, asteroid belt, neutrino field, atomic nucleus, DNA strand, and even the event horizon of a black hole. The experience is compelling even when Tyson explains that we have no idea where black holes lead or what happens to the matter and light captured there. The computer-generated graphics, animation, and the use of photographic images from telescopes and probes are outstanding.

The viewer is invited similarly to the visceral witness of the Big Bang when Tyson stands on the January 1 square of the cosmic calendar, puts on his sunglasses, and looks toward a pulsing fireball to stage right. When it explodes, Tyson's suit jacket is blown back. The scene is both arresting—we are virtually "blown away"—and comical, as it evokes memories (among older viewers, at least) of the Maxell audiotape advertisement in which a sunglass-wearing man's hair and clothes are blown back by the sound coming from his speakers.[40] (That ad was effective, too.)

The final aspects of the emotional work done by the program are sentimentality and haunting, related mechanisms. The first episode begins with Tyson at the seashore, where Sagan stood to introduce the first series. During the introduction, Tyson holds Sagan's daybook, where there is a notation from 1975 reading, "Neil deGrasse Tyson." Tyson recounts meeting Sagan, who welcomed Tyson to his home in Ithaca, New York, and offered him an overnight stay due to inclement weather. Tyson comments that Sagan was "the kind of person I wanted to be." On this point, a reviewer of the show in the *Atlantic* commented, "Cue the waterworks." Another member of the interview team responded, "I actually gasped when Tyson pulled out Sagan's calendar to show their appointment, marked down."[41] Druyan and Tyson have commented on how important it is that the show "touch you" with "uplifting themes" and "calls to action."[42]

Sagan's voice occurs many times across the episodes, most extensively in the conclusion in his exhortation to be "good strong links in the chain of life." Tyson often uses Sagan's language verbatim in certain segments, for example, "at" the great library of Alexandria. These echoes are more than sweetly sentimental. Rhetorical scholar Joshua Gunn has noted the particular, eerie affective register of haunting: "Beyond mere metaphor, the idiom denotes a conceptual repertoire for listening to and speaking about the dead, literally and figuratively, as well as a considered attempt to orient the critic in a position of hospitality, open to the other."[43] While Gunn is speaking of how the theoretical critique of the humanist subject (i.e., the troubling of the idea that we are each whole and willful persons) leaves us open to the voices of others,

I believe that Sagan's voice does eerily similar work, asking viewers to notice that neither Tyson nor any of us is unique; none of us can control the cosmos; we have no recourse to the comforts of magic or superstition. Sagan's ghost is thus part of the critique of arrogance, fear, parochialism, and mysticism the show puts forward.

These insights comport perfectly with Sagan's continual exhortation to cosmopolitanism and humility. Gunn's essay continues with language that evokes this point: "Insofar as the specter"—that is, the object/past/voice whose ghostly presence is troubling—"neither 'is' nor 'is not,' it is a figure that represents past and future temporalities."[44] The (non)presence of the specter is uncanny, traumatic, and sublime. And along with the sound track, Sagan's voice reminds us that emotion work is often sonic, or aural.

Spectacle

There is not much left to say here about spectacle. The word's root—from Latin, *specere*, to look—of course, is tied to the visual, as in *spectacles* (eyeglasses), *spectatorship, speculation, prospect, inspect,* and so on. Every instance of narrative, myth (especially myth), emotion, and embodiment (including immersion) employed as described above contributes to the series as a spectacular phenomenon that compels watching. In its mythic incarnations, spectacle invites awe and wonder. It matters, however, what we are being invited to find awe-some. I will discuss the implications of the spectacle of *Cosmos* with regard to the concept of fidelity—the degree to which an appeal is aligned with the interests of those exhorted to identify with it—below.

Closely related to spectacle is *celebrity*. Celebrities are cultural constructs whose highly publicized bodies and identities mediate our understanding of realities.[45] The process of filtering social problems through the bodies and voices of individual celebrities can discourage critique and political engagement in favor of personalism and consumerism (for example, when celebrities champion a charity or hold a relief concert or encourage particular consumer choices).[46] However, this outcome is not guaranteed.

Scientific celebrities are interesting cases in point. In his book *Celebrity Scientists,* Declan Fahy argues that celebrity is a result of personal attractiveness and charisma, the commodification of science in cultural products, and the capacity of the person to embody ideas and ideologies.[47] While media attention hooks audiences with an emphasis on a celebrity's private life, the "stars" can come to symbolize wider cultural issues.[48] With regard to Tyson,

Fahy argues, the scientist's persona is a focal point for understanding not only science but also race and representation.

Fahy writes, "You can think of Neil deGrasse Tyson as the Carl Sagan of the 21st century—as long as you envision a Sagan who's muscular, African-American, and as cool as his predecessor was geeky." This description highlights Tyson's race and (unfortunately) ties his identity to an athletic stereotype, both "muscular" and "cool."[49] According to Fahy, the most significant achievement of Tyson for civil rights is that he is an example of a black intellectual with "an influential position in public life."[50] Fahy highlights the capacity of such celebrity to mediate public issues:

> Tyson's media driven celebrity has ultimately earned him social power and influence not only over nonspecialist publics, but also over science policy, the U.S. space program, the categorization of the planets, and the future of his scientific field. His stardom has allowed him to glide between these realms.[51]

Along with Bill Nye and Richard Dawson, Tyson has provoked conservatives by asserting the facticity of evolution and anthropogenic global warming. It is the tension between the assertion of facts alongside the self-conscious attention to communication strategies that makes the show's rhetoric a case study in progressive mediation.

NUCLEAR CONTRADICTIONS

Cosmos offers its publics science lessons in every episode—about physics, evolution, light, biology, archaeology, geology astronomy, geography, climate, and history. On several occasions, the hosts make bald statements of fact, for example, "Evolution is a fact." In episode 9, in a discussion of global warning, Tyson refutes each of the opposition's arguments with points of scientific evidence. The writers have included earnest policy proposals to adopt plant-based and other solar energy; to end the use of fossil fuels; to restore the polar ice caps; and to address poverty, education inequality, and other social problems. Both Sagan and Tyson urge viewers to identify with figures who confront corporate interests. Sagan, especially, sought to divorce scientific inquiry from greatness. And, as noted previously, the narrative and visual techniques of the episodes construct a holistic, coherent, and comforting model of the cosmos. Yet at key moments, the show interrupts its earnestness and coherence. The examples I will discuss might seem to counter the producers' claims to be offering audiences a body of unmanipulated scientific knowledge. I will suggest, however, that something else is going on.

Myth, Naturalization, and Denaturalization

The semiotician Roland Barthes defines myth slightly differently than I have, but in a related way. Myth, he says, is a story that structures human understanding of the world in such a way that it has become invisible common sense. Mythic discourse is for him a closed system that works by making its frames seem natural. Myth *naturalizes* ideas that are not natural at all. It makes inequality, competition, and patriotism seem like features of nature when they are constructs of society. The critical response should be, then, to *denaturalize* what has become naturalized and thus invisible.[52] This mode of critique seems somewhat ironic when examining a text that is primarily concerned with describing nature itself. But as the scholars of the rhetoric of science have argued, there is no bare communication or experience of nature. Every act to educate and inform is mediated. The programs create elegant mythic narratives, but they also disrupt the cosmic storyline; they engage in denaturalization.

The Reflexive Function of Animation

Cosmos repeatedly calls attention to the process of mediation even as it asserts what seem to be plain facts. The most significant and protracted example of this contradiction is the animation of the biographical narratives of scientists. In Sagan's version, these narratives were reconstructed as realistic reenactments. But as a number of critics have pointed out, the animations in the 2014 *Cosmos* are strangely flat and choppy—they are cartoonish. The cartoons do not aspire to realism, or the appearance of being seamless and true reenactments of something that actually happened exactly in this way. They literally denaturalize the people represented.

On the one hand, this mode of representation potentially allows for broad viewer identification with these figures because they are abstract. In addition, the use of animation may effectively engage children and youth.[53] On the other hand, the cartoons distance viewers and the rest of the program's content from the stories being told. Audiences are told, "We're going to teach you the truth about the cosmos," and then are poked to realize, "Hey, we're constructing the version of the truth you're getting."

These animated sequences interrupt the immersion in images and sound that assert the coherence—that might evince a cosmic designer—of the cosmic order: the galaxy and the shell, the impossibly perfect moth for the impossible orchid, the elegance of DNA. About images, Barthes observed that most of the time photographic or video images are persuasive because they appear to be real and unquestionably representative of the persons, objects, and actions depicted. He described the flow of such images as *studium*, a Latin term for the standard cultural interpretation of a photographic image. In contrast, Barthes appreciated the *punctum*, referring to the ways that photographs can call attention to their construction to interrupt the usual process of meaning making and to invite emotional investment and response.[54] The moment of *punctum* is a moment of reflexive contemplation and questioning.

For Barthes, the *punctum* is a personal experience. However, it is worth noting that the word comes from the Latin, meaning "point" or "mark," and is the root of the words *puncture* and *punctuation*. Punctuation is the interruption of the flow of prose and meaning for audiences beyond the individual. *Cosmos: A Spacetime Odyssey* contains moments of *punctum* or critical interruption of the order and flow of narrative and image. The animated biographies constitute one of those marks, indicating to the viewer that what is being presented is a *version* of history.

Another moment of animation also plays the role of *punctum*. Both series include the same forty-second time-lapsed line drawings in white on black that summarize the course of human evolution. Starting with pre-cellular life, then a single cell, the image morphs into a ring of dancing cells, to sponges and fish and the like, to amphibians, then dinosaurs and other land animals, to small mammals, to arboreal animals and apes, to hominids walking upright, to a modern woman. It is simple and elegant, set to an excerpt from Vivaldi's "Four Seasons" (*Spring*).[55]

Given the program's commitment to establishing the facticity of evolution, this animated sequence is strange. It is visually arresting and easily grasped. Its strongest feature is the illustration of the continuity of the shapes of evolving life forms. It is easy to see how, on the one hand, each form transitions to the next in a smooth process. On the other hand, it is a cartoon, leaving the possibility open that audiences will read it as an imaginative exercise rather than scientific explanation. Sagan runs it twice in his episode; the 2014 version plays it exactly as it is in the original, a moment of intertextuality that calls attention to itself even more pointedly. This segment points to how all of the writers and producers are aware of themselves as communicators. They are faced with the awesome responsibility of mediating some of the most important and most difficult knowledge of all.

Part of that responsibility is to own up to the process of mediation. The risk of doing so, taken in these animated sequences, is leaving the narrative presented as radically open to question; the beauty of doing so is leaving the narrative presented as radically open to question. *Cosmos* creates a mythic vision of the universe, the Earth, and the past, present, and future of life, but unlike the mythos of creationists, there are moments of punctuation that interrupt the story and ask the viewer to pause and reflect. Sagan seems to verbally "wink" when he says, "Let's look at it *again*: compressing four *billion* years of evolution into 40 seconds."

Playing God

Playful moments also interrupt the flow of information on *Cosmos*. For example, when discussing neutrinos (nanominute subatomic particles caused by radioactive decay), Tyson tells viewers that they are almost impossible to detect. However, he says, there are detectors that use spheres of matter to see the charge that is made when the neutrino hits them. He explains this process to the audience while sitting in a small yellow dinghy (and he is not a small person) floating in a room full of gold spheres, also floating. He resembles a large child in a funhouse ball pit. The lights are shut off. "We are lying in wait," he says. There is a periodic flash of light: "There!" he says.[56]

Surprisingly, this ball pit is really the subterranean Japanese neutrino detection chamber Super Kamiokande. Rowing the dinghy, Tyson whispers, "Stalking the wild neutrino is the rarest of sport. The lengths one must go to track them down is nothing short of astonishing." It is "the most elusive prey in the cosmos." This commentary and scene are funny in a way that, as in the case of animation, winks at viewers. The image of Tyson in a tiny boat stalking wild neutrinos is playfully absurd, even as the phenomenon observed—the flash of light—actually happens. While amusing, this scene positions Tyson as somewhat godlike: Alone in the dark, he commands the neutrinos to appear on cue.

There is another moment when this maneuver is even more arresting. In episode 12 ("The World Set Free," the second to last episode), Tyson explains how coral reefs and limestone rock, like those making up the White Cliffs of Dover, store carbon dioxide in harmless non-atmospheric form. He stands before the cliffs to explain how much carbon dioxide humans add to the atmosphere every year: the equivalent mass of the cliffs. As he speaks, the cliffs rise up behind him to illustrate the massive shift. It looks as though he can command the earth, a bit like an image of Moses parting the waters.

Taking the spaceship of the imagination anywhere is a godlike act, but none more so than the ride up to and over the event horizon of an imagined black hole in episode 4 ("A Sky Full of Ghosts"). The episode actually starts with a warning and an invitation from Tyson:

> Seeing is not believing. Our senses can deceive us. Even the stars are not what they appear to be. The cosmos as revealed by science is stranger than we ever could have imagined. Light, and time space, and gravity conspire to create realities which lie beyond human experience. *That's* where we're headed. Come with me.

This paragraph is internally contradictory: There are realities beyond our experience. We're going to go experience them. And I, Neil deGrasse Tyson, have the power to reveal them to you.

As the spaceship approaches the black hole, Tyson says, "The magic show of space-time really is crazy." This statement is preceded by a discussion of how movement close to light-speed, when time and aging slow down, could be a source of quasi-immortality, something only a deity could promise until now. The hole sits in the center of a red ring of gas, with a stream of particles flowing from its center. The ship "shakes." "That was us," says Tyson, "resisting a few million g's of gravity." Again, this is a moment of punctuation, a wink acknowledging that this is still an impossible imaginary voyage. After a lecture on how black holes form and how they can be detected (during which Tyson manipulates an animated black hole on the deck of the spaceship as a god may appear to be sculpting the cosmos), Tyson says that if one were to go to the event horizon, she would disappear instantly. The ship then is riding the turbulence. Tyson squints against the light of the hole's stellar corona. "If you somehow survive the perilous journey across the event horizon, you'd be able to look back out and see the entire future history of the universe unfold before your eyes." Significantly, he adds, "Before we go there, I should tell you, we are entering uncharted scientific territory. . . . But let's perform a thought experiment." The ship is pulled, blurring, into the hole; Tyson's visage warps as the music swells. We cut to an image of the ship skating along in deformed space to the sound of electronic music. It disappears. After a break, Tyson explains, "You might end up in a different place and time than our own universe. . . . Black holes may very well be tunnels through the universe . . . an intergalactic subway system. . . . Or we may find ourselves into an entirely different universe. . . . It's another magic trick of space-time." Tyson appears suddenly in a used car parking lot in a move that seems like street magic. He explains that if we want to know what's inside a black hole, we should simply look around, since our own universe could be one of many inside of a black hole.

Thus, the show puts Tyson in a position to reveal the cosmos's darkest secrets while also admitting that the exercise is speculative, a "thought experiment." The scene enacts the science-persuasion "contradiction," which, as I have argued in chapter 2, is not a contradiction at all if one recognizes the role of mediation in conveying critical knowledge.

The capacity of video graphics today to move a viewer through sequences of images that construct a magnificent and coherent totality may, to some extent, work against the program's stated mission. Human eyes come into being over eight minutes; the evolution of the species happens in forty seconds. We can see and explain objects at great distances and those too tiny to see with our most sophisticated technology. The repetition of spiral shapes and the universal life language of DNA convey a sense of design that almost seems magical. Are the producers of *Cosmos* simply replacing one compelling but problematic mythic narrative with another?

I want to suggest a different way to understand the apparent contradiction between a commitment to scientific fact and the tools of mediation that are so self-consciously employed by the creators of *Cosmos*. First, the "facts" of the cosmos are so immense and total as to make mythic narrative unavoidable. But rather than let the gorgeous and tightly woven story proceed in an even, uncontested, and perfect way—the way of *studium*—these points of surprise and reflection invite questioning. The *punctum* asks us to pause and laugh, or find something strange, or wonder how exactly persuasive the case is.

In this way, the method of the program enacts the shorthand version of the scientific method it sets out: Make observations. Build on the knowledge that you have. Recognize that that knowledge could be wrong. Acknowledge that you could be wrong. Be unafraid to admit what you don't know. Don't believe something someone else tells you without questioning her authority and testing her claims against observation. From my analysis, I'll add, have a sense of humor.

Mediation is core to introducing information in persuasive terms. The argument that cuts across this book is that facts do not stand by themselves and that mediation is inevitable—but there is good mediation, by which I mean the framing and interpretation of information in ways faithful to the interests of its audiences, and bad mediation, which is mystification and manipulation that convinces people to make decisions and to elect leaders who are not in their best interests. Far from weakening its internal case, *Cosmos*'s incongruous moments of denaturalization, excess, and humor demonstrate the features of a productive rhetorical realism as I laid them out in chapter 2. American rhetorical theorist Kenneth Burke wrote that myth was a powerful rhetoric tool. What remains to be understood, he argued, is that there are good myths and bad myths. The question is how to tell the difference.[57]

Let's take up this question of good and bad mediation in the context of the controversy over creation and evolution, a struggle that has played itself out in the context of U.S. public schools.

AN EXCURSUS ON RHETORICAL AND SCIENTIFIC EDUCATION

Ideologies of Education

The French revolutionary and scientist Antoine deStutt de Tracy realized, just as I am arguing, that no information circulates without mediation, no education happens outside ideology.[58] He coined the term *ideology* not to describe a set of dogmatic lies or mystifications of the truth, but rather to appreciate the role of education in teaching the young the moral and political principles and the habits of citizenship guiding the society as a whole. Both functions, however, occur at the same time: What to revolutionaries looks like the liberation of thought from the monarchs is to future generations an education in conformity and obedience. The democratizing function and indoctrination function are one and the same. (Indeed, Marx condemned Tracy's rhetoric as bourgeois doctrine.) In any case, Tracy argued that *ideology* was a positive term: the propagation of new ways of being and thinking in the new society. Given that mediation—or the ideological framing of information—is inevitable and necessary, the question becomes not what is a good instance of persuasion or a bad one, but rather *whose knowledge is getting circulated, and on whose terms?* If the choice is between feudal ignorance and liberal universal schooling, then the schools are doing democratic, emancipatory work.

After the revolution and through the reign of Napoleon and into the modern era, public education became an ideological battleground between the left and the monarchist right. The same can be said about public education in the United States. A system of universal schooling has become the site of struggle over education in science and history, especially.

It was not until the Progressive Era of the 1910s and 1920s that a clear rationale for and practice of ideally free, universal public schooling (which was real only for some portions of the population even so) became widely spread. The pragmatist philosopher John Dewey expressed the concern that ignorance, and especially technical and scientific ignorance, was a barrier to full participation in decision making in an increasingly technological society (and this was well before the development and use of nuclear weapons). Moreover, he feared that an atomized (no pun intended) population could not form what he envisioned as a Great Community, in which democratic deliberation happened in the common interest of all.[59]

Critics of Dewey have noted the ideological character of this vision, which denies differences of interest and access by class, race, and gender to both education and civic forums. Dewey and other progressive educators believed that all Americans shared the same interests and that in the Great Community, antagonism would have no place. Universal ideals have not prevailed because this approach to education cannot fully engage the question I raised above: Whose mediation is it? In other words, in whose interests and on whose terms are whose knowledges circulated as true and necessary to democracy? Starting points for this inquiry are three political perspectives or approaches to the mediation of information in the public schools. Here I will attempt a brief sketch.

Liberal Education

First, in the tradition of the French Revolution and the Progressive Era, a liberal approach to education affirms the values of cooperative citizenship and national belonging while continually presenting knowledge as neutral. Liberals deny that education—or good journalism, for that matter—mediates information in ideological ways. Like the fact-checkers of chapter 3, they panic over "fake news" and politicians' lies but do not generally question the political or economic system, the norms of civility or national citizenship. The norms of family and personal responsibility are assumed as well. The celebrations of Thanksgiving, Veterans', and Memorial Days convey these lessons. Assignments asking students to construct their "family trees" are fraught when students are in non-normative (although statistically normal) family forms, or are immigrants, refugees, and so on. It is common for teachers to use reward (i.e., money or object)-based methods of classroom discipline, preparing children for life as workers in capitalism: do your job and get toys. Faith in the transparency and security of factual knowledge is itself an ideological outcome of liberal education. Students graduate believing that it is easy to tell the difference between truths and lies or distortions.

The expectation of family prosperity can come under strain in the public schools. I read recently in the *New York Times* about a school in Brooklyn in which half of all students are homeless—in and out of school, often hungry, and often traumatized by a precarious existence.[60] Information in such a setting cannot be neutral. The context of its delivery is far from equal, to begin with. And knowledge about social problems and U.S. and world history, in addition to science and the arts, cannot proceed as if all schoolchildren had equal stakes in social competence and belonging. Teachers and administrators at School 188 feel the strain at having to provide a normative curriculum with test-based assessments when there are other, more urgent lessons, to be understood. Children learn to write letters to the president pleading with him to address homelessness, or to Santa asking for money for a down payment on a house.

In this context, charter schools represent neoliberalism's—hyper-privatized capitalism's—crystallization. If public resources cannot educate students, perhaps the market and profit-driven schools can fill the gaps. However, these schools most often fail the most vulnerable children, hyper-exploit teachers, and reinforce rote knowledge that leads to strong test scores. "Facts" are commodities in a commercial learning environment.[61]

Conservative Education

Private schools, accessible only to elites in the United States, naturally cultivate a view of the world in which the wealthy deserve their prosperity. In addition, conservative schooling can be rigorous because the youth there have grown up in houses with books; they are not generally too hungry to learn. The curriculum in many of these schools is based on "great books," largely written by men, accounting for history, literature, and the arts. Allan Bloom and William Bennett advocated this mode of education in their argument that in the education system, pupils were losing sight of basic moral knowledge based on biblical principle or the ideology of personal responsibility.

Conservative Christians have started charters and curricula for home-schooling children in the context of religious faith and morality. Along with other conservatives, they do not deny the propaganda function of primary education. With basic literacy and math skills comes the fallback to scripture as the absolute authority. Deep questions have a single answer. These schools attempt to create a closed universe of learning in which children will not find their faith or their ideals challenged. Nor will they need to encounter social and economic or ideological differences, which are the source of another kind of education entirely.

In the conservative context, facts are neither neutral nor commodities: They are weapons in the broader culture war. It is in this context that science education, particularly on the topic of biological evolution, becomes part of this battleground. Although advocates of creationism have not yet succeeded in their efforts to have public schools teach creationism or intelligent design alongside the theory of evolution, liberals and progressives alike have reason to worry as the current presidential administration includes fundamentalists who will lead the charge; it will also likely put in place justices on the Supreme Court who might rule for creationists in new cases to come.[62]

Creationists adopt the language of liberalism in advocating the intrusion of religion into a secular (on the basis of the Establishment Clause of the First Amendment to the U.S. Constitution) public education system. As in the case of Creation.com, they attempt to make a case for a supernatural designer in scientific language. They also argue for inclusion of creationism as a form of intellectual pluralism, arguing that evolution is "only" a theory (which, of course, misunderstands the status of theory in scientific inquiry) and that other theories (hypotheses or speculations) should have a place alongside the prevailing content.[63]

On this point, they argue that their perspective is marginalized or oppressed, potentially invoking liberal sympathy and an openness to inclusion of other (their) voices. The main buttress of the (neo)liberal school system against creationism is, ironically, the belief that the knowledge produced in mainstream schools is non-ideological, so that the intrusion of any propagandistic agenda, especially religion, cannot be admitted. Weirdly, the courts have affirmed the principle of neutrality, which in turn wins teachers, students, and bodies of citizens to the ideal of neutral, nonpartisan knowledge. The ideology of the system is that the system that exists is ideology free.

Critical and Radical Education

I am not advocating the inclusion of an argument for divine creation and design in the teaching of science in public schools. However, neither am I arguing for an education that is naïve about the perspectival partisanship of knowledge.

There is a substantial tradition of critical and radical pedagogy to draw from to give shape to a curriculum that raises such questions.[64] There are at least four principles that can be drawn from this literature. First, acknowledge the lived experiences of students and their communities and use them as a basis for curriculum. A student who writes the president asking for help with the mortgage needs to be told that it is unlikely, given at least recent historical patterns, that the president will be willing or able to do that. Raise the question: What has it taken and what will it take to demand accountability from a society founded on inequality?

Second, and relatedly, encourage students to create curriculum based on questions arising from their lived experiences. Possible themes include histories of oppressed people and the words of silenced voices, the diversity of the world's people and their practices, and a sense of commonality, not with all other people but with the majority of humanity living without the resources and agency to thrive. Third, equip students with basic skills and knowledge, not so that they can become compliant citizens but so that they can use these tools to build movements for social change and to run a sustainable society based on the liberated interests of ordinary people. This knowledge includes the best scientific understandings available as well as information and practice in the skills of organizing, persuasion, leadership, and compassion—that is to say, rhetoric. Fourth and finally, engage social movement struggles as sites of education and transformation. Participation in movements against racism, imperialism, economic exploitation, misogyny, and all other oppressions puts into practice lessons learned and provides incalculable new ones as the transformation of consciousness is accelerated in struggle.

Radicals are not antiscience. As Marx and Engels and many critics before and since have argued, however, it is crucial to apply the basics of scientific investigation to society itself rather than seeing the tools of inquiry as transcendent and neutral. It is important that we develop analyses of the system as a whole, where it came from, and what caused it to be the way it is, so that we can take steps to change it. We need to develop clear social theories that are built by and for the working class and all of the communities of the oppressed who compose it. Such theories start with the collective rather than the individual, but not the Great Community imagined by liberals.

We can study ants, but we could also wonder what the ant observes. People are not ants, but the outcome of any scientific inquiry is shaped first by one's vantage point. Feminists and Marxists call this idea "standpoint epistemology." The idea is that in a kingdom ruled by a giant, the giant can hardly see the little people under his feet. It depends upon their labor and cooperation, but he has little idea about their experience.

However, if you are one of the little people underfoot, and you look up, you get a very clear view of the entire giant. The system of his foot on your back is crucial information about how society works. To be safe for the future and all those who are with you and will come after, you must take down the giant. Since you are too small, as the Ewoks in *Star Wars* realized, to bring him down by yourself, you must get together with as many other people as you can to share experience, to theorize, to ask, What happened the last time the giant nearly fell? How many sticks will we need and how sharp must they be to puncture his skin and make him fall? Can we make ourselves larger? Can we do anything to make him sick and weak? Can he be killed? How can we do that? When that happens, how can we move him out of the way? How do we inspire others to stay with us in this process? What do we need to know to make and sustain a society without giants?

All of this knowledge needs to be systematically and accurately gathered if your people are not to be crushed. It is a scientific process of observation, experimentation, questioning, theorizing, testing, assessing, and being accountable. It involves not only facts but also the organization of facts and the practices of collective organizing, argumentation, and inspiration. The process builds upon the history and experience of those who came before, but their offerings should not be taken on authority alone.

The advocates of radical pedagogy have shown how experiential learning can generate critical consciousness, and that critical consciousness can be shared and generalized, producing new practices and ways of being in the world. Carl Sagan understood the potential of involving young people in science. There are two scenes in the first *Cosmos* series where he shares his ideas with a diverse classroom of public school students in Brooklyn, where he was raised. He passes out photographic images taken by *Voyager* as if they are trading cards. Students excitedly examine and exchange them while Sagan tells them about what *Voyager* has helped scientists to discover. In the second segment, he asks for volunteers to wheel a model of the solar system around to demonstrate the orbits of the planets. He gets the students up and moving, involving their bodies in the practice of learning. He takes numerous questions and does his best to answer them. These students may not have been inspired every day, but the looks on their faces on this day reveal what happens when they are engaged honestly and with humility.

COSMIC PEDAGOGY

As I mentioned above, both *Cosmos* and its creationist opponents have produced study guides for the episodes. I'll take the ones for the first episode as examples to show their profound differences. What they share is the awareness that the program's longest-term and most profoundly important audience will be children. The authors at the disingenuously titled website "Evolution News" worry that the new *Cosmos,* with its flashy graphics and compelling stories, will become a staple in science classrooms.

David Klinghoffer writes,

> Despite its increasingly undisguised axe-grinding, history-befogging, and faith-baiting excesses, there's no question that the rebooted *Cosmos* series with Neil deGrasse Tyson will be turning up in classrooms as a "supplement" to science education. I mentioned this earlier today, but it is not simply a matter of my speculating. The Internet is abuzz with talk by teachers and others who are excited about the prospect.[65]

The page quotes teachers who had posted their enthusiasm about the program on other websites:

> Neil deGrasse Tyson, Cosmos is amazing! **I can't wait to buy it on DVD so that I can show it to my 8th grade science class during our universe section!!** My students do a lab on the universal timeline (much like the calendar you speak of in Cosmos). I can't wait to add the explanation for Cosmos into the lab! Thank you for inspiring a new generation of scientists! (emphasis in original)

> Teachers looking for an excellent television show to help drive home various science information to your students should look no further. The television station Fox has done society a great service by putting "Cosmos: A Spacetime Odyssey" hosted by Neil deGrasse Tyson on the air. Tyson delivers the often-complicated ideas in a way that all levels of learners can understand and still be entertained by the stories. Episodes of this show make great supplements in the science classroom and also can be used as a reward or movie day.

> While Carl Sagan premiered a similar "cosmic calendar" back in 1980, the one on display last night was really incredible. **I've no doubt this part of "Cosmos" will be replayed countless times in science classes around the world for decades to come.** (emphasis in original)

There is evidence that teachers are using the series. At the blog LessonPlans.com, Monica Fuglei praises *Cosmos* for building scientific literacy, encouraging scientific analysis, prodding debate about scientific concepts, and sparking intellectual curiosity and inquiry.[66] The site encourages having students design their own lesson plans around the content.

The study guides at the *Cosmos* site also demonstrate a tone of openness. Aimed at students in grades six to twelve, they are written by Ann Druyan. They summarize the episodes, but most notably, they focus on student-driven content:

- Find your own birthday on the Cosmic Calendar.
- Earn a learner's permit to drive your own Ship of the Imagination [by explaining the rules of exploring the cosmos—the scientific method].
- Select a destination in the cosmos, giving the coordinates in space and time. Present your research and write or draw a vision of what it would be like.[67]

Another exercise involves students' history and experience:

> On the Cosmic Calendar, we see how the chance gravitational jostling of an asteroid an inch to the left has the most profound consequences for the existence of our species. Imagine a contingency that led to your own existence: for example, the chance meeting of your parents, historical factors that may have driven one of your grandparents to leave his or her home country and venture to another to meet your other grandparent. Encourage students to develop their own causality chain of events.

In contrast, Ken Ham's guides are motivated by defensiveness: "I expect that an anti-biblical American TV series will soon be used in public schools across the country, and I want parents to be prepared to counter the series' evolutionary arguments from a biblical standpoint."[68] For episode 1, Dr. Elizabeth Mitchell calls attention to how much of the episode involves imagination and speculation and argues that the aim of scientific literacy would be served by engaging other "scientific" viewpoints. In a smart move, she notes that Tyson admits that we do not know the answers to the biggest questions: What caused the Big Bang and how did life begin? I believe that those are the openings for faith that make the most sense as a matter of metaphysics or philosophy rather than science. However, Ham's mission is to convince followers that the young-earth creationist account is backed by its own science, of a particular kind. Thus, the leader discussion guide contrasts experimental science and origins science, the latter of which

> attempts to discover the truth about the unobservable past by interpreting scientific observations in light of what the scientist believes about the past (presuppositions or starting assumptions). These beliefs about the past may

include eyewitness testimony of someone who was there—namely, God our Creator—or uniformitarian or materialistic evolutionary beliefs that substitute man's fallible ideas for what God has told us about our origins.

The guide suggests an experiment in which a student lights one candle and lets it burn itself out. Then the student is asked to light a candle, marking the time, then blow it out, marking the time. In only one scenario will another person know how long the candle burned: the one with the record of an eyewitness. (In this experiment, the child is God.) The test's only point is that we can only have certain knowledge about the past if we have an eyewitness record, and that the Bible is that record. Not only does this lesson mistake eyewitness evidence for the only authoritative evidence, but it also makes the Bible the ultimate and only fallback authority. It is not a system that encourages questioning; there is nothing new under the sun, in the sun, or beyond the sun. There is no need to go looking.

The guides lead to a site called "Kid's Answers," and there is a companion magazine.[69] Each subtopic, "Evolution," "Science," "Creation," and so on, gives very little time to questions. One question, "Are people just animals?" gets the terse reply, "The Bible teaches that people are made in God's image. Animals were not made in God's image; only people were!"[70] Enough said—the less, apparently, the better. One can only hope that many children find this answer unsatisfying.

The answer to those living under the giant's heel who might ask, "Why is the giant standing on us?" would be "because God made it so." Thus, the debate over science education is relevant to human emancipation. Accepting a closed explanatory system with no evidence aside from scripture is a recipe for passivity and incuriosity at best; at worst, as *Cosmos* points out, knowledges outside of authorized accounts, and their discoverers, are subject to repression and persecution. Returning to the questions *Whose knowledge is it? Who is it by, and who is it for? Who is left out?*, we might simply observe, in response, that creationism is not for the oppressed.

Radicals reject creationism as a curriculum not because of its persuasive strategies, especially not because its discourse is mythic in character. Any attempt to systematize knowledge—scientific, historical, or social—will have a mythic component if it hopes to inspire engagement. Kenneth Burke regarded myth as essential as "a means of affecting social cohesion" and "a bridging device to relate humanity to the earth and the wider university—in short, the cosmos."[71] Burke claimed that there are accurate myths and inaccurate ones. By accurate, he meant descriptive of the reality of ordinary people and faithful to their interests. By inaccurate, he meant characterized by dogmatic mystification.[72] Who gets to tell the stories, whose are they, and who benefits from the telling? Whose stories are left out? These are the important questions when considering the crucial mediating role of education. And in a literal sense, it is a religious calling. The word *religion* has as its root, according to the dictionary, the Latin word *religare*, meaning "to tie" or "to bind." In this sense, religion is merely a system of ideas and practices that tie a community together. If we choose those ideas and practices in alignment with an obligation to the interests among the oppressed and exploited in emancipation, then we could say that we would have put into place an accurate religion.

Even more interesting is research into the Latin roots of the word *religion* that traces it not to *religare* but to *relegare*, derived by the Roman rhetorician Cicero, to mean "to go through or over again in reading, speech, or thought."[73] This derivation is exciting from the perspective of radical pedagogy, whose practices encourage the rethinking and analysis of received knowledge in light of experience and the goals of liberation.

I confess that I have not always taught in the ways practiced by and advocated by the radical pedagogues whose work I admire. There are occasions when I have tried to and other occasions when I should have done so. One obstacle to experience-based, resistance-oriented pedagogy is the inaccessibility of higher education—and equal quality primary education—to increasing numbers of people without the means to pay outright or the ability to carry a huge burden of debt. One consequence of this situation is that my students are more likely to be the children of giants than of the oppressed and exploited. Their experience would not be a critical base for generating questions and insights.

There are other, better, places for revolutionary education than the college classroom as it currently is configured. Among those sites are the organizing spaces of social movements and radical political parties who encourage historical, scientific, and theoretical education for the purpose of human liberation.

Inviting viewers to investigate the universe, Neil deGrasse Tyson says, "Come with me." Inviting readers, scholars, and activists to recognize the necessity of mediation to radical learning and emancipatory practice, I say, "Come with us."

CHAPTER 6

From Thomas Paine to #BlackLivesMatter

The Tasks of Making Revolutionary Common Sense

SO FAR in this book I have argued that the responses by liberals and progressives to the crisis of truth in U.S. political culture have been mistaken in their focus on the minutiae of fact-checking. Those farther on the Left still tend to hold the position that in a controversy, the better argument with the best empirical evidence will win out against lies and mystification. While I practice and teach (and believe in the importance of) evidence-based reasoning and communication practice, my experience and research have led me to realize that we must attend more thoughtfully to the processes of mediation—the role of communicators to intervene in the circulation of knowledge, especially the knowledge based on the interests and experiences of the oppressed and exploited—in the interpretation and shaping of political ideas.

I have discussed the importance of the "big five" rhetorical strategies that have been embraced by champions of ordinary people. However, I also have pointed to the risks and limitations of those strategies, including the political compromises one must make (for example, cooperation with a heteronormative, masculinist narrative frame in publicizing whistleblowers) and the constraining role of historical moment, as in the case of the failure of the second *Cosmos* in reaching the same audiences as its forbearer. With regard to *Cosmos*, I noted the ethical quality of reflexivity and contradiction—*punctum*—in what would otherwise potentially be an exercise in standard mythmaking (*studium*).

In this chapter I raise the same questions and possibilities about the role of truth claims in a special case: a revolution. I was drawn to the American Revolution for two reasons, the first being that it is an accessible example for U.S. reading audiences, and the second being the figure of Thomas Paine. Pushing the left edge of the revolution, Paine put himself in a position to circulate revolutionary ideas in such a way that they became "common sense." The name of his famous pamphlet speaks to my primary concern about how we can bring knowledges of subordinated groups into popular consciousness such that they become commonsensical, challenging or replacing previous dogmas. A revolutionary situation is unique in this regard—relatively rare but also momentous in its significance. As a socialist and a lifetime activist, I, and I think many others at our historical juncture, am interested in how communicators inject new political truths into a society in the midst of major crisis.

There is some controversy about whether the American War for Independence represented a significant or radically transformative revolution. Neil Davidson explores the distinction between political and social revolutions: In the former, transformation seeks to change political ideology and shape the form of government without altering the fundamental economic structures and hierarchies of power in place.[1] He and Eric Foner both conclude that the American Revolution occupies the category of political revolution, Davidson noting that since the United States had no feudal remnants in its structure, it did not actually require an anti-feudal struggle.[2] Foner, in later work, makes the argument that the U.S. Civil War completed that revolution. Before then, the continuance of slavery in the United States after the War for Independence challenged any idea that the economic and power relations in the United States had been fundamentally altered in the first round. However, even if the revolution were not a deep-reaching social revolution, it did require a war, and motivation for that war required a new political language. And as Herbert Aptheker argues, the pressure on the merchant class from below articulated revolutionary ideas not because of the economic situation, but in spite of it.[3] Although the immature colonial bourgeoisie chafed against monarchical rule and sought control of its fortunes, the active involvement of workers, farmers, and craftspeople amplified the revolution's truly democratic content.[4]

Having to motivate Americans unfamiliar with the language of democracy and independence to support a decolonizing war required rhetorical work. In a specifically revolutionary situation, timing, the quality of the intervention, and the capacity of the communicator to make the right intervention at the right time are crucial. In the rhetorical theory of the ancient Greeks, this idea of using well-timed situated political judgment (or *phronesis*) in the context of crisis is called *kairos*.[5]

In what follows I will provide brief background on Paine and his role in the American Revolution. Then I will perform an analysis of *Common Sense* that identifies features of its political ideology and the strategies through which they are mediated. While Paine did not employ the resource of spectacle (as did the activists in the Boston Tea Party, for example), he used an emerging form of media—the pamphlet, following the development of the newspaper from a mercantile tool to a disseminator of politics. His was a vernacular, or bottom-up, production similar to the efforts of many social movements throughout U.S. history up to today. In *Common Sense,* he develops narratives, including mythic ones, to describe the heroes, villains, values, responsibilities, and destinies of the revolution. His use of emotional appeals is notable as well. The most important aspect of his intervention into the revolution as a mediator is how, at exactly the right moment, he moved the leftmost edge of liberalism into intelligibility for large parts of the population, who would not necessarily fight for free trade but who would fight for the ideas of democratic representation and equal rights. I will close out the analysis of the pamphlet by observing its implicit theories of ideology, mediation, and social change. The chapter then turns to the question of whether we have mediators of revolutionary struggle among us today, arguing for a possibility in the #BlackLivesMatter movement.

COMMON SENSE: NEW FORM, NEW VISION

When Paine crafted and published the pamphlet *Common Sense* in 1776, he had been in Philadelphia for just over a year. The war was a long shot for the Patriots, and many colonists were neutral on the question of independence or loyal to the Crown. The elite discourses of the intellectual leaders of the revolution, including John Adams and Thomas Jefferson, did not reach the mass of colonists, most of whom were artisans—craftspeople and owners of small, home-based businesses—and laborers. The artisans had already become politically active, having formed the Patriotic Society and a militia. Open military engagement with the British had begun the year before at Lexington and Concord. General George Washington struggled with low troop morale.

It was into this context that Paine introduced *Common Sense,* to explosive effect. It articulated some of the most radical ideas of the Enlightenment about liberty and was shocking in its intensity regarding the despotism of monarchical rule. In spite of—or because of—its radicalism, it went through two dozen editions and sold hundreds of thousands of copies in its first year, reaching many thousands more as it was read aloud in taverns, in coffeehouses, at street fairs, and on battlefields. Commentators at the time credited the pamphlet with playing a pivotal role in winning the population and the troops in favor of independence, at any cost. As Dennehey, Morgan, and Assenza observe, "Paine was able to encourage the coming together of the thirteen diverse colonies, and helped sustain this energy even during the harsh and demoralizing winter of 1776, when Washington's troops were ready to quit."[6]

The content of the pamphlet was informed, according to historian Bernard Bailyn, by several traditions: Enlightenment rationality, Deist theology, Newtonian science—with its appreciation of reason, natural order, and observation—and the legacy of antimonarchical agitation in Paine's home, England. The pamphlet, shorter and less expensive than a book, longer and more detailed than a broadside, was a new medium of communication, one well suited to Paine's democratizing purposes. According to Edward Larkin, the content of the pamphlet cannot be separated from its democratic style: both form and content expressed a new vision of the access of ordinary people to the political process and to representation in it.

Common Sense contains three sections after an introduction in which Paine encourages readers to consider new ideas with open minds and to refuse to be ruled by their preconceptions:

> Perhaps the sentiments contained in the following pages are not *yet* sufficiently fashionable to procure them general Favor; a long Habit of not thinking a Thing *wrong*, gives it a superficial appearance of being *right*, and raises at first a formidable outcry in defence of Custom. But the Tumult soon subsides. Time makes more Converts than Reason.[7]

This passage is as astonishing as it is brief, for Paine has in short form established what it means to critique dominant ideology. He expresses his understanding that people who are used to one way of thinking may find it difficult to accept the new. He breaks the connection between the familiar and the true. And he calls attention to how experience and the passage of time will prove him right.

The next paragraph of the introduction is interesting in the same way, arguing that by inflicting violence and abuse upon the oppressed, the powerful call their own privilege into question—"and in matters too which might never have been thought of, had not the sufferers been aggravated into the inquiry." In one sentence, Paine has defined standpoint epistemology, or the idea that the experience of oppression leads sufferers (aggravates them) to engage in critique and resistance. He also here alerts readers that they are well within their rights to question the king and the Parliament. Moreover, the passage encourages readers to relate what Paine is about to argue to their personal experience.

In the rest of the introduction, Paine (writing anonymously) tells readers that he has left his own personal life out of the text in favor of the description of universal principles, ending with a lyrical call for attention: "The laying a country desolate with fire and sword, declaring war against the natural rights of all mankind, and extirpating the defenders thereof from the face of the earth, is the concern of every man to whom nature hath given the power of feeling."

The body of the pamphlet contains three sections, the first being "On the Origin and Design of Government in General, with Concise Remarks on the English Constitution." It is important to note that Paine does not open with a call to support independence; that idea is not introduced until the final section. This first section identifies government itself as perhaps a necessary evil that becomes "intolerable" when it encroaches upon society. Paine here defines and defends the idea of civil society, a domain of positive and productive, voluntary social interaction (which he calls "intercourse") outside of the domain of government influence. Paine rejects the idea that human nature is base and therefore requiring rule. "Government," he writes, "like dress, is the badge of lost innocence." Because he argues for a vision of human nature not defined by sin, even that badge, he suggests, is unnecessary.

The second section ("On the Monarchy and Hereditary Succession") explains that to the extent that people in collective societies need some organizing form, it should be of a kind closest to a state of "natural liberty," in which society is the people's "first thought." Paine envisions a government with a unicameral legislature of recallable delegates elected proportionally from the colonies. He continues by condemning the English Constitution for enshrining the hereditary right of monarchs and aristocrats to rule. Even though there is a form of checks and balances in the constitution, the king is immune from such oversight; moreover, he writes, if the king's rule is so just, why should a system of checks be required? In arguing that those dependent on the king should not be the ones to judge the fitness of the monarchy, he compares a bad constitution to a prostitute whose clients would not be able to judge a wife; thus those dependent on a rotten constitution are not in a position to weigh in on its merits. Here and elsewhere, metaphorical allusions to marriage and relations between men and women in general arise in ways that are quite sexist (in this case, that a sexually active woman is like a corrupt government), a feature upon which other critics and historians have not extensively commented.

The section continues with an argument that division of society into classes of kings and subjects is not natural. Paine's evidence is that throughout the greatest part of human history, and in many contemporary nations, there had been no kings. He turns to the Old Testament to note the folly of the Israelites in choosing first Saul and then David as their king when scripture commanded otherwise. In two pages filled with italic emphasis he occupies the implied voice of God describing what a king would do to the people: He will reign over you; he will take your sons as servants; he will steal the harvest; he will use the loot to make war; he will take your daughter to work in his household; he will take over your land and your livestock. "AND THE LORD WILL NOT HEAR YOU ON THAT DAY."[8] In this allegory, God is the stand-in for natural rights, which should be the only ruler over humanity, with the acceptance of any other rule as unnatural. For a Christian reader, the extended venture into Old Testament history connects the idea of natural rights with godliness.

This analogy supports his next argument against hereditary succession as unjust, unnatural, and fueled by habit and superstition. He compares the right of succession to original sin: One bad decision echoes across history as depraved monarchs follow the corrupt and incompetent. He calls monarchs depraved ruffians, savages, and plunderers who leave the people to be ruled by minors and any other manner of the unfit. At the end of this section, he makes a transition by stating that the closer a government comes to a republic, the less it needs a king.

Then he moves into the third and longest section, "On the Present State of American Affairs." Notably, this section returns to the call for readers to overcome their prejudices and preconceptions. He calls into being a set of readers who, in this way, are empowered to "suffer his reason and his feelings to determine for themselves, that he will put on, or rather that he will not put off, the true character of a man, and generously enlarge his views beyond the present day."

Although the colonies could decide to negotiate with the Crown at any point, he presents the taking up of arms as a *fait accompli*: "The period of debate is closed," and "reconciliation, like an agreeable dream, hath passed away." Having oriented his audience to a present-moment point of view, he refutes a number of arguments in favor of remaining under British rule. Notably, he makes his call for natural rights and civil and religious liberty a global one by invoking the people of multiple nations who emigrated to come to America's shores. He details the infringements of the British on commerce, arguing that its outdated mode of government is an impediment to free trade. This argument captures the significance of this writing as an expression of a new set of economic arrangements, whose entrepreneurs chafed against the royal bit.

At this point, Paine launches into an extended and lyrical rationale for independence: "Every thing that is right or reasonable pleads for separation. The blood of the slain, the weeping voice of nature cries, 'TIS TIME TO PART." Rather than delay and bring debt and ruin upon our children, he argues, "We ought to do the work of it." He urges distance from those with interests in the power and profit of reconciliation, moderates who dangerously delay the inevitable, and the willfully ignorant (prejudiced) and then appeals to his readers' emotions:

> Hath your house been burnt? Hath your property been destroyed before your face? Are your wife and children destitute of a bed to lie on or bread to live on? Have you lost a parent or a child by their hands, and yourself the ruined and wretched survivor? If you have not, then are you not a judge of those who have. But if you have, and can still shake hands with the murderers, then are you unworthy the name of husband, father, friend, or love, and whatever may be your rank or title in life, you have the heart of a coward, and the spirit of a sycophant.

In a heavily gendered appeal, he states his goal as not to inflame or exaggerate, but rather "to awaken us from fatal and unmanly slumbers, that we may pursue determinately some fixed object. . . . The present winter is worth an age if rightly employed, but if lost or neglected the whole Continent will partake of the misfortune. . . . Reconciliation is *now* a fallacious dream. Nature hath deserted the connection and art cannot supply her place." References to nature and art here are meaningful: Natural law favors independence and therefore "hath deserted" the goal of reconciliation. Art in this context seemingly refers to the artifice of politics; no adjustments within the political order will suffice. With these words, Paine escalates the call for immediate action for independence, rejecting lesser measures.

In response to any potential insecurities arising from the fact that the colonies had no plan as to what sort of government to form, Paine proposes a minimal government consisting of delegates to a unicameral congress with a president elected by those delegates and rotating in representation among the colonies. He concludes with a rousing call, (which ironically features a bit of the colonial "white man's burden" argument about Africa and Asia):

> O! Ye that love mankind! Ye that dare oppose not only the tyranny but the tyrant, stand forth! Every spot of the old world is overrun with oppression.

Freedom hath been hunted round the Globe. Asia and Africa have long expelled her. Europe regards her like a stranger, and England hath given her warning to depart. O! receive the fugitive and prepare in time an asylum for mankind.[9]

In an appendix, Paine offers an optimistic summary of the available resources for war (munitions, troops, and treasure) and the capacity of the colonies to sustain it.

PAINE AND THE BIG FIVE

Scholarly research on Paine's rhetorical efforts has identified how, in a crucial moment, Paine used new and vernacular media to reach broad audiences with the most radical ideas of the Enlightenment. In the process, he constituted a public sphere of ordinary people. About the use of an emerging medium, Craig Nelson writes,

> *Common Sense* appeared in the form of a pamphlet, the most popular style of eighteenth-century publishing, as it offered a medium for anyone who could afford the cost of paper and a print shop's fees. With no binding or cover, consisting of between twenty and eighty loosely sewn pages, with costs affordable for almost any would be author, the longest pamphlets were about the length of today's romance novels or classic mysteries. Costing about a shilling and therefore far less expensive than books, pamphlets were just the right length for explaining a position in detail, as well as for being read aloud to the illiterate, an important consideration for those wanting to reach the widest of audiences.[10]

Paine used this emerging and broadly accessible medium to spread crystallizing Enlightenment ideas. Eric Foner summarizes:

> Paine was one of the creators of this secular language of revolution, a language in which timeless discontents, millennial aspirations and popular traditions were expressed in a strikingly new vocabulary. The very slogans and rallying cries we associate with the revolutions of the late eighteenth century come from Paine's writings: the "rights of man," the "age of reason," the "age of revolution" and "the times that try men's souls." Paine helped to transform the meaning of the key words of political discourse.[11]

These words included *democracy, equal rights,* and *republic,* invoking the founding myths of the republic, which operated simultaneously as revolutionary ideals, and, in the more traditional meaning of myth, ideological cover for capitalism as it emerged as a mode of production. Paine's rhetoric forefronts "equality" over and above the other God-term of liberal ideology, "liberty." That choice marks him as invested in the more radical adjustment of social relations to level access to resources and representation.

Foner also points out that Paine's style matched the ideological import of his writing:

> He forged a new political language. He did not simply change the meanings of words, he created a literary style designed to bring his message to the widest possible audience. His rhetoric was clear, simple and straightforward; his arguments rooted in the common experiences of a mass readership. . . . Through this new language, he communicated a new vision—a utopian image of an egalitarian republican society.[12]

An intriguing dimension of that vision came from Paine's and other revolutionaries' investment in developments in science, from Newtonian theories of gravity to the image of the solar system as a regular, ordered whole. Not only could ordinary people understand science, society could be governed and move according to natural law, as well.[13] In this way, Paine demonstrates how the science emerging during the Enlightenment was closely tied to the project of democracy, as I noted in the previous chapter.

Research in rhetorical studies has identified a number of persuasive strategies employed by Paine. Hogan and Williams argue that Paine constructed a new kind of charisma: "grounded in the mundane, empirical, natural, and pragmatic, and in a new passionate self-revelatory style in which the leader is not charismatic due to greatness but due to the resonance with 'universal sentiment' of the people."[14]

Affect and emotion were also central to Paine's efforts. Michelle Kennerly notes how emotional language and vivid metaphor were mechanisms of "transport" enabling audiences to move toward formerly unknown or unintelligible concepts.[15] On the subject of emotional appeals, Edward Gallagher argues that Paine "wrapped people in the comfort of time" in response to their anxieties.[16] Larkin describes how allegories drawn from nature and (unfortunately) from the relations between men and women concretized abstract concepts.

More broadly, these scholars emphasize how Paine's writings invented and cultivated a public sphere that extended beyond the merchant elites of colonial society. Larkin writes,

Instead of subscribing to the traditional binary that counterpoised the mob and the elite, he created an idiom where politics could be simultaneously popular and thoroughly reasoned. His writing made it possible to think of a public sphere that could be democratized outside the narrow confines of a literate bourgeoisie. . . . Paine turns the people into thoughtful participants in the affairs of the nation and transforms democracy from a political system into a more broadly conceived social and cultural phenomenon involving the dissemination of ideas. . . . This process of making politics accessible to ordinary people involved not only the invention of a new political language but, just as importantly, the fashioning of a new kind of political actor.[17]

Foner likewise notes that Paine's texts circulated not only in coffeehouses and salons, but also in taverns and street fairs, making something of a spectacle of the text.

In addition to challenging the divide between popular (low) culture and political discussion, Paine explodes other dichotomies. He found the distinctions between public and private, entertainment and instruction, theoretical science and applied mechanics, and elite genres and popular culture to serve the exclusions of the masses from politics.[18]

Most importantly for my purposes, the scholarship repeatedly recognizes the pivotal role in history effected by *Common Sense*. The immediate military and constitutional crisis was set in the context of nascent capitalism, which encouraged the wide debate of the principles of democracy, for it was those principles that would shore up the rising merchant class's economic and political position. The efforts of elites toward a new kind of society needed a push from below, couched in terms of equality and rights. Paine himself represents the contradiction between a shift toward exploitative economic relationships and that shift's promotion of new, egalitarian ideas.[19] He supported laissez-faire economics as counterpart to and regulator of the natural political order.

Davidson explains how even bourgeois revolutions require the investment of the "lower orders," although elites are likely to put on the brakes after the revolution's initial goals are won.[20] Other intellectual leaders of the revolution welcomed Paine's effective intervention at first and came to revile him and his radicalism later. Hogan and Williams quote John Adams as saying, "Without the pen of the author of Common Sense, the sword of Washington would have been raised in vain."[21] Later, Adams would call Paine a satyr and a mongrel.[22]

But every revolutionary crisis finds a point at which its ideals and contradictions find pivotal expression. About Paine's intervention, Foner writes, "Paine was precisely the right man at the right time: articulating ideas which were in the air but only dimly perceived by most of his contemporaries, helping to promote revolution by changing the very terms in which people thought about politics and society."[23]

PAINE'S IMPLICIT THEORY OF IDEOLOGY AND MEDIATION

David Hoffman argues that Paine cut against readers' caution and loyalty by reframing tradition and prior belief as "prejudice," which at the time did not have the connotation of discrimination, but rather meant prejudgment or established belief.[24] Then "common sense" was counterpoised to "prejudice," encouraging readers to break with the familiar in favor of new ideas more fitting to their identities and situations. To have one's commitments framed as prejudgments invites identifying with the goal of reasoned judgment of present facts and arguments.

Hoffman's insight resonates with the idea of Paine as a self-conscious mediator of political crisis. Paine's redefinition of prior commitment as "prejudice" indicates a sophisticated theory of ideology. Rather than ascribing loyalty to the Crown as having bought into a pack of lies, Paine implies that beliefs are a product of the times. His statement about time in part 1 of the pamphlet resonates here: "Time makes more Converts than Reason." One can read this statement as indicating how a moment in time, a situation of crisis, may open the way for people to come to new ways of seeing more quickly than preaching ideology at them would. People cannot help but internalize prevailing ideas at the time of their circulation during periods of relative stability.

Revolutionary crisis upsets the hegemony of those ideas, which could provoke anxiety among citizens and a retreat to their comfort. However, new times require new ideas, pitched as not merely a set of facts but as a reasoned set of interpretations and principles to explain society's functioning afresh. Although Paine wanted to call his pamphlet *Plain Truth,* the purpose of mediation is to offer audiences a coherent articulation of counterhegemonic ideas in connection with audience members' experience. It is far from offering the "plain truth." Political activists, commentators, and leaders today should understand that this role requires something besides fact-checking. In addition to its historical influence, Paine's work teaches us that meeting citizens in their own language without disdain for the common, understanding the crucial component of timing or *kairos,* employing narrative, myth, and emotion, and setting forth a set of principles and proposals that connect with the experience of ordinary people will do far better service to social change than the iteration of old prejudices.

There is a bit of an irony in this analysis, since Gramsci referred to "common sense" as the naturalized set of beliefs of a society during a time of stability. On that argument, it is common sense that needs countering. But he also observed that every epoch throws up a new set of ideas that are put into place as old ones are denaturalized. This new ideological frame then becomes common sense—in Paine's terms, it will become the next generation's "prejudice," a force of stability and cohesion that itself will need challenging when it conflicts with the interests of those living under its assumptions. *Common Sense* is not "the plain truth." It is ideology. And regarding ideologies, we can say that there are "their" ideologies—those of the ruling class—and "our" ideologies—the knowledge, including facts, interpretation, and analysis—that can guide social change even unto revolution with fidelity to the interests of those it hails.

THE PAINE OF OUR TIME: PUBLIC INTELLECTUALS, #BLACKLIVESMATTER, AND SOCIAL REVOLUTION

Reading Paine's *Common Sense* at our historical, political, economic, and social moment naturally provokes the question of whether we have any Thomas Paines among us doing this timely work of reaching mass audiences with political clarity and motivation. I argue that we do in the #BlackLives-Matter movement. This movement involves public intellectuals who have created and sustained new publics through the use of emerging media and who understand and communicate about injustice in new, compelling, and condensed language. They employ narrative, myth, embodiment, affect, and spectacle to tremendous effect. The crisis they have entered into with perfect timing may be more urgent even than Paine's. The leading voices in this movement have begun to describe what it would take to mount a social revolution that can address the deep causes of racist brutality in the United States.

Public Intellectuals as Mediators

In Gramsci's terms, Paine was an organic, public intellectual. Without access to higher education, he steeped himself in public lectures on science and philosophy. In the eighteenth-century context of a blossoming set of publics and counterpublics—spaces in civil society for people of all ranks to collect to discuss science, politics, and the arts—he participated in debates over the most pressing questions of his day. He learned the concerns and the language of the people who would be among his readers. When he intervened, he did so not as an elite figure speaking to the masses, but as one of the people. A public intellectual, according to Richard Posner, is a person with intellectual resources who writes for broad public audiences on issues of political import.[25] Public intellectuals can operate from outside the communities for whom they speak, but Gramsci argued for the importance of what he called *organic* intellectuals, who emerge as leaders in struggle and are members of the communities they organize. Pundits and scholars can do good work mediating political information, but the most vital work happens from inside communities and movements.

Public intellectuals have been important to social movement causes, both revolutionary and modest. They arise out of collective experience and agitation and attempt to generalize and synthesize a political voice that can capture the interests of those seeking change. They do not always do so with fidelity to the people whose struggle they have leveraged, as when media empire owner Oprah Winfrey advises self-help for suffering Americans and distances herself from the civil rights movement.[26] Although they appear to be individual pundits, gurus, prophets, artists, or other celebrities, it would be wrong to credit any solo effort with a cause's success.[27] (On this point, the lionization of Paine as an individual deserves question; if he were not the one to condense and translate the ideals of the revolution from below, it might have been someone else—his friend Benjamin Rush or perhaps Ben Franklin.)

There are a number of public intellectuals in the United States, many of them black: from Neil deGrasse Tyson to Henry Louis Gates, Angela Davis, Michelle Alexander, Cornell West, Keeanga Yamahtta-Taylor, and Michael Eric Hall. Most of these scholar-activists operate from home bases in the academy. All of them do incredible work as researchers, teachers, translators of ideas, public speakers and writers, and activists. They have been mediators of the crises of racialized poverty and the abuses of the U.S. criminal justice system. Each has been a crucial voice in the movement against the police murders of black people. Outspokenness can be punished as white supremacist and other right-wing organizers make blacklists and hit lists containing the names of those who speak out. Their work refutes the common claim that public intellectualism is "in decline."[28] Their audiences belie any claim that the quality of public life is diminished from some historical ideal moment. Black feminist scholar (and public intellectual) Patricia Hill Collins traces some of the ancestry of U.S. black public intellectuals to W. E. B. Du Bois and Ida B. Wells.[29] She criticizes the ways in which and the extent to which elite, male public intellectuals rise to the forefront of U.S. politics and culture, while black women like Wells are rendered marginal.[30]

The marginalization of women as public intellectuals has been challenged forcefully since 2014. So has the notion of the public intellectual as a "special" individual. The movement that resonates most with the intervention made by Paine was sparked when a simple slogan appeared on Twitter: #BlackLives-Matter. Using an emergent medium with a unique capacity to aggregate vernacular voices in the millions, a group of women put a piece of explosive common sense into the political world.

#BlackLivesMatter

As the story is usually told, activist Alicia Garza first used the statement "black lives matter" on Facebook in response to the acquittal of George Zimmerman in the shooting death of black teen Trayvon Martin. On Twitter, Garza's friends Patrice Cullors and Opal Tometi repeated the slogan with the hashtag: #BlackLivesMatter.[31] Any denunciation of Twitter culture as debasing political conversation withers in the wake of this moment. The phrase lay dormant for a while. However, after the November 2014 court decision not to indict police officer Darren Wilson, the man who shot to death Michael Brown in Ferguson, Missouri, the use of the hashtag exploded. The court decision about Wilson was quickly followed by news of the police murder of Tamir Rice, a boy of twelve, in Cleveland, and the crescendo continued.

The Pew Research Center charted the hashtag's fortunes from its first mention on July 12, 2013, until March 31, 2016, finding that it was used 13.3 million times. (If you take into account related hashtags #Ferguson, #SayHerName, #ICantBreathe, #HandsUpDontShoot, and others, the number is much higher.) Peaks in its circulation included the murder of Tamir Rice; the announcement in 2014 that Darren Wilson would not be indicted; again in April 2015 when Freddie Gray died in police custody in Baltimore; when Bernie Sanders announced his (belated) support for the movement; and in July 2015 when Sandra Bland was found hanged in her Texas jail cell.[32]

Twitter as Modality of Mediation. The phrase itself is a condensation of an argument: Police killings of black people are wrong; they are happening; they are an indication that black lives do not matter; but black lives do matter. Like Paine's argument for natural rights, it sets forth very plainly a message that galvanized millions of people in a short period of time, not only to circulate information with the hashtag but also to get involved in movement organizing. The women who initiated the #BlackLivesMatter tag created the organization Black Lives Matter, and numerous others followed suit. Pew notes that much of the time, users of the hashtag linked it to antiracist news, news of other cases of police murder of black people, or movement events. Activists used the hashtag to organize protests; users could search the hashtag along with tags for their cities or dates of protest to stay in constant touch with events. Quoted in Pew, analyst Lee Raine told the *New York Times*: "This is a very powerful example of how a hashtag now is attached to a movement, and a movement, in some ways, has grown around a hashtag—and a series of really painful and really powerful conversations are taking place in a brand new space."[33]

The #BlackLivesMatter hashtag's occurrence far exceeded the frequency of the counterhashtag #AllLivesMatter. A team of researchers in quantitative science at the University of Vermont recently noted that those using #BlackLivesMatter more often connected the label with "informationally rich conversations" than did those engaged in its counterpoint.[34] Compiling huge amounts of quantitative data on the association of words with the hashtag at key moments in time, they also describe how the hashtag was closely connected to movement beyond the web. They observe that the hashtag #Ferguson was more widely used before the murder of Tamir Rice and the Darren Wilson non-indictment. Intriguingly, the #BlackLivesMatter hashtag had many co-occurrences with #Beyoncé and #QueenBey, indicating the singer's role as a different kind of public intellectual in the critique of police racism.

The hashtag has also enabled some conversations criticizing and expanding the scope of the movement. Importantly, feminists and queer scholars and activists are articulating #BlackLivesMatter to the police murders specifically of black women and to the contributions and challenges feminists and queer activists are making to the struggle.[35] Treva Lindsey argues for a "herstorical" approach to "Black violability," which "offers an expansive lens that renders visible Black women and girls and trans*, genderqueer, gender nonconforming, and queer people as victims and survivors of anti-Black racial terror."[36] Sarah Jackson and her coauthor, Brooke Foucault Welles, have described the affordances of Twitter in this and other emerging social movements. They argue that Twitter activism, circulating out from opinion-leader hubs, catalyzes online counterpublics that can contest mainstream framings—or conduct frame-checking and rekeying—of racism, policing, and violence.[37]

The capacity of Twitter and similar online tools to aggregate and coordinate publics, create networks of associations and meanings across topics, and condense meaningful entries into public discourse makes the medium different from non-computer-mediated and longer-form Internet vehicles. In a way, Twitter is like Paine's pamphlet—smaller than a book and accessible to millions of people in a way that even blogs and newspapers are not. The platform enables links to longer narratives and additional information and conspires to conjoin one conversation with others. Yarimar Bonilla and Jonathan Rosa describe specifically how hashtags work:

The hashtag symbol is often used as a way of making a conversation within this platform [Twitter]. The hashtag serves as an indexing system in both the clerical sense and the semiotic sense. In the clerical sense, it allows the ordering and quick retrieval of information about a specific topic. . . . In addition to providing a filing system, hashtags simultaneously function semiotically by marking the intended significance of an utterance . . . to performatively frame what these comments are "really about."[38]

As with narrative metaphors in the abortion videos or the persona crafting of Edward Snowden and Chelsea Manning, hashtags create interpretive frames within which to understand the meaning of the verbal content of the message. They tell readers to read a statement in terms of the tag such that an item of news about the destruction of public housing concluded with #BlackLivesMatter encourages the reader to understand the destruction of the housing as akin to or the same as racialized violence of other kinds. In addition, Bonilla and Rosa note, hashtags create extended intertextual chains of meaning by tying the one hashtag to others, such as #Palestine, linking racial violence in the United States with the cause of Palestinians. They create complex publics ranging from brief engagement to the formation of group identities, communities, and activism—much as Paine's pamphlet did. However, they do so in a multivocal and dialogical way that enables readers to engage multiple streams and comments from almost anywhere, creating a "shared sense of temporality."[39]

The Rhetoric of #BlackLivesMatter. In spite of its condensed, indexical modality, Twitter does not foreclose upon familiar rhetorical strategies of movement discourse, including the "big five." For example, media researcher Guobin Yang describes how hashtag activism enables "narrative agency" in the construction of ritualized "contentious collective events."[40] Yang argues that hashtags express and tie sharers to forceful action: "petitioning, demanding, appealing, and protesting. They express refusals, objections, and imperatives to take immediate action. They often challenge narratives in mainstream media."[41]

Rhetorical scholarship has identified the profound affective or emotional power of the movement around #BlackLivesMatter. Kashif Jerome Powell ties the activist performances of death scenes (in organized die-ins) as invoking not only the terror of present police abuse but of the terror of the middle passage of the North Atlantic slave trade.[42] He writes,

The unexhausted catalogue of police-involved killings exemplifies a continuation of mourned inexpression, which results in the incessant repetition of the atrocities of the Transatlantic Slave Trade through political and social (which always implies visual and performative) processes of projecting the density of that memory onto black bodies.[43]

Protesters "place their bodies in performative opposition to the rule of law to make visible the absences constructed by dense affects of nonexistence that devalue life to the point of death."[44]

The movement has also used visual media in spectacular ways, circulating images and videos of the dead body of Michael Brown and the killing of Tamir Rice, among many others. As Bonilla and Rosa write,

> The death of Michael Brown quickly captured the imagination of thousands across and beyond the United States. Protestors from around the nation flocked to Ferguson to participate in demonstrations calling for the arrest of the officer responsible for the fatal shooting. Television viewers tuned in across the country to watch live news coverage of the violent confrontations between the protestors and the highly armed local police. Images of these confrontations circulated widely in national and international news coverage, and news of these events quickly went "viral" across social media.[45]

Photographs circulated of protestors confronting militarized police, of youth wearing hoodies to stand in for Trayvon Martin, and of ralliers marching with their hands raised to say, "Hands up—don't shoot."

Finally, with regard to rhetorical strategies, Foner and others observed that Paine's outlook was utopian. Similarly, Glenn Mackin has argued that the Black Lives Matter movement, while communicating in propositional form, "introduces new perceptions into the field of sensory experience" to invoke a counterworld.[46] The activist performances are more than what some theorists would celebrate as disruptive, incomprehensible, destructive interruptions; they introduce a competing world, in which racist injustice becomes visible and intelligible. That world is invoked in the simple sentence, "Black lives matter." According to Mackin, it provokes the question of whether a world in which black lives matter does, in fact, exist. If not, to state the claim is to insist on the possibility of a counterworld.[47] For example, the image of protestors with raised hands in the "hands up, don't shoot" gesture affirms both the rationality and the outrage of black activists in struggle.[48] Mackin concludes, "The activists enact modes of freedom and equality that the dominant order of sense denies—above all, the freedom to engage in practices in which one steps out of one's assigned roles and reconfigures the sensory world."[49] The same claim might be made about Thomas Paine's reconfiguration of the dominant order of sense.

CONCLUSION: THE REVOLUTIONARY INTERVENTION OF COMMON SENSE

Like Paine's *Common Sense*, #BlackLivesMatter is a timed, crafted, strategic set of actions. As founder Alicia Garza wrote, "Black Lives Matter is an ideological and political intervention in a world where Black lives are systematically and intentionally targeted for demise. It is an affirmation of Black folks' contributions to this society, our humanity, and our resilience in the face of deadly oppression."[50] This intervention has put out an analysis and spread it globally and almost instantaneously—or, over many instants—with political clarity and directness. Like Paine, its millions of authors describe the utter corruption of systemic autocratic power and the threats and realities it enacts. Although radical and confrontational, those circulating the hashtag have touched the reality of hundreds of thousands of black people's experience, making the movement and its demands "common sense" even as the explosion of conversation around the slogan followed a long period of quietude.

Unlike Paine, however, #BlackLivesMatter demands more than a political revolution in which basic structures of class and race and gender remain even as political reforms are undertaken. The movement identifies a need for a thoroughgoing social revolution. It is clear that the use of the hashtag mobilized people to become involved in self-education and embodied public protest. Educational projects like the #BlackLivesMatter syllabus have been circulated by radical educators in primary, secondary, and higher education.[51] This fact brings me back to the insight about common sense and ideology that Paine also understood. Gramsci argued that political education—in the workplace, in the schools, in meetings, in coffee shops, in bars, and in the streets—must challenge the "hegemonic position," the position of unquestioned political legitimacy, of those who control society and its resources. That hegemony is sustained by common sense, which "represents the place from which any genuine political education must depart."[52]

On this point, Walter Adamson argues, "From the point of view of political education, then, common sense is not only its necessary starting point but also its most formidable obstacle. To supersede common sense, the 'man-in-the-mass' must somehow be led to a series of negations which expose and repudiate the prevailing common sense."[53] When workers, including every category of diversity and oppression, face the concrete reality of their experience of exploitation and oppression, and collective, organized political discourse and action put language to that experience, workers experience a "catharsis," in which doubts about the necessity of change are overcome by rationality and agency.[54]

It is easy to see how Paine's *Common Sense*, and the organizing and rhetoric of #BlackLivesMatter, have served the purpose of catharsis and the replacement of existing common sense—in Paine's terms, "prejudice"—in favor of an analysis of abusive power and a strategy to defeat it. Adamson's discussion does not highlight how, when a new class assumes power, its common sense, established and developed in the struggle, becomes hegemonic—if there is a revolution.

The new networks, protest repertoires, and perspectives can embolden and enable a real fight against racist violence and an economic system that depends upon it to discipline black bodies in what Michelle Alexander calls "the new Jim Crow."[55] Keeanga-Yamahtta Taylor has argued that the #BlackLivesMatter movement represents a black awakening after the murders of Mike Brown, Eric Garner, Trayvon Martin, Sean Bell, Amadou Diallo, and the accumulation of many others.[56] The explosion of protests shattered the illusion of a "postracial" society. Just as the open-casket funeral of teenage lynching victim Emmett Till did in 1955, the image of Mike Brown's body left in the street sparked an uprising that has grown into a movement characterized by multiple organizations and demands. Their efforts are marked by internationalism—for example, in solidarity with Palestine liberation—and sensitivity to the interlocked oppressions of race, gender, sexuality, nation, citizenship, and political orientation. The invigoration of this movement, Taylor argues, will require a deepening of solidarity and demands, tying the struggle for higher wages, housing justice, education justice, and union struggles if it is to get at not only the expressions of racism but its deep causes in our economic system.

Taylor also takes a position on the American Revolution and the Civil War. She argues that a vision of freedom imagined as inclusion in mainstream political and financial institutions is an impoverished one. Not only did the emancipation of slaves fail to end even the most brutal expressions of racist injustice, but the election of the nation's first black president corresponded to an escalation of racist violence on the part of the carceral state. Inclusion has come—and failed.[57]

Black liberation therefore requires a strategy to organize across difference to understand the origins and nature of black oppression and to fight more broadly in the struggle for human liberation. Taylor returns to the voices and struggles of the post–World War II black radicals like C. L. R. James, Malcolm X, Stokely Carmichael, Angela Davis, and others, who named the economic system that generated and benefitted from racist oppression: capitalism.[58]

Sean Monahan observed that in his writings *Rights of Man* and *Agrarian Justice*, Paine moved in a similar direction to make more radical challenges to inequalities in the ownership of property, to condemn profit as the product of taking more value from labor than one pays the laborer, and to call for a revolution in the "state of civilization"—in other words, a social revolution.[59] The task of black liberation requires a social revolution through and through. The organizers of #BlackLivesMatter, whose timing, platform, and message have sparked a new militancy, are the exact right voices at the exact right time. What remains is to solidify solidaristic militancy for the fight to come.

Paine successfully tapped similar outrage and made a similar call:

> Hath your house been burnt? Hath your property been destroyed before your face? Are your wife and children destitute of a bed to lie on or bread to live on? Have you lost a parent or a child by their hands, and yourself the ruined and wretched survivor? . . . Reconciliation, like an agreeable dream, hath passed away. . . . Every thing that is right or reasonable pleads for separation. The blood of the slain, the weeping voice of nature cries, 'TIS TIME TO PART.

The Fact of Our Crisis

ON NOVEMBER 16, 2016, the Oxford Dictionaries declared that *post-truth* would be its 2016 "word of the year."[1] Journalist Amy Wang clarified, "The dictionary defines 'post-truth' as 'relating to or denoting circumstances in which objective facts are less influential in shaping public opinion than appeals to emotion and personal belief.'" The word's use increased 2,000 percent since 2015, mostly in response to Donald Trump's tendency to tell untruths.

It is unclear whether Trump's capacity to lie is objectively greater than that of any other previous U.S. politician. Journalist Alexios Mantzarlis argues, "No, we're not in a post-fact era," noting many headlines announcing the same malady—from 2007, 2008, 2011, 2012, and from the Reagan era, thirty years ago.[2] Notably, Mantzarlis is a professional fact-checker. But he knows that *truthiness* is a term coined by Steven Colbert not in 2016 or even 2010—but in 2005. *Truthiness* was *Merriam-Webster's* word of the year in 2006, not 2016.

I believe that the insights of this book will apply to political culture and consciousness into the foreseeable future. But in the wake of Donald Trump's election, the *New Yorker* published an essay on the Enlightenment philosopher Rousseau's take on facts. Rousseau condemned the elitists of rationalism and their disdain for the uneducated. The *New Yorker*, however, draws the wrong conclusion. Rather than embrace Rousseau's democratic insight, author Pankaj Mishra lumps Rousseau and Trump together in the club of narcissists who only like regular people because they (Trump and Rousseau) want to be adored.[3]

This elitism, as I have argued, is not helpful. If we are, and maybe always were, in a post-fact universe, in which the powerful get to decide what is true—then let the Left be post-fact: post-fact in the way that postmodernists claim that they are not "after" or "against" modernism, but rather play a "complicating" role with modernist thought. Let us be post-fact, not to reject facts but to complicate them and to enlarge our understanding of the complexity of the rhetorical mediation of knowledge. Let us leave behind the idea that there are universal truths in favor of the idea that whose truth gets to count as truth is always a contestation among classes with contending interests in an unequal society.

In the case studies, I have developed an overarching argument: Although we should not reject realist foundationalism, our perceptions of the realities of both science and our experience are mediated by rhetors employing frames of meaning and powerful rhetorical strategies such that our beliefs cannot possibly "correspond" to an objective reality; instead, they can be assessed as matters of fidelity, or faithfulness, to our interests and aspirations. Much of what passes for common sense in mainstream political culture is dominated by powerful interests and shaped by oppressive frames of meaning. However, radical, experience-based education, timely interventions in public controversy, and political organization may serve as sites of consciousness-raising and the production of liberatory thought.

In support of this argument, I have performed critical interpretations of a set of documents and videos in various domains. In addition, I have offered up a range of conceptual tools both to help us critique and understand efforts at mediation in the interest of working class people and to inspire us to be inventive, to produce rhetoric that is timely in the struggles that lie ahead.

In chapter 1, I made the basic case for a rhetorical realism, by which I mean an approach to reality and truth that does not suppose that they are hiding about in the bushes waiting to be discovered, photographed, and revealed unvarnished to an ignorant world. After a discussion of the controversy between realist and relativist thinkers and noting the limitations of each, the chapter looked to scholars who study the rhetoric of science; it is there that we find the most robust theories of mediation about matters of life and death.

Mediation is the core concept of this book. It refers to how, always and necessarily, human beings and their ideologies, biases, interpretive fames, talents or lack thereof, emotional state, values, interests, and commitments all get in the middle of the process of knowing. Inquiry and facts are crucial to the longevity of the Earth and the human race, but they are also subject to the vagaries of history and power. There are no neutral facts once they enter the world of communication, which is to say, ever. We can critique the abuses of knowledge and its complicity in ideology and atrocity without giving up on the project of inquiry or the idea of an informed, democratic civil society in which people are armed with the knowledge they need to survive and struggle.

In chapter 2, I laid out rhetorical resources that progressives and the Left have held suspect, which I have called "the big five": narrative, myth, affect, embodiment, and spectacle. These strategies are incredibly powerful, and the Right knows that in a debate between statistics and the story of a crime victim, the story will win. The concept of fidelity is important in order to assess the work of the big five. Rather than asking, "Are we being manipulated?" or "Does this spectacle get the facts right?" we might instead ask whether the texts exhibit fidelity, or faithfulness, to the interests and goals of the people addressed by and constituted in them. We have an obligation to present the narrative—and every other modality available to us—alongside other kinds of support in order to use the big five in non-cynical ways faithful to the interests of working class and oppressed communities.

Chapter 3 demonstrated the limits of fact-checking in the case of the video series casting abortion providers as opportunist, profiteering monsters. The responses of Planned Parenthood and other abortion-rights organizations feebly resorted to nitpicking the videos' dishonest and manipulative moments. How could such efforts even dent the viewer's memory of fetal parts being pulled with tweezers from a tray or of a provider talking about crushing heads to extract fetuses from the birth canal while consuming salad and Chardonnay? Even I, among the most vocal and confident supporters of women's right to abortion, had difficulty watching and analyzing the videos. They need to be taken seriously. In order to take them seriously, I introduced the concept of frame analysis and media framing and created the concept of "frame-checking" as a counter to fact-checking.

Hermagoras's *stasis* system is helpful in the task of frame-checking. Hermagoras taught that arguers' claims each occupy one of several different places or "levels" of a case. When a persuader makes a proposition describing reality—for example, "Police regularly murder Black people"—that is a claim at the *stasis* of conjecture. When the same person claims, "It is wrong for police to regularly murder Black people," that statement is located at the *stasis* of quality, or value. "Murder is the deliberate killing of another person" is a statement at the *stasis* of definition. "This crisis of police murder of Black people is caused by systemic institutional racism" is a claim at the *stasis* of causation. And, "We should challenge the system of institutional racism in order to stop the regular police murder of Black people" is a claim at the *stasis* of policy or proposal. When progressives obsess over fact-checking, they are limiting their responses to conjectural claims, failing to respond to opponents at other meaningful levels.

The chapters then moved in order from cases that I found to be less faithful to ordinary people's interests to those that exhibited the greatest fidelity. In chapter 4, I analyzed the differential framing of Chelsea Manning and Edward Snowden, both of whom exposed large volumes of national security secrets. In the narrative media frames of major news media and popular culture, Snowden was cast in his own spy-hero action film. In contrast, Manning's sexual orientation and gender identity influenced framing of her disclosures; she did not have access to the dominant frames that situated Snowden as a hero and her as a victim. In this chapter, queerness is an important concept to describe a state of being defined by what Michael Warner terms "nonstandard intimacies" and fluidity of gender identity and expression.[4] While some critical scholars embrace the queer refusal to live standard lives according to heteronormative timetables, national belonging, and family forms, all as manifestations of resistance, the consequences of being queer in Manning's case suggest caution about welcoming failure: a sentence of thirty-five years in a prison system that does not recognize her right to exist.

Chapter 5 engaged issues of nature and scientific knowledge in an examination of the 2014 version of the series *Cosmos*. It is the epitome of a progressive discourse—insisting on inclusion, reason, the democratization of knowledge, and pure curiosity pitched for mass audiences—that embraces the big five (bang). Two very intriguing patterns emerge from my analysis, the first being that the producers thoroughly embraced the tools of myth, narrative, affect, embodiment, and spectacle. In particular, the producers and host conjured up some mythic narratives like Harry Potter, locating viewers in an awesome cosmos with the answers to our questions about both our origins and our destinies. However, the program winks at the viewer in its visual rhetoric so that audiences may not take even this scientific mythic narrative on faith. Host Neil deGrasse Tyson can assert scientific facts while his surroundings undergo massive, impossible transformation, while biographies of beleaguered scientists who went up against the powerful to engage in new discovery depict them as flat animations—not anything like realism. The genius of these nods to the seemingly improbable world of the cosmos is that they alert the viewer to the constructed and mediated nature of the very program that is attempting to convey scientific truths. While telling viewers not to accept what passes for truth blindly, it also tells viewers not to automatically accept that *the program* is passing for truth.

This is an ethical move that prompted me to introduce the concepts of *naturalization, studium,* and *punctum.* Roland Barthes was concerned with the capacity of images to appear as natural, given reality. The standard, commonsense understanding of an image or photograph is not interrupted by contradiction or complexity. The easy flow of such images can be described as *studium*. By *punctum*, Barthes meant the punctuation, the interruption, the invitation to see something more complex in what we thought was true. *Cosmos* engages in *punctum*, denaturalizing even its own arguments about what is natural and real.

In that chapter, I also engaged the rhetoric of creationism and its efforts to get a toehold in the American public education system. There is more at stake in preventing the religious Right's agenda from passing as science, however. The Establishment Clause of the First Amendment to the U.S. Constitution does forbid the imposition of religion in any government setting, including the schools. However, a better reason for preventing pseudo-science from taking a place in the schools is that it is not good for ordinary people, for the exploited and oppressed, for workers and the poor, whose interests are not served by supernatural accounts of and justifications for their suffering. This insight means that we have to understand public (and all) education as inherently mediated—in other words, as inherently ideological. Our standard for evaluating a curriculum is not limited to whether it is true in some factual sense. More importantly, the question is whether it is *faithful* or exhibits fidelity toward the people whose minds it seeks to shape. Traditions in radical pedagogy urge educators to see our role as not merely or primarily vehicles for facts but also as mediators of knowledges with profound stakes for young people who take on the burden of changing a vastly unjust and unequal society.

The question of education arises again in chapter 6, which considers the mediation of radical ideas by the American revolutionary Thomas Paine alongside the Black Lives Matter movement of our own day. Schools are not the only sites for political education: Pamphlets and hashtags—and picket lines, organizing meetings, consciousness-raising groups, quilting circles, protests, and anywhere people share their experiences—can also do this crucial work. This chapter argues that the push for truly radical change happens from below, by people whose commitment to the Enlightenment ideas of equality and liberty is not a matter of lip service. At key moments in history, public intellectuals—organizers, teachers, pundits, and other celebrities—face opportunities to mediate public understanding of the basic flaws and antagonisms inherent in the social system. The ability to leap into such a moment of crisis with a fitting intervention is called *kairos*. In those moments, received wisdom, prevailing common sense, or what Paine called "prejudice," all can fall away in favor of new interpretations of reality and motivations to act on behalf of the ideals that our "Founding Fathers" and subsequent political leaders failed to cherish. In Marx's terms, "All that is solid melts into air."[5]

There are two additional threads that pull through the book. The first is how claims to nature and the natural appear in each case study. In the case of the "Human Capital" abortion videos, the nature of the fetus is at stake: Determining its personhood then determines the nature of abortion providers as monstrous and unnatural. With regard to Edward Snowden and Chelsea Manning, Snowden's gender, sexuality, and masculinity appear as natural, making it easy for the media to slot him into the role of hero. In contrast, Manning's queerness and gender transition challenge what is taken for granted as natural, enabling the treatment of her as both a gender and a national traitor. *Cosmos* prompted a debate about the nature of nature; while creationists seek to naturalize the idea of a cosmic designer, the creators of *Cosmos* denaturalize even their own efforts to describe the natural.

Finally, the chapter about Thomas Paine and Black Lives Matter showed how the question of human nature influences radical politics and the fortunes of citizens. For Paine, the ideals of the Enlightenment include an optimistic vision of human nature as essentially good rather than craven, an argument invoking natural law (with the support of Enlightenment science) to justify democratic revolution, and the idea that the monarchy or any form of autocratic rule is unnatural—indeed, monstrous. In a reverse case, the history of racist brutality since Paine's invocation of a democratic common sense dehumanizes black people and naturalizes the policing and imprisonment of people defined, in the nation's founding documents and carried forward until now, as less than fully human.

The second thread is about critical consciousness: Where does it come from, and how? Key to the process of consciousness-raising, which is another way of saying the mediation of experience and belief, is denaturalization: the making of what seemed to be natural common sense subject to questioning so that it ceases to fall into the category of "nature." Then received ideas and social practices are revealed to be human, social constructs, subject to critique and revision. The practice of denaturalization is emancipatory.

One irony in the process, however, is the necessary establishment of a new, naturalized common sense. Every new ruling class generates ideas legitimating its rule and attempts to universalize those ideas as serving the interests of all of the people. This irony, according to Gramsci, is in the nature of hegemony. Even if we sustain a healthy skepticism toward appeals to the natural in politics, we must have some criteria by which to discern whose common sense is operating and in whose interests. Following work undertaken with my colleague Kathleen Feyh, I have proposed the standard of fidelity to a class's interests rather than correspondence to "objective" reality as the measure of whose *sense* is actually in the interest of the *commons*—the majority of humankind who own no part of the means of producing and distributing the necessities of life, the majority of humankind who must work for others for a wage, and all of the oppressed. The resources of nature have been devastated by capitalism; science has been used to justify atrocity and discrimination in health, nutrition, labor, and housing. However, some invocations of nature and uses of science, if freed for human need, are not and will not be the material or ideological tools of the oppressors.

Political education through pedagogy and struggle—in which the people articulating critique social analysis and plans for change—has actively and collectively produced common sense based on experience and aspirations. Teachers and intellectuals in the academy and other established institutions (think tanks, media networks) must work in solidarity with the organic intellectuals, organizers, and activists who are cultivating new knowledge about the giant of a system and how to take it down. Public intellectuals like Thomas Paine, Neil deGrasse Tyson, Alicia Garza, and Glenn Greenwald play an important mediating role, sometimes sparking new clarity about the need for change.

I have hoped to reach five overlapping audiences with the arguments in this book. The first consists of communities of progressives and liberals who, I believe, have put too much blame and too much attention on mere facts. I hope that I have convinced you that throwing facts at malignant power is a limited strategy, in favor of articulating broader truths that can organize people collectively in struggle in their own interests.

The second audience for this work includes journalists and political communication scholars who have embraced fact-checking as a radically democratic practice. Fact-checking is not an example of public intellectual work unless combined with a coherent framing of what those facts mean and for whom. Intellectuals *mediate* between facts and understanding. We must not dismiss or malign the mistaken or believe that we are the carriers of unquestionable truths. In its story of the triumph of women against brutality, *Mad Max: Fury Road* may tell the truth better than any lecture, satirical mockery, or fact-checking column. Where does critical consciousness come from? Not merely, or even primarily, from "facts." Therefore, I call on my colleagues and comrades who report and analyze political news to move beyond fact-checking to frame-checking.

It does matter when a politician lies to us—but it is also crucial to understand why large numbers of people find ideas contrary to not only reality but also to their better interests compelling. Journalists and commentators could step up to the question of *doxa*. How might they help actively to shape common sense in ways more accountable to their publics? Trying to distinguish between "fake" news and "objective" information is unhelpful because there is no objective representation of information. Everything is mediated from a perspective. The idea of objectivity is itself a frame that makes the existing organization and priorities of society seem natural. In this sense, coverage that is conducted in reputable ways by reputable organizations about U.S. wars, when it establishes the necessity of those wars as common sense, is "fake" news. What is "true" is information that informs, engages, and enables the capacity of ordinary people to transform society and their lives. We should elevate artisan, vernacular, activist, and investigative journalism in our esteem and develop the habit of reflecting upon our practices of framing and mediation.

My third audience consists of academics with whom I have argued over the past few decades about the implications of poststructuralist relativism for political judgment and action. They have made a case that Marxist scholars and critics in general should get past representational or correspondence-based theories of truth. My position is that it is possible to construct a sophisticated realism that does not give ground to relativism while recognizing the rhetorical character (i.e., mediation) of all knowledge. It has been my goal to construct a standpoint-based theory of truth as fidelity working from the theories of Lukács and Gramsci. I look forward to ongoing dialogue on these theoretical points.

Fourth, my conclusions have implications for educators. Teachers are among the most important mediators of knowledge, but too often in settings that do not enable engaged pedagogy for liberation. We teachers in primary education and in colleges and universities should, where we can, develop strategies for building curriculum based on the voices and experiences of our students and designed to educate them as engaged citizens and activists.

Finally, I hope that this book is interesting to activists and others who are not necessarily scholars or journalists. The case I am making is relevant across many professions and domains, from the classroom to the newsroom, from our televisions and computers to political organizations.

In short, I am arguing that we do not face a crisis of facts. We face the fact of a crisis.

The Trump regime has emboldened bigots across the country. White supremacist groups are marching openly in our streets and on our campuses. On August 12, 2017, during a rally of open neo-Nazis in Charlottesville, Virginia, a white supremacist drove his car into a crowd of antiracist demonstrators, killing one principled activist and wounding many others.[6] The *New York Times* acknowledged that "many of these groups have felt emboldened since the election of Donald J. Trump as president."[7] During the span of one week, the news included these headlines: "Homophobic Man Beats Lesbian Unconscious on Brooklyn-Bound Q Train," "White Supremacist Arrested in Fatal Stabbing of Two Men after Anti-Muslim Rant in Portland," "Campus Killing: Suspect Is a Member of an 'Alt-Reich' Facebook Group," "Noose Found at Exhibit in African American Smithsonian Museum," and "LeBron James' Los Angeles Home Vandalized with 'N-word' Graffiti."[8] Black Lives Matter leader and Princeton professor Keeanga-Yahmatta Taylor was forced to cancel a speaking tour due to racist and homophobic death threats.[9] The perpetrators of such abuse ascribe to the xenophobia and bigotry of the Trump administration, which has effectively given them permission to give open expression to their ideas and translate them into violence.

Meanwhile, in the United States (and around the world), the gap in wealth between the richest and poorest in society is at its ever-rising peak. There are more empty homes, hotels, and apartment buildings than there are homeless people, yet thousands are left to endure the bitterness of winter without adequate shelter.[10] Unemployment has decreased over the past several years, but most new jobs are precarious, part-time, and subject to a paltry minimum wage.[11] The wealthiest sixty-two people own the same amount of wealth as half of the world's population.[12]

The climate is heating up, and we are past the tipping point of whether we face cataclysm to wondering when, and how bad, it will be.[13] We can guess that it will be not so bad for the Donald Trumps of this world, and horrific for ordinary people facing climate-related disasters without shelter, transport, or wealth.

Because of the Black Lives Matter movement, many people have become "woke" to the reality of vicious and unrelenting police violence against black Americans, and organizations and individuals are rising up to demand that black lives matter. But the violence is unremitting and its perpetrators are unrepentant. Racist scapegoating targets immigrants and Muslims, among others, such that white supremacists and Islamophobes have emerged with Trump's implicit blessing to harass, injure, vandalize, and kill people who are increasingly defined as (literally) outside the pale.

Sexual assault affects, in conservative estimates, one in five women in the United States and one in thirty-three men; the rates are much higher on college campuses,[14] while perpetrators often go unpunished, as administrators and juries worry about the impact prosecution will have on the rapists while slut-shaming the survivors.[15] Sexism is such a pervasive feature of social life that women still underearn men,[16] street harassment passes as natural, and our president can grope women at will without consequence. Of course, racism, queerphobia, and other interlocking oppressions complicate that reality in devastating ways.

The right to marry has not ended the discrimination against and bashing of LGBTQ* persons.[17] The massacre at the Pulse nightclub on June 12, 2016, was not only the deadliest mass shooting by a single (nonmilitary/nonpolice) shooter in U.S. history but also the deadliest hate crime committed against LGBTQ* people.[18] Trans* persons are the most vulnerable victims of hate crimes. Legal reforms like marriage equality are crucial and hard-won, but the realities facing queer workers and youth require our ongoing activism.

Again: We are not facing a crisis of facts. We are facing the fact of a crisis. Throwing facts at the crisis will not prevent Trump from enacting his racist, misogynistic, anti-immigrant, Islamophobic agenda. However, as Gary Younge argued recently, "Donald Trump Is Not Too Big to Fail."[19]

> Trump's victory illustrates the weakness of the Republican Party's leaders, not their strength. . . . His agenda is no more unassailable than his victory was unfathomable. But there is nothing inevitable in his demise. If the liberal left is going to challenge him effectively in the coming years, then it must learn the lessons of its defeat. The Democratic machine does not need a tune-up—it needs a complete overhaul. For far too long, it has been too arrogant, complacent, or contemptuous (and sometimes all three) to make an argument beyond "at least we're not them."

These are revolutionary sentiments, and revolutionary change is a logical conclusion to draw from the facts that we are facing a number of large crises, that they are systemic, and that the mainstream electoral process cannot fix the problems. Revolution is not a far-flung prospect; it happened in our own front yard. And it was a good thing.

Revolutionary or no, the solution to the crisis of the economic and political system lies in building struggles against Trump's agenda, countering the hegemony of a pro-corporate, racist, sexist common sense, and entering the streets in large enough numbers to make it difficult, if not impossible, for him and his cronies to rule. Building struggle means mediating: getting involved in organizations to generate, interpret, debate, and act on collective knowledge about our experience and the system that produces it.

Teresa Shook, a retired attorney and grandmother, understood this process. She got on Facebook and posed a question: "What if women marched on Washington around Inauguration Day en masse?"[20] With those words, Shook leapt into the void of crisis to crystallize public debate and will. Like Tom Paine's, her call went viral. That moment of *kairos* generated the involvement of hundreds of thousands of people who marched on Washington to declare, as organizer Tamika Mallory stated, "that we will not be silent and we will not let anyone roll back the rights we have fought and struggled to get." Like Paine's, the Women's March platform declared commitments more radical than mainstream liberalism. Organizers express solidarity against racism and exploitation and for equal pay and full equality for immigrants and LGBTQ* persons. The platform called for economic and environmental justice and vows to protest the persecution of immigrants and Muslims. This is a vision worth marching for.[21] Indeed, half a million people marched against Trump on January 21, 2017, in Washington, DC, the largest protest march in U.S. history. More than four hundred smaller marches were held in cities across the country, and worldwide, more than 5 million people participated in the collective refusal of Trump's agenda.

Since Inauguration Day, there have been mass marches for science, against climate denial, for LGBTQ* rights, and more. There has been a surge of activism involving hundreds of thousands of people. Social movement researchers at the University of Maryland surveyed protesters who participated in these movements. They found that the actions so far have built a base for what will likely be consistent protest activity across the foreseeable future. The resistance to the imperatives of Trump's regime has drawn thousands of new and diverse activists, and most participants are "repeat protesters."[22]

All of these events featured activists who were carried away by emotion, narrative, myth, spectacle, and above all, embodiment. Now and any time people rise to fight exploitation and oppression, let us be moved to greater critique and solidarity in the knowledge that we will make a difference.

Because when *their* reality bites, *our* reality bites *back*.

NOTES

NOTES TO THE PREFACE

1. Hall et al., *Policing the Crisis,* 20–35, 316–19, 392–95.
2. Zimdars, "False, Misleading, Clickbait-y, and Satirical 'News' Sources."
3. Reader, "How We Got to Post-Truth."
4. See Selfa, "Trump's Middle Class Army"; Henley, "White and Wealthy Voters Gave Victory to Donald Trump, Exit Polls Show."
5. Stack, "Yes, Trump Really Is Saying 'Big League,' Not 'Bigly,' Linguists Say." See also Waldman, "The Accidental Brilliance of Trump's Speaking Style."
6. Foster, "What is Covfefe? Donald Trump's Bizarre Tweet Confuses the World as Typo Mocked Online."
7. Tavernise, "As Fake News Spreads Lies, More Readers Shrug at the Truth."
8. Thanks to John Lyne for this insight.
9. Qiu, "Fact-Checking President Trump through His First 100 Days."

NOTES TO THE INTRODUCTION

1. A phrase attributed to radical civil rights activist Bayard Rustin in 1942.
2. Suskind, "Faith, Certainty and the Presidency of George W. Bush."
3. This book does tremendous work in sorting debates on the status of truth in philosophy, journalism, and politics. While upholding the need for political accountability to a rational standard (as public sphere theory would advise), the book's contributors describe the complexity and partiality of categories of knowledge.
4. Aune, "Cultures of Discourse: Marxism and Rhetorical Theory," 169.
5. For example, see David Zirin on radical politics and sport, *People's History of Sports* and *Brazil's Dance with the Devil: The World Cup, the Olympics, and the Fight for Democracy*; see the poetry of South African poet Dennis Brutus, *Poetry and Protest*; the music and insight of hip-hop artist Boots Riley, in his foreword to Vincent, *Party Music: The Inside Story of the Black Panthers' Band and How Black Power Transformed Soul Music*; the astonishing visual artwork of Sara Levy, who made the infamous *Bloody Trump* (https://sarahlevyart.wordpress.com); and all of the creative song, dance, puppetry, and theatre that have distinguished activist traditions around the world.
6. Cook et al., "Quantifying the Consensus on Anthropogenic Global Warming in the Scientific Literature."

7. Eilperin, "The Public's Interest in Climate Change Is Waning"; Pew Research Center, "Keystone XL Pipeline Draws Broad Support."

8. Lakoff, *Moral Politics*.

9. Foucault, *Discipline & Punish*, 30.

10. Nietzsche, *Will to Power*.

11. Greene, "Another Materialist Rhetoric"; Greene, "Rhetoric and Capitalism: Rhetorical Agency as Communicative Labor."

12. McGee, "In Search of 'the People': A Rhetorical Alternative"; Charland, "Constitutive Rhetoric: The Case of the Peuple Québécois"; Laclau, *On Populist Reason*.

13. Bourdieu, *Outline of a Theory of Practice*; Lukács, *History and Class Consciousness*; Gramsci, *Selections from the Prison Notebooks of Antonio Gramsci*.

14. Hall, "The Problem of Ideology." See also Larrain's critique of Hall's revision of the concept of ideology to mean articulation rather than falsehood, "Stuart Hall and the Marxist Conception of Ideology."

15. Cherwitz and Hikins, "Rhetorical Perspectivism."

16. Triece, *Tell It Like It Is*.

17. Plato, *Sophist*; Jarratt, *Rereading the Sophists*; Hesk, *Deception and Democracy in Classical Athens*.

18. Geuss, *Philosophy and Real Politics*, 4.

19. See Jarman, "Motivated to Ignore the Facts: The Inability of Fact-Checking to Promote Truth in the Public Sphere."

20. Burke, *The Philosophy of Literary Form: Studies in Symbolic Action*, 171.

21. Ibid., 175.

22. Triece, *Tell It Like It Is*.

23. Savage, "Bradley Manning Admits Providing Files to WikiLeaks"; Thompson, "Early Struggles of Soldier Charged in Leak Case."

24. See Warner, *Publics and Counterpublics*.

25. Foucault, "Two Lectures," 81.

26. National Center for Science Education, "Ten Major Court Cases about Evolution and Creationism."

27. Paine, *Common Sense*.

28. Hodson, *Language and Revolution*; Hogan and Williams, "Republican Charisma and the American Revolution: The Textual Persona of Thomas Paine's Common Sense"; Larkin, *Thomas Paine and the Literature of Revolution*; Loughran, "Disseminating Common Sense: Thomas Paine and the Problem of the Early National Bestseller."

NOTES TO CHAPTER 1

1. Colbert, "The Word—'Truthiness'"; Zimmer, "Truthiness"; Merriam-Webster, "2006 Word of the Year: Merriam-Webster Announces 'Truthiness' as 2006 Word of the Year." See also Gilbert, "#NotIntendedToBeAFactualStatement," in Hannan, 93–113.

2. Davies, "The Age of Post-Truth Politics."

3. Backer, "Toward an Activist Theory of Language," in Hannan, 3–21, makes a similar case for understanding "truth-as-correctness," in which activist groups vie for establishing alternative truths in a struggle over hegemony.

4. For a critique of a simple version of false consciousness, see Jameson, *The Political Unconscious*, 281.

5. Hall, "The Problem of Ideology"; Larrain, "Stuart Hall and the Marxist Conception of Ideology."

6. Jarratt, *Rereading the Sophists*.

7. Ibid., 123.

8. Althusser, "Ideology and Ideological State Apparatuses."

9. Saussure, *Course in General Linguistics*; Althusser, "Ideology and Ideological State Apparatuses."

10. Wachowski and Wachowski, *The Matrix*; Wachowski and Wachowski, *The Matrix Reloaded*; Wachowski and Wachowski, *The Matrix Revolutions*; Cloud, "The Matrix and Critical Theory's Desertion of the Real."

11. Foucault, *The History of Sexuality: An Introduction*.

12. Ham, "As Hiroshima Smouldered, Our Atom Bomb Scientists Suffered Remorse."

13. Baudrillard, *Simulacra and Simulation*; Lyotard, *The Postmodern Condition*.

14. Baudrillard, *Simulacra and Simulation*, 6.

15. For another critique of Habermas, see Lewis A. Friedland and Thomas B. Hove, "Habermas' Account of Truth in Political Communication," in Hannan, 23–39.

16. Plato, *Gorgias*; Plato, *Phaedrus*.

17. Haskins, *Logos and Power in Isocrates and Aristotle*; Jarratt, *Rereading the Sophists*.

18. Aristotle, *Aristotle: Art of Rhetoric*; Isocrates, *Isocrates II*.

19. Scott, "On Viewing Rhetoric as Epistemic."

20. Brummett, "Some Implications of 'Process' or 'Intersubjectivity': Postmodern Rhetoric"; Schiappa, *Defining Reality*; Cherwitz and Hikins, *Communication and Knowledge*; Cherwitz, *Rhetoric and Philosophy*.

21. McGee, "A Materialist's Conception of Rhetoric."

22. Cherwitz and Hikins, "Rhetorical Perspectivism."

23. Cloud, "Materiality of Discourse as Oxymoron."

24. Cloud, "The Matrix and Critical Theory's Desertion of the Real"; Greene, "Another Materialist Rhetoric."

25. McKerrow, "Critical Rhetoric: Theory and Praxis."

26. Requarth, "Scientists, Stop Thinking Explaining Science Will Fix Things."

27. Coppola, "Science Hasn't Been This Controversial Since 1676."

28. Bernstein, *Beyond Objectivism and Relativism*, 48. Bernstein works from Gadamer's hermeneutics, which Bernstein regards as navigating the realism-relativism binary, to conceptualize truths as dialogic and communicative in ways that generate practical judgment and action.

29. Kuhn, *The Structure of Scientific Revolutions*.

30. Treichler, *How to Have Theory in an Epidemic*, 152.

31. Ibid., 173.

32. Gross, *Starring the Text: The Place of Rhetoric in Science Studies*.

33. Bazerman, "Codifying the Social Scientific Style: The APA Publication Manual as a Behaviorist Rhetoric."

34. Mike Shapiro, "The Rhetoric of Social Science: The Political Responsibilities of the Scholar," 363.

35. John S. Nelson, Megill, and McCloskey, *The Rhetoric of the Human Sciences*, ix.

36. Leff, "Modern Sophistic and the Unity of Rhetoric," 35.

37. Rorty, "Science as Solidarity," 43.

38. Ibid., 44.

39. Rosaldo, "Where Objectivity Lies: The Rhetoric of Anthropology," 87.

40. Gross, *Starring the Text*, 42.

41. Ceccarelli, *Shaping Science with Rhetoric*; Ceccarelli, "Science and Civil Debate: The Case of E. O. Wilson's Sociobiology."

42. Ceccarelli, *On the Frontier of Science*.

43. Ibid., 3–4.

44. Ibid., 91–110.

45. Gaonkar, "The Idea of Rhetoric in the Rhetoric of Science."

46. Gross, *Starring the Text,* 143; see also Ceccarelli, "Science and Civil Debate."

47. Habermas, *The Structural Transformation of the Public Sphere.*

48. See Nancy Fraser, "Rethinking the Public Sphere: A Contribution to the Critique of Actually Existing Democracy."

49. Eberly, *Citizen Critics*; Warner, *Publics and Counterpublics.*

50. See Aune, "Cultures of Discourse: Marxism and Rhetorical Theory," 72.

51. Gramsci, *An Antonio Gramsci Reader,* 72.

52. Ibid., 197.

53. For an elaboration of this perspective on class, see German, *A Question of Class*; Michael Zweig, *The Working Class Majority: America's Best-Kept Secret.*

54. Karl Marx, "Commodities." See also Ricard Gunn, "Marxism and Mediation"; Mike Wayne, *Marxism and Media Studies.*

55. Engster, "Subjectivity and Its Critics: Commodity Mediation and the Economic Constitution of Objectivity and Subjectivity."

56. Negt and Kluge, *Public Sphere and Experience,* 250.

57. On the idea of the organic party organization, see Antonio Gramsci, "The Modern Prince," in *Selections from the Prison Notebooks.* http://www.marxists.org/archive/gramsci/editions/spn/modern_prince/ch15.htm. See also Negt & Kluge, *Public Sphere and Experience,* 258–63, 54–95; and Lukács, *History and Class Consciousness,* 295–342.

58. This idea resonates with the deconstructive psychoanalytic critique of subjectivity, seeking an encounter with the sense that I am not I, and to even try to say so is impossible. Psychoanalysis would have us reject the idea of that contradiction as a springboard for organized schemata of consciousness. Simon Skepton articulates the concept of alienation to the deconstructive project. It might be productive to articulate the concept of standpoint to the experience of the subaltern.

59. Hartsock, *Money, Sex, and Power,* 285. See also her collection *Standpoint Theory Revisited.*

60. In response to the post-Marxist argument that there are no class interests before their articulation in discourse, I suggest *standpoint* as a substitute term with objective status even before the idea of interests is articulated. See Laclau and Mouffe, *Hegemony and Socialist Strategy* and Laclau, *On Populist Reason.* For Laclau, rhetoric is what links the particularity of individual psychic drives to a universalizing demand in populist discourse. For Lukács, the particularity of the workers' experience is not just any position but one particular to the worker as commodity.

61. Karlyn Kohrs Campbell has argued that consciousness-raising is the development of theory from experience and practice based on women's marginalized epistemic stance. Campbell, "Consciousness-Raising: Linking Theory, Criticism, and Practice."

62. As Lise Vogel argues in *Marxism and the Oppression of Women,* the objectification of women's labor in and outside of the home under capitalism positions women as objects in both domains (but only constitutes their labor as a commodity in the domain of paid work). Another practice of the consciousness-raising project is Paolo Freire's "pedagogy of the oppressed," which starts the educational experience with the experience of the oppressed and works from there toward an understanding of the systematicity of oppression and, ultimately, of the system itself. See Freire and Macedo, *Pedagogy of the Oppressed.* Analyses of neo/postcolonial subjectivities might provide other examples. However, there is something specific about working class subjectivity: It gets to the core motive of the entire system such that consciousness-raising founded on this standpoint could lead toward revolutionary conclusions.

63. Cloud and Feyh, "'Reason in Revolt Now Thunders': Emotional Fidelity and Working Class Standpoint in the 'Internationale.'"

64. McGee and Lyne, "What Are Nice Folks Like You Doing in a Place Like This? Some Entailments of Treating Knowledge Claims Rhetorically," 389; emphasis added.

65. Bernstein, *Beyond Objectivism and Relativism.*

66. Ibid., 12.

NOTES TO CHAPTER 2

1. Hess, "That Cute Whale You Clicked On? It's Doomed."
2. Bell, "Aww-Some Animals: Why Do Baby Mammals Melt Our Hearts?"
3. Hedges, *Empire of Illusion*, 5.
4. Ibid., 45.
5. Ibid., 49.
6. Gajanan, "Colin Kaepernick and a Brief History of Protest in Sports."
7. Ahmed, *Cultural Politics of Emotion*.
8. Laclau, *On Populist Reason*.
9. Hawhee, *Bodily Arts*, 10.
10. Hawhee, *Bodily Arts*.
11. Coupe, *Kenneth Burke on Myth: An Introduction*.
12. Beyoncé, "Formation," *Lemonade*, 2016.
13. Thank you, Bill Rawlins.
14. Spanos, "Beyoncé: 'The War on People of Color Needs to Be Over.'"
15. Lewis, "'Formation' Exploits New Orleans' Trauma."
16. Kellner, *Media Spectacle*, 2.
17. Two representative works in this area are Hariman and Lucaites, *No Caption Needed*; Finnegan, *Making Photography Matter: A Viewer's History from the Civil War to the Great Depression*.
18. Cloud, "'To Veil the Threat of Terror': Afghan Women and the <Clash of Civilizations> in the Imagery of the US War on Terrorism."
19. Sontag, *On Photography*.
20. Edelman, *Constructing the Political Spectacle*, 1.
21. Ibid., 3.
22. Ibid., 9.
23. Gabler, "Toward a New Definition of Celebrity."
24. Ibid., 109.
25. Hesford, *Spectacular Rhetorics: Human Rights Visions, Recognitions, Feminisms*.
26. Debord, *Society of the Spectacle*.
27. Kellner, *Media Spectacle*, 177.
28. Cloud, "The Irony Bribe and Reality Television: Investment and Detachment in *The Bachelor*."
29. See Matt Stopera, "The Pepper Spraying Cop Meme."

NOTES TO CHAPTER 3

1. Jackie Calmes, "Planned Parenthood Videos Were Altered, Analysis Finds," *New York Times*, August 27, 2015, http://www.nytimes.com/2015/08/28/us/abortion-planned -parenthood-videos.html.
2. Levitan, Dave. "Unspinning the Planned Parenthood Video." FactCheck.org, July 21, 2015, http://www.factcheck.org/2015/07/unspinning-the-planned-parenthood-video/.
3. Burke, *The Philosophy of Literary Form: Studies in Symbolic Action*, 171.
4. Graves, Nyhan, and Reifler, "The Diffusion of Fact-Checking: Understanding the Growth of a Journalistic Innovation."
5. Ibid.
6. Stuart Hall et al., *Policing the Crisis: Mugging, the State, and Law and Order*, 116.
7. Cheryl Gay Stolberg, "Many Politicians Lie. But Trump Has Elevated the Art of Fabrication," *New York Times*, August 7, 2017, https://www.nytimes.com/2017/08/07/us/politics/lies -trump-obama-mislead.html?_r=0. See also Linda Qio, "Fact Check: Trump's Account of

His First 100 Days in Office," *New York Times*, April 30, 2017, https://www.nytimes.com/2017/04/30/us/politics/fact-check-trump-100-days.html?mcubz=0.

8. Andrejevic, *Infoglut*, 5–10.

9. Geuss, *Philosophy and Real Politics*.

10. Elster, *Making Sense of Marx*.

11. Eugene Kiely, "IG Report on Clinton's Emails," FactCheck.org, May 27, 2016, http://www.factcheck.org/2016/05/ig-report-on-clintons-emails/.

12. Nadeau, "Classical Systems of Stases in Greek: Hermagoras to Hermogenes"; Bennett, "Hermagoras of Temnos," 190.

13. George Kennedy, *A New History of Classical Rhetoric*, 97–99. While the original theory explicated by Hermagoras, Hermogenes, and Cicero was designed for invention in a forensic setting, modern scholars have extended the category of jurisdiction into the deliberative, or policy, domain to encompass questions of future action: What should be done? See Hoppman, "A Modern Theory of Stasis" for this argument and for an expanded set of categories of engagement.

14. Robert Farley, "Expert Voice Analyst: It's Trump," FactCheck.org, June 2, 2016, http://www.factcheck.org/2016/06/expert-voice-analyst-its-trump/.

15. Egan, "Lord of the Lies."

16. Burke, *Attitudes toward History*, 102–8.

17. Gitlin, *The Whole World Is Watching*.

18. Kuypers, "Framing Analysis from a Rhetorical Perspective," 300; Kenneth Burke introduced a similar concept in the idea of "terministic screens," which, like frames, are strategies of selection and emphasis that shape perception. Burke, *Language as Symbolic Action*, 44–75. See also Reese et al., *Framing Public Life: Perspectives on Media and our Understanding of the Social World*.

19. Goffman, *Frame Analysis*, 35.

20. Ibid., 177.

21. Entman, "Framing: Toward Clarification of a Fractured Paradigm."

22. Scheufele and Iyengar, "The State of Framing Research: A Call for New Directions"; see also Iyengar, *Is Anyone Responsible: How Television Frames Political Issues*. Scheufele and Iyengar express the concern that the concept of framing has been too loosely applied and conflated with other media strategies like agenda setting.

23. Karl Marx, "The German Ideology"; Burke, *The Philosophy of Literary Form*, 171.

24. Goffman, *Frame Analysis*, 45, 426.

25. Mollie Hemingway, "A Quick and Easy Guide to the Planned Parenthood Videos," *Federalist*, September 29, 2015, http://thefederalist.com/2015/09/29/a-quick-and-easy-guide-to-the-planned-parenthood-videos/.

26. The Center for Medical Progress, "Human Capital."

27. Sontag, *On Photography*, 110.

28. Editorial Board, "The Campaign of Deception Against Planned Parenthood," *New York Times*, July 22, 2015, https://www.nytimes.com/2015/07/22/opinion/the-campaign-of-deception-against-planned-parenthood.html.

29. Condit, *Decoding Abortion Rhetoric*, 79–95.

30. Levitan, "Unspinning the Planned Parenthood Video."

31. David A. Graham, "What Does the Planned Parenthood Video Show?" *The Atlantic*, July 15, 2015, http://www.theatlantic.com/politics/archive/2015/07/planned-parenthood-abortion/398558/.

32. Ross Douthat, "Lies, Carly Fiorina, and Abortion," *New York Times*, September 28, 2015, https://douthat.blogs.nytimes.com/2015/09/28/lies-carly-fiorina-and-abortion/.

33. Hunter Schwartz, "What the Planned Parenthood Video Means to the Abortion Debate," *Washington Post*, July 16, 2015, https://www.washingtonpost.com/news/the-fix/wp/2015/07/16/

what-the-planned-parenthood-video-means-to-the-abortion-debate/?utm_term=
.f939a8bffb83.

34. "An Overview of Abortion Laws."

35. Emily Crockett, "Attacks on Abortion Providers Have Increased since the Planned Parenthood Videos," Vox.com, November 28, 2015, https://www.vox.com/2015/11/28/9810572/abortion-attacks-planned-parenthood-colorado; The Center for Medical Progress, "Human Capital"; see also Samantha Allen, "Planned Parenthood Smear Videos Caused Nine Times More Threats," *Daily Beast*, December 2, 2015, http://www.thedailybeast.com/articles/2015/12/02/planned-parenthood-vids-sparked-threats.html.

36. Burke, *Attitudes toward History*, 102.

37. Goffman, *Frame Analysis*, 177.

38. Greene, "Another Materialist Rhetoric," 37.

39. Scott, "On Viewing Rhetoric as Epistemic."

NOTES TO CHAPTER 4

1. National Public Radio, "Bradley Manning Had Long Been Plagued by Mental Health Issues."

2. Fishman, "Bradley Manning's Army of One."

3. Cloud, "Hegemony or Concordance? The Rhetoric of Tokenism in 'Oprah' Winfrey's Rags-to-Riches Biography."

4. Stoeckley and Assange, *The United States vs. Private Chelsea Manning*; Madar, *The Passion of Bradley Manning*; Nicks, *Private*; Mitchell and Gosztola, *Truth and Consequences*; Greenwald, *No Place to Hide*; Lucas, *The Snowden Operation*; Harding, *The Snowden Files*; Gellman, *Dark Mirror*; Rall, *Snowden*; Snowden, *Everything You Know about the Constitution Is Wrong*.

5. Gitlin, *The Whole World Is Watching*.

6. Roy Greenslade, "Edward Snowden's Leaks Cause Editorial Split at the Washington Post," *Guardian*, July 5, 2013, https://www.theguardian.com/media/greenslade/2013/jul/05/edward-snowden-washington-post.

7. See Jim Rutenberg, "Data Breaches Change the Rules."

8. Glenn Greenwald, Ewen MacAskill, and Laura Poitras, "Edward Snowden: The Whistleblower behind the NSA Surveillance Revelations," *Guardian*, June 11, 2013, https://www.theguardian.com/world/2013/jun/09/edward-snowden-nsa-whistleblower-surveillance.

9. Greenwald, *No Place to Hide*, 924–28.

10. Discussion at *Rancid Honeytrap*'s "Confronting Edward Snowden's Remarks on Bradley Manning" is interesting in featuring a debate over Snowden's purpose in putting down Manning. This blog consistently defends Manning's process as both careful and meticulous. The posts and discussions here are massive on the theme of "Good Whistleblower/Bad Whistleblower." See also Tracy, "Is Edward Snowden the Anti-Bradley Manning?"; Hedges, "'Shooting the Messenger': The media and Snowden are using diminishing Manning and WikiLeaks to elevate Snowden's leaks."

11. Peterson, "Snowden, Wikileaks Clash over Leaked DNC Emails," *Washington Post*, July 28, 2016, https://www.washingtonpost.com/news/the-switch/wp/2016/07/28/a-twitter-spat-breaks-out-between-snowden-and-wikileaks/?utm_term=.1b55434e7da8.

12. Greenwald, *No Place to Hide*, 321–26.

13. Ibid., 907–11.

14. Ewen MacAskill, "Edward Snowden, NSA files source: 'If they want to get you, in time they will,'" *Guardian*, June 10, 2013, https://www.theguardian.com/world/2013/jun/09/nsa-whistleblower-edward-snowden-why.

15. Robert O'Harrow, "Post-9/11 Outsourcing of U.S. Intelligence raises risks," *Washington Post*, June 9, 2010, https://www.washingtonpost.com/world/national-security/the-outsourcing -of-us-intelligence-raises-risks-among-the-benefits/2013/06/09/eba2d314-d14c-11e2-9f1a -1a7cdee20287_story.html?utm_term=.fb7da48d094b. There is an interesting twist on the concepts of public interests and private lives insofar as Snowden was able to retrieve so much information without oversight because he worked for a *private* contractor, the corporation Booz Allen Hamilton. The *Washington Post* reported on a National Intelligence briefing that read, in part, "We Can't Spy . . . If We Can't Buy!"

16. Phoebe Greenwood, "Edward Snowden Should Have Right to Legal Defence in US, Says Hillary Clinton," *Guardian*, July 4, 2014, https://www.theguardian.com/world/2014/jul/04/ edward-snowden-legal-defence-hillary-clinton-interview.

17. Severin Carrell, "Edward Snowden in Running to Be Glasgow University Rector," *Guardian*, January 21, 2014, https://www.theguardian.com/world/2014/jan/21/edward-snowden -glasgow-university-rector-vote.

18. Mark Rice-Oxley, Leila Haddou, and Frances Perraudin, "Edward Snowden Voted Guardian Person of the Year," *Guardian*, December 9, 2013, https://www.theguardian.com/world/ 2013/dec/09/edward-snowden-voted-guardian-person-of-year-2013.

19. Jim Dwyer, "A Removed Snowden Sculpture Inspires a Hologram in Its Place," *New York Times*, April 7, 2015, https://www.nytimes.com/2015/04/08/nyregion/a-removed-snowden -sculpture-inspires-a-hologram-in-its-place.html.

20. Ed Pilkington, "Edward Snowden Did This Country a Great Service. Let Him Come Home," *Guardian*, September 14, 2016, https://www.theguardian.com/us-news/2016/sep/ 14/edward-snowden-pardon-bernie-sanders-daniel-ellsberg.

21. Ibid.

22. There is a good if hagiographic summary at https://www.wired.com/2014/08/edward-snowden/. NBC published a timeline at http://www.nbcnews.com/feature/edward-snowden-interview/ edward-snowden-timeline-n114871.

23. Rall, *Snowden*, 18.

24. Ibid., 20.

25. Ibid., 23.

26. Ibid., 27.

27. Ibid., 47.

28. Ibid., 191.

29. Greenwald, MacAskill, and Poitras, "Snowden: The Whistleblower behind the NSA Leaks."

30. Ibid.

31. Ewen MacAskill, "The NSA's Bulk Metadata Collection Authority Just Expired: What Now?," *Guardian*, November 28, 2015, https://www.theguardian.com/us-news/2015/nov/ 28/nsa-bulk-metadata-collection-expires-usa-freedom-act.

32. Danny Yardron, "Edward Snowden: 'I'm Not an Unhappy Ending for Whistleblowers,'" *Guardian*, April 2, 2016, https://www.theguardian.com/us-news/2016/apr/01/edward -snowden-whistleblower-russia-exile.

33. *Guardian* Editorial Board, "Edward Snowden: More Conscientious Objector than Common Thief."

34. Greenwald, *No Place to Hide*, 121–22, 315.

35. Ibid., 116–21.

36. Ewen MacAskill, "Edward Snowden: How the Spy Story of the Age Leaked Out," *Guardian*, June 12, 2013, https://www.theguardian.com/world/2013/jun/11/edward-snowden-nsa -whistleblower-profile.

37. Cass, "Who Is Edward Snowden? Many Questions Remain."

38. "Timeline: Edward Snowden's Journey," *Star Tribune*, August 1, 2013, http://www .startribune.com/timeline-edward-snowden-s-journey/217930921/.

39. Jeremy Ravinsky, "Snowden Saga in Overdrive after Flight to Russia," *Christian Science Monitor*, June 24, 2013, https://www.csmonitor.com/World/Global-Issues/2013/0624/Snowden-saga-in-overdrive-after-flight-to-Russia.

40. Rall, *Snowden*, 143.

41. Ibid., 106.

42. Ibid., 153.

43. Harding, *The Snowden Files*, 217.

44. Ibid., 253.

45. John Bolton, "Edward Snowden's Leaks Are a Grave Threat to US National Security," *Guardian*, June 18, 2013, https://www.theguardian.com/commentisfree/2013/jun/18/edward-snowden-leaks-grave-threat.

46. Lucas, *The Snowden Operation: Inside the West's Greatest Intelligence Disaster*, 794–97.

47. Ibid., 939–42.

48. Harding, *The Snowden Files*, 7.

49. Glenn Greenwald, "Edward Snowden: US Surveillance 'Not Something I'm Willing to Live Under,'" *Guardian*, July 8, 2013, https://www.theguardian.com/world/2013/jul/08/edward-snowden-surveillance-excess-interview.

50. Rusbridger and MacAskill, "I, Spy: Edward Snowden in Exile."

51. Cloud and Gatchet, "David, Goliath, and the Black Panthers: The Paradox of the Oppressed Militant in Rhetoric of Self-Defense."

52. See a summary of polls at https://en.wikipedia.org/wiki/Commentary_on_Edward_Snowden's_disclosure.

53. Steven Nelson, "Edward Snowden Unpopular at Home, a Hero Abroad, Poll Finds."

54. Haroon Siddique, "Edward Snowden's Girlfriend Is 'As Well as Can Be Expected,' Says Father," June 12, 2013, https://www.theguardian.com/world/2013/jun/12/edward-snowden-lindsay-mills-father.

55. Richard Roeper, "In *Snowden*, Oliver Stone Depicts the NSA Leaker as Pure Hero," *Chicago Sun-Times*, September 14, 2016, http://chicago.suntimes.com/entertainment/in-snowden-oliver-stone-depicts-the-nsa-leaker-as-pure-hero/.

56. Paul Lewis and Karen McVeigh, "Edward Snowden: What We Know about the Source behind the NSA Files Leak," *Guardian*, June 10, 2013, https://www.theguardian.com/world/2013/jun/11/edward-snowden-what-we-know-nsa.

57. "ICYMI: Brian Williams Breaks Down the Snowden Interview," *NBC News*, May 29, 2014, http://www.nbcnews.com/watch/nbc-news/icymi-brian-williams-breaks-down-the-snowden-interview-269157955565.

58. Greenwald, *No Place to Hide*.

59. Peter Bradshaw, "Citizenfour Review—Gripping Snowden Documentary Offers Portrait of Power, Paranoia and One Remarkable Man," *Guardian*, October 16, 2014, https://www.theguardian.com/film/2014/oct/16/citizen-four-review-edward-snowden-documentary.

60. Stuart Dredge, "Edward Snowden? There's a Temple Run-Style Endless Runner App for Him," *Guardian*, August 9, 2013, https://www.theguardian.com/technology/appsblog/2013/aug/09/edward-snowden-iphone-ipad-android-game.

61. John Broder and Scott Shane, "For Snowden, A Life of Ambition, Despite the Drifting," *New York Times*, June 15, 2013, http://www.nytimes.com/2013/06/16/us/for-snowden-a-life-of-ambition-despite-the-drifting.html.

62. Peter Rainer, "'Citizenfour': Director Laura Poitras Shares the Rage of Her Subject Edward Snowden," *Christian Science Monitor*, October 24, 2014, https://www.csmonitor.com/The-Culture/Movies/2014/1024/Citizenfour-Director-Laura-Poitras-shares-the-rage-of-her-subject-Edward-Snowden.

63. A. O. Scott, "Review: 'Snowden,' Oliver Stone's Restrained Portrait of a Whistle-Blower," *New York Times*, September 15, 2016, https://www.nytimes.com/2016/09/16/movies/snowden-review-oliver-stone-joseph-gordon-levitt.html.

64. Tracy, "Is Edward Snowden the Anti-Bradley Manning?"

65. Tim Grieving, "Chelsea Manning as Opera: Story of Transgender WikiLeaks Figure Unfolds in 'The Source,'" *Los Angeles Times*, October 14, 2016, http://www.latimes.com/entertainment/arts/la-ca-cm-source-opera-chelsea-manning-20161016-snap-story.html.

66. Cloud, *Control and Consolation in U.S. Political and Popular Culture: Rhetorics of Therapy.*

67. Thompson, "Early Struggles of Soldier Charged in Leak Case."

68. Ellen Nakashima and Julie Tate, "Soldier's Gender Identity Issues Are Raised in WikiLeaks Case," *Washington Post*, December 17, 2011, https://www.washingtonpost.com/world/national-security/soldiers-gender-identity-issues-raised-in-wikileaks-case/2011/12/17/gIQAXxlC1O_story.html?utm_term=.1bc96obbcef9.

69. Ed Pilkington, "Adrian Lamo Tells Manning Trial about Six Days of Chats with Accused Leaker," *Guardian*, June 4, 2013, https://www.theguardian.com/world/2013/jun/04/adrian-lamo-testifies-bradley-manning.

70. Manning, "The Fog Machine of War."

71. Pilkington, "Chelsea Manning Writes Bill to Protect Journalism and Curb Espionage Act," May 6, 2015, https://www.theguardian.com/us-news/2015/may/07/chelsea-manning-bill-journalism-espionage-act.

72. Ed Pilkington, "Edward Snowden Sends Birthday Greeting to 'Extraordinary' Chelsea Manning," *Guardian*, December 16, 2014, https://www.theguardian.com/us-news/2014/dec/16/edward-snowden-birthday-greeting-chelsea-manning.

73. "The Iraq Archive: The Strands of a War," *New York Times*, October 22, 2010, http://www.nytimes.com/2010/10/23/world/middleeast/23intro.html?mtrref=www.google.com&gwh=EC75B36ADA3798D169C91A1FCD421134&gwt=pay. See also Tavernise and Lehren, "A Grim Portrait of Civilian Deaths in Iraq."

74. Neely Tucker, "Bradley Manning: How Do We Weigh His Crimes?," *Washington Post*, August 1, 2013, https://www.pressreader.com/usa/the-washington-post/20130801/282222303382037.

75. Ellen Nakashima and Julie Tate, "Army Private to Face Hearing in Leak of Government Documents," *Washington Post*, December 16, 2011, https://www.pressreader.com/usa/the-washington-post/20111216/294733542327178.

76. Eugene Robinson, "Give Manning a Plea Deal," *Washington Post*, June 3, 2013, https://www.washingtonpost.com/opinions/eugene-robinson-give-manning-a-plea-deal-in-classified-leaks-case/2013/06/03/3d2a7578-cc8b-11e2-8845-d970ccb04497_story.html?utm_term=.1e541dc858b1.

77. Amanda Holpunch, "Chelsea Manning: 'It is Terrifying to Face the Government Alone,'" *Guardian*, August 2, 2016, https://www.theguardian.com/us-news/2016/aug/02/chelsea-manning-interview-amnesty-international.

78. "Bradley Manning: Cruel and Unusual," *Guardian*, March 14, 2011, https://www.theguardian.com/commentisfree/2011/mar/15/bradley-manning-prison-treatment-wikileaks. See a similar narration of this in Bruce Ackerman, "Bradley Manning's Inhumane Treatment."

79. James Ridgeway and Jean Casella, "The Lonely Battle against Solitary Confinement," *Guardian*, January 19, 2011, https://www.theguardian.com/commentisfree/cifamerica/2011/jan/19/bradley-manning-wikileaks.

80. Ed Pilkington, "Stripped Naked Every Night, Bradley Manning Tells of Prison Ordeal," *Guardian*, March 10, 2011, https://www.theguardian.com/world/2011/mar/11/stripped-naked-bradley-manning-prison.

81. Johnson, *The Lavender Scare.*

82. Nicks, *Private,* 119.

83. Ibid., 138–39.

84. Ibid., 195.

85. Ibid.

86. Ibid., 162–63.

87. Ed Pilkington, "Chelsea Manning Supporters Condemn Threat of Indefinite Solitary Confinement," *Guardian*, August 13, 2015, https://www.theguardian.com/us-news/2015/aug/13/chelsea-manning-indefinite-solitary-confinement-petitions; see also Pilkington, "Chelsea Manning May Face Solitary Confinement for Having Jenner Vanity Fair Issue."

88. Charlie Savage, "Manning, Facing Prison for Leaks, Apologizes at Court-Martial Trial," *New York Times*, August 14, 2013, http://www.nytimes.com/2013/08/15/us/manning-apologizes-for-leaks-my-actions-hurt-people.html.

89. Maggie O'Kane, Chavala Madlena, and Guy Grandjean, "WikiLeaks Accused Bradley Manning 'should have never been sent to Iraq,'" *Guardian*, May 27, 2011, https://www.theguardian.com/world/2011/may/27/bradley-manning-wikileaks-mentally-fragile.

90. See also Broder and Thompson, "Loner Sought a Refuge, and Ended up in War." Here he's called a violent misfit. Also, Nakashima and Finn, "Lawyer: Leaks Suspect's Mental Health Doubted."

91. Charles Davis, "The Liberal Betrayal of Bradley Manning," Salon.com, April 10, 2012, http://www.salon.com/2012/04/10/the_liberal_betrayal_of_bradley_manning/.

92. Glenn Greenwald, "Bradley Manning: The Face of Heroism," *Guardian*, February 28, 2013, https://www.theguardian.com/commentisfree/2013/feb/28/bradley-manning-heroism-pleads-guilty.

93. Glenn Greenwald, "US Investigates Possible WikiLeaks Leaker for 'Communication with the Enemy,'" *Guardian*, September 27, 2012, https://www.theguardian.com/commentisfree/2012/sep/27/wikileaks-investigation-enemy.

94. *Washington Post* Editorial Board, "Leaks and Democracy," *Washington Post*, August 2, 2013, https://search-proquest-com.libezproxy2.syr.edu/docview/1416507392?accountid=14214.

95. Ed Pilkington, "Manning Says He First Tried to Leak to Washington Post and New York Times," *Guardian*, February 28, 2013, https://www.theguardian.com/world/2013/feb/28/manning-washington-post-new-york-times; also Pilkington, "Manning Chose Leaks That Would Not Harm US, Lawyer Says."

96. Scott Shane and Charles Savage, "In WikiLeaks Case, Defense Puts the Jailers on Trial," *New York Times*, December 7, 2012, http://www.nytimes.com/2012/12/08/us/in-private-bradley-manning-case-jailers-become-the-accused.html.

97. Ginger Thompson, "Last Witness for Military Takes the Stand," Dispatch.com, December 20, 2011, http://www.the-dispatch.com/news/20111220/last-witness-for-military-takes-stand-in-leak-case/1.

98. Dominic Rushe and Matt Williams, "Bradley Manning Hearing-Tuesday 20 December," *Guardian*, December 20, 2011, https://www.theguardian.com/world/blog/2011/dec/20/bradley-manning-hearing-live-updates.

99. Esther Addley, "Bradley Manning: The Angry Young Man Who Turned Whistleblower," *Guardian*, July 30, 2013, https://www.theguardian.com/world/2013/jul/30/bradley-manning-angry-young-man.

100. Nicks, *Private*, 131.

101. Monica Hesse, "Manning's Transgender Declaration Proves Complicated," *Stars and Stripes*, August 23, 2013, https://www.stripes.com/news/army/manning-s-transgender-declaration-proves-complicated-1.236891#.WYzUAoqQyew; see also *Washington Post* Editorial Board, "The Manning Moment."

102. Trevor Timm, "Don't Punish Chelsea Manning, Release Her," *Guardian*, September 13, 2016, https://www.theguardian.com/commentisfree/2016/sep/13/release-chelsea-manning-wikileaks-hunger-strike.

103. Martin Pengelly, "Chelsea Manning Was Transgender 'in Secret,'" *Guardian*, December 8, 2014, https://www.theguardian.com/us-news/2014/dec/08/chelsea-manning-transgender

-secret-us-army; see also Pilkington, "Chelsea Manning Allowed to Have Hormone Therapy"; Londoño, "Chelsea Manning Wins Change of Legal Name to Chelsea Elizabeth Manning."

104. Jennifer Finney Boylan, "Longing for When 'I'm Trans' Brings Nothing but 'Ho-Hum,'" *Washington Post*, August 23, 2013, https://www.pressreader.com/usa/the-washington-post/20130823/282295317855451.

105. Lenny Bernstein and Julie Tate, "Bradley Manning Says He Will Live as a Woman and Seek Hormone Therapy in Prison," *Washington Post*, August 22, 2013, https://www.washingtonpost.com/world/national-security/bradley-manning-says-he-will-live-as-a-woman-and-seek-hormone-therapy-in-prison/2013/08/22/8f2fb2a8-0b5f-11e3-b87c-476db8ac34cd_story.html?utm_term=.e20448f9cf7f.

106. Glenn Greenwald, "Bradley Manning Is off Limits at SF Gay Pride Parade," *Guardian*, April 27, 2013, https://www.theguardian.com/commentisfree/2013/apr/27/bradley-manning-sf-gay-pride.

107. *Teen Vogue* celebrates Manning's release and transformation in an article on her fashion choices (photographed by Annie Liebovitz), pointing out how even in freedom, gender normativity enables sympathetic framing of Manning as foremost a feminine woman: "A very natural, very beautiful little girl." Nathan Heller, "Chelsea Manning Changed the Course of History. Now She's Focusing on Herself," *Teen Vogue*, August 10, 2017, http://www.vogue.com/article/chelsea-manning-vogue-interview-september-issue-2017.

NOTES TO CHAPTER 5

1. Burke, *The Rhetoric of Religion.*
2. *Cosmos: A Personal Voyage*; *Cosmos: A Spacetime Odyssey.*
3. Genzlinger, "Hitchhiking in a Starry Reboot of a Journey through the Universe, *New York Times*, March 7, 2014, https://www.nytimes.com/2014/03/08/arts/television/neil-degrasse-tyson-hosts-cosmos-a-spacetime-odyssey.html.
4. Aune, *Rhetoric And Marxism.*
5. *Cosmos: A Personal Voyage.*
6. *Cosmos: A Spacetime Odyssey.*
7. Rick Kissell, "'Cosmos' Draws Biggest Global Audience Ever for National Geographic Channel," *Variety*, July 7, 2014, http://variety.com/2014/tv/news/cosmos-draws-biggest-global-audience-ever-for-national-geographic-channel-1201257111/.
8. Jenkins, "After One Brief Season, Cosmos Makes Its Final Voyage."
9. Kissell, "'Cosmos' Draws Biggest Global Audience Ever for National Geographic Channel."
10. "Cosmos: A Spacetime Odyssey on FOX."
11. Hank Campbell, "Five Things Neil deGrasse Tyson's 'Cosmos' Gets Wrong." See also Richards, "How Cosmos Does Religious History Badly." Most critics found the cosmic calendar to be a useful device to manage the scale of cosmic history.
12. Enns, "'Cosmos' and Christianity (or Any Religion, for That Matter)."
13. Crugnale, "'Cosmos' Evolution Segment Cut Out of Fox Affiliate Broadcast."
14. Bynum, "TV Networks Refuse to Renew Neil deGrasse Tyson's Cosmos." Catholics embraced the show; see Connolly, "Is It Okay for Catholics to Watch Cosmos: A Spacetime Odyssey?"
15. Creation Ministries International, "About Us—Creation.com."
16. Creation Ministries International, "Cosmos Neil deGrasse Tyson Review—Creation.com."
17. A strategy common in Holocaust denial discourse; Lipstadt, *Denying the Holocaust.*
18. Answers in Genesis, "*Cosmos* Review: 'Unafraid of the Dark'"; for all of Answers in Genesis's reviews of *Cosmos*, see "Cosmos: A SpaceTime Odyssey Review."

19. For example, this passage makes no scientific sense: "No particle is fast enough to travel from p to q—this would require infinite speed, which would require infinite energy in the classical limit. Event p is not simultaneous with event r because a particle of the right velocity could travel from p to r. Neither is event s simultaneous with p since a particle can travel from s to p. Moreover, there is no ambiguity about which events have happened first. Clearly, events below p and q have happened before p and q, and events higher on the vertical axis have happened later. Any point with the same ct value as p and q is simultaneous with p and q. Thus, in a Newtonian universe with two dimensions of space and one of time, all events concurrent with p are represented by the horizontal plane that passes through p. All observers, regardless of their location or velocity in the universe, would agree on both the relative and absolute timing of these events."

20. Answers in Genesis, "Anisotropic Synchrony Convention—Distant Starlight Problem."

21. Answers in Genesis, "Questioning Cosmos."

22. According to its website, 200,000 people subscribe to its "Acts and Facts" newsletter, with hundreds of thousands of others who tune in to daily web "devotionals" and radio programs. Institute for Creation Research, "Who We Are."

23. Institute for Creation Research, "Guide to the Universe."

24. Thomas, "Cosmos: A Series Created to Counter Creation."

25. Arel, "13 ways Neil deGrasse Tyson's 'Cosmos' Sent the Religious Right off the Deep End."

26. Horst, "'Cosmos' Writer Ann Druyan on Science and Seth MacFarlane."

27. Ibid.

28. Wiener-Bronner and Ohlheiser, "What Does Neil deGrasse Tyson's 'Cosmos' Say about Religion?"

29. McClure, "Resurrecting the Narrative Paradigm: Identification and the Case of Young Earth Creationism."

30. Ibid., 206.

31. Ibid., 207.

32. Brummett, "The Representative Anecdote as a Burkean Method, Applied to Evangelical Rhetoric"; Burke, A Grammar of Motives, 59–62.

33. Burke, A Grammar of Motives, 61.

34. Bland and Morrison, "The Experimental Detection of an Emotional Response to the Idea of Evolution."

35. Cloud and Feyh, "Reason in Revolt: Emotional Fidelity and Working Class Standpoint in the 'Internationale.'"

36. Kelly and Hoerl, "Genesis in Hyperreality: Legitimizing Disingenuous Controversy at the Creation Museum."

37. Lynch, "'Prepare to Believe': The Creation Museum as Embodied Conversion Narrative."

38. Ibid., 2.

39. The sound track can be heard at Epic Step, Cosmos: A Spacetime Odyssey—Alan Silvestri—Soundtrack.

40. Audiophile Vintage, Famous Maxell Blown Away Guy over 500 Plays Tape C.

41. Wiener-Bronner and Ohlheiser, "What Does Neil deGrasse Tyson's 'Cosmos' Say About Religion?"

42. Ibid.

43. Joshua Gunn, "Review Essay: Mourning Humanism, or, the Idiom of Haunting," 79.

44. Ibid., 82.

45. See Cashmore, Celebrity Culture. Nayar, Seeing Stars: Spectacle, Society and Celebrity Culture; Marshall, The Celebrity Culture Reader.

46. Cloud, "Shock Therapy: Oprah Winfrey, Celebrity Philanthropy, and Disaster 'Relief' in Haiti."

47. Fahy, The New Celebrity Scientists, 7.

48. Ibid.

49. Ibid., 90.
50. Ibid., 201.
51. Ibid.
52. Barthes, *Mythologies*.
53. See literature on animation in science education, Barak and Dori, "Science Education in Primary Schools: Is an Animation Worth a Thousand Pictures?" On the potential of animation to foster denaturalization or reflexivity, see Stabile, *Prime Time Animation*, 154–61.
54. Barthes, *Image-Music-Text*.
55. You can see the segment here: Santorsola, *Carl Sagan-Cosmos-Evolution into 40 Seconds*.
56. "Stalking the Wild Neutrino."
57. Burke, *Permanence and Change: An Anatomy of Purpose*.
58. Eagleton, *Ideology: An Introduction*, 2, 5, 99, 178, 188. Also Head, *Ideology and Social Science*.
59. Dewey and Rogers, *The Public and Its Problems*; Dewey, *Democracy and Education*; Garrison, Neubert, and Reich, *Democracy and Education Reconsidered*; Jenlink, *Dewey's Democracy and Education Revisited*; Johnston, *Deweyan Inquiry*.
60. Harris, "Where Nearly Half of Pupils Are Homeless, School Aims to Be Teacher, Therapist, Even Santa."
61. See critique in Bale and Knopp, *Education and Capitalism*.
62. For summaries of the history of the law and teaching of evolution and creationism in public schools, see Moore, Jensen, and Hatch, "Twenty Questions: What Have the Courts Said about the Teaching of Evolution and Creationism in Public Schools?"; Humes, *Monkey Girl*; Miller, *Only a Theory*; Adam R. Shapiro, *Trying Biology*; Moran, *American Genesis*.
63. For other analysis of core arguments and rhetorical strategies of creationism, see Tierney and Holley, "Intelligent Design and the Attack on Scientific Inquiry"; Carbonell, "Intelligent Design Creationism and the Mechanisms of Postmodernity."
64. There are multiple traditions of critical pedagogy that share a general approach of situated working class anti-oppression education pioneered by Paulo Freire; see Freire and Macedo, *Pedagogy of the Oppressed, 30th Anniversary Edition*; Irwin, *Paulo Freire's Philosophy of Education*; Freire, *Paulo Freire* (Freire was influenced by the Marxist tradition, which also informed the efforts of the Birmingham School for Cultural Studies); Cole, *Marxism and Educational Theory*; Macrine, McLaren, and Hill, *Revolutionizing Pedagogy*. Recently, Henry Giroux has taken up the banner of radical education in the context of the critique of neoliberalism; see Giroux, *Schooling and the Struggle for Public Life*; Giroux, *On Critical Pedagogy*; also Hill, *Contesting Neoliberal Education*. There is an important argument between critical pedagogy and Dewey's perspective; see Irwin, *Paulo Freire's Philosophy of Education*, 6–8. Dewey and other progressives share "a modernist (and romantic) faith in individual reason and democratic community"; pedagogies based on the pragmatists have become "instrumentalist."
65. Klinghoffer, "There's No Question 'Cosmos' Is Coming to Public School Science Classrooms." For a response to Klinghoffer, see Arel, "Why Neil deGrasse Tyson Has Creationists so Thoroughly Petrified."
66. Fuglei, "Five Ways Neil deGrasse Tyson and Bill Nye Can Help Teachers Improve Science Literacy."
67. Druyan, "Quest for Students, Episode 1."
68. Answers in Genesis, "Questioning Cosmos."
69. Answers in Genesis, "Kids Answers."
70. Answers in Genesis, "Creation for Kids."
71. Coupe, *Kenneth Burke on Myth: An Introduction*, 3.
72. Burke, "Revolutionary Symbolism in America," 267–74.
73. Hoyt, *The Etymology of Religion*.

NOTES TO CHAPTER 6

1. Davidson, *How Revolutionary Were the Bourgeois Revolutions?*, 443; Foner, *Reconstruction*; Foner, *Slavery, the Civil War, and Reconstruction*.
2. Davidson, *How Revolutionary Were the Bourgeois Revolutions?*
3. Aptheker, *The American Revolution, 1763–1783*, 14. For additional history from the Left on the revolution, see Smith, *A People's History of the United States* and Raphael, *A People's History of the American Revolution*. Raphael's book contains excerpts from people—slaves, workers, women, pacifists, and Native Americans—whose voices have been excluded from traditional histories. Raphael argues that one should appreciate the militancy of ordinary people in the revolution without overestimating its gains. See also Raphael's *The First American Revolution*, about militant conflict before 1775, and his *Founding Myths: Stories That Hide Our Patriotic Past*. Also Holton, *Forced Founders*.
4. Aptheker, *The American Revolution*, 22. For Aptheker's discussion of class divisions in the colonies and the organizing efforts of the masses, see 46–57. On Thomas Paine, see 96–97; see also Nash, *The Unknown American Revolution* on the militant origins and eventual taming of the revolution. See also Bouton, *Taming Democracy*.
5. On *kairos*, see Cloud, Feyh, and McCann, "Kairos of the Vanguard," 147–57; Kinneavy and Eskin, "Kairos in Aristotle's Rhetoric."
6. Dennehy, Morgan, and Assenza, "Thomas Paine: Creating the New Story for a New Nation," 184.
7. Paine, *Common Sense*.
8. Foner, *Tom Paine and Revolutionary America*, 80. Paine was not a Christian; scholars have argued that he adopted the religious argument as way of reaching his audiences in the context of the American Great Awakening.
9. I hope that it is clear here that I am not excusing Paine's sexism or racism.
10. Craig Nelson, "Thomas Paine and the Making of 'Common Sense,'" 237.
11. Foner, *Tom Paine and Revolutionary America*, xxxi. See Rosenfeld on the "epistemological history" of the idea of common sense in the context of the Enlightenment: *Common Sense: A Political History*; Goetzmann, *Beyond the Revolution: A History of American Thought from Paine to Pragmatism*.
12. Larkin, *Thomas Paine and the Literature of Revolution*, 118; Hoffman, "Paine and Prejudice" 388.
13. Ibid.; ibid.
14. Hogan and Williams, "Republican Charisma and the American Revolution: The Textual Persona of Thomas Paine's Common Sense."
15. Kennerly, "Getting Carried Away: How Rhetorical Transport Gets Judgment Going."
16. Edward J. Gallagher, "Thomas Paine's CRISIS 1 and the Comfort of Time."
17. Larkin, *Thomas Paine and the Literature of Revolution*, 4.
18. Ibid., 10.
19. Foner, *Tom Paine and Revolutionary America*, 66.
20. Davidson, *How Revolutionary Were the Bourgeois Revolutions?*
21. Hogan and Williams, "Republican Charisma and the American Revolution," 5.
22. Foner, *Tom Paine and Revolutionary America*, 8.
23. Ibid., xii.
24. Hoffman, "Paine and Prejudice."
25. Posner, *Public Intellectuals: A Study of Decline, with a New Preface and Epilogue*, 123.
26. Cloud, "Hegemony or Concordance? The Rhetoric of Tokenism in 'Oprah' Winfrey's Rags-to-Riches Biography."
27. Young, *Prophets, Gurus, and Pundits*.
28. Posner, *Public Intellectuals*; Jacoby, *The Last Intellectuals*.
29. Collins, "Black Public Intellectuals: From Du Bois to the Present."

30. Ibid.
31. Chokshi, "How #BlackLivesMatter Came to Define a Movement."
32. Anderson and Hitlin, "The Hashtag #BlackLivesMatter Emerges: Social Activism on Twitter."
33. Chokshi, "How #BlackLivesMatter Came to Define a Movement."
34. Ryan J. Gallagher, Reagan, Danforth, and Dodds, "Divergent Discourse between Protests and Counter-Protests: #BlackLivesMatter and #AllLivesMatter."
35. Cohen and Jackson, "Ask a Feminist: A Conversation with Cathy J. Cohen on Black Lives Matter, Feminism, and Contemporary Activism." See also Lindsey, "Post-Ferguson: A 'Herstorical' Approach to Black Violability." Garza, "A Herstory of the #BlackLivesMatter Movement by Alicia Garza."
36. Lindsey, "Post-Ferguson: A 'Herstorical' Approach to Black Violability."
37. Jackson and Welles, "#Ferguson is Everywhere: Initiators in Emerging Counterpublic Networks"; Jackson and Welles, "Hijacking #MyNPD: Social Media Dissent and Networked Counterpublics."
38. Bonilla and Rosa, "#Ferguson: Digital Protest, Hashtag Ethnography, and the Racial Politics of Social Media in the United States."
39. Ibid., 7.
40. Yang, "Narrative Agency in Hashtag Activism: The Case of #BlackLivesMatter."
41. Ibid., 15.
42. Powell, "Making #BlackLivesMatter: Michael Brown, Eric Garner, and the Specters of Black Life—Toward a Hauntology of Blackness."
43. Ibid., 255.
44. Ibid.
45. Bonilla and Rosa, "#Ferguson," 4.
46. Mackin, "Black Lives Matter and the Concept of the Counterworld."
47. Ibid., 473.
48. Ibid., 477.
49. Ibid., 479.
50. Garza, "A Herstory of the #BlackLivesMatter Movement by Alicia Garza."
51. See *Radical Teacher*, vol. 106 (2016). All articles in this volume focus on teaching materials about and engaging students in the movement. Sarah Dowling, Marcus Johnson, and Ron Krabill assess their attempts to integrate movement knowledge into the neoliberal college classroom, with mixed success: "Teaching Ferguson: Can #BlackLivesMatter in the Neoliberal University?"
52. Quoted in Adamson, *Hegemony and Revolution*, 151.
53. Ibid., 151–52.
54. Ibid., 153.
55. Alexander and West, *The New Jim Crow*.
56. Taylor, *From #BlackLivesMatter to Black Liberation*.
57. Ibid., 217.
58. Ibid., 195–205.
59. Monahan, "Reading Paine from the Left."

NOTES TO THE CONCLUSION

1. Wang, "'Post-Truth' Named 2016 Word of the Year by Oxford Dictionaries."
2. Mantzarlis, "No, We're Not in a 'Post-Fact' Era."
3. Mishra, "The Anti-Élite, Post-Fact Worlds of Trump and Rousseau."
4. Warner, *Publics and Counterpublics*, 199.

5. Marx and Engels, *Manifesto of the Communist Party.*

6. Sheryl Gay Stolberg and Brian M. Rosenthal, "Deadly Chaos after White Nationalist Rally in Virginia," *New York Times*, August 12, 2017, https://www.nytimes.com/ 2017/08/12/us/charlottesville -protest-white-nationalist.html?hp&action=click&pgtype=Homepage&clickSource=story -heading&module=a-lede-package-region&region=top-news&WT.nav=top-news&mtrref= www.nytimes.com&gwh=6756AED1AB830B56213AD58401C2EE01&gwt=pay.

7. Ibid.

8. Blankstein and Silva, "LeBron James' Los Angeles Home Vandalized"; Williams and McGlone, "Noose Found at Exhibit in African American Smithsonian Museum"; Schmid, "White Supremacist Arrested in Fatal Stabbing of Two Men after Anti-Muslim Rant in Portland"; Yan, Simon, and Graef, "Campus Killing"; Riese, "Homophobic Man Beats Lesbian Unconscious."

9. Savali, "Princeton Professor Keeanga-Yahmatta Taylor Cancels Public Appearances."

10. National Alliance to End Homelessness, "The State of Homelessness in America"; Neate, "Scandal of Europe's 11m Empty Homes."

11. Bernick, "The Jobs Perplex: With US Unemployment So Low, Why Is Job Dissatisfaction and Anxiety So High?"; Economic Policy Institute, "The Top Charts of 2016."

12. Elliott, "Richest 62 People as Wealthy as Half of World's Population."

13. Kahn, "The World Passes 400 PPM Threshold. Permanently." That threshold was probably passed several years ago: Michael D. Lemonick, "Global Warming: Beyond the Tipping Point."

14. National Sexual Violence Resource Center, "Statistics About Sexual Violence."

15. Kingkade, "Prosecutors Rarely Bring Charges in Campus Rape Cases"; LaFrance, "What Makes the Stanford Rape Case So Unusual."

16. Economic Policy Institute, "The Top Charts of 2016."

17. Park and Mykhyalyshyn, "L. G. B. T. People Are More Likely to Be Targets of Hate Crimes Than Any Other Minority Group."

18. Ravitz, "Before Orlando."

19. Younge, "Donald Trump Is Not Too Big to Fail."

20. Stein and Somashekhar, "Women's March on Washington Is Poised to Be the Biggest Anti-Trump Demonstration."

21. Cauterucci, "The Women's March on Washington Has Released an Unapologetically Progressive Platform."

22. Fisher, Down, and Ray, "The Demographics of the #Resistance."

GLOSSARY OF KEY TERMS

Affect: the sensory feelings that are interpreted to become emotions that we can express and understand

Agency: the capacity to exert one's will over one's present and future

Aristotle: Ancient Greek teacher of rhetoric

Belief: a rhetorically and socially constructed statement about reality

Big five: key rhetorical strategies more embraced by the Right than the Left, including affect, embodiment, myth, narrative, and spectacle

Black Lives Matter / #BlackLivesMatter: a movement, significantly organized on Twitter, against police brutality and other racist aggression against black Americans

Burke, Kenneth: influential American rhetorician who criticized debunking and described how identification works as persuasion

Capitalism: an economic system based on competition and profit that relies on extracting value from the labor of the working class

Celebrities: people whose bodies, image, and character become linked to ideas and values so that people can relate to them

Common Sense: pamphlet by Thomas Paine encouraging support for the American Revolution

Common sense: following Gramsci, hegemonic discourses that can be supplanted through resistance and the installation of a new set of truths as prevailing belief

Culture of critical discourse (CCD): a scholarly perspective that valorizes facts and rational argument without attention to mediation; the "reality-based community"

Denaturalization: a form of criticism that takes apart beliefs that appear to be natural and noncontroversial to show how they were socially constructed; rekeying

Dewey, John: American pragmatist philosopher who discussed the role of education in democracy

Doxa: received wisdom, prevailing belief, common sense

Embodiment: the strategy of making an audience feel as if they are physically experiencing a situation, space, event, or body of knowledge

Enlightenment: a body of philosophical and political thought and scientific progress that emerged in concert with mercantile capitalism that expressed faith in reason, observation, empiricism; also human rights, liberty, and equality as values

Enthymeme: a form of reasoning that relies upon shared common ground in the form of values

Episteme: baseline knowledge or experience

Epistemic: pertaining to how we know

Epistemology: the branch of philosophy concerned with how people know

Exploitation: the extraction of profit from a worker's labor, directing value produced to the employer rather than the employee; the attendant processes of alienation and oppression

Fact-checking: a journalistic practice that compares what a politician says to a belief assumed to be true

Fidelity: perspectival resonance of a message (in narrative or other form) with the shared experiences and interests of those whose identities are called into being by the discourse

Frame analysis: how discourses selectively direct attention, involve audiences intimately with the matter at hand, and construct coherent and non-contradictory schemes of making sense of the world

Frame-checking: an alternative to fact-checking; evaluates the narrative and other meaning making that couches information in context

Frankfurt School: group of Jewish academics who fled fascism in Europe and founded a school of critical inquiry in the United States

Gramsci: Italian Marxist who described the importance of culture in maintaining power

Habermas: contemporary scholar of the public sphere

Hegemony: the maintenance of power through both force and the rhetoric of a ruling class

Idealism: the idea that ideas and values determine the shape of society

Ideology: system of ideas that justifies and naturalizes the status quo

Interests: a social group's needs and desire for a better future

Isocrates: Ancient Greek teacher of rhetoric

Kant: an Enlightenment philosopher

LGBTQ*: a shorthand naming communities defending nonstandard sexualities and gender identities against oppression; the list often includes lesbian, gay, bisexual, transgender, queer, intersex, questioning, asexual, pan- or omni-sexual, and more (hence the need for shorthand, which will always be inadequate; sometimes substituted with "queer")

Lukács: Hungarian Marxist who invented standpoint epistemology

Manning, Chelsea: whistleblower who exposed classified information about U.S. wars in 2008

Marxism: body of theory associated with Karl Marx, a nineteenth-century philosopher, critic, and activist who was concerned with the liberation of ordinary people

Materialism: idea in philosophy that the embodied practices and social organization of humans drives changes in ideas rather than the other way around (idealism)

Media frames: concept developed by Todd Gitlin to describe how reporters mediate information to shape public perception of events

Mediation: the process of intervening between *episteme* and *doxa* with rhetoric that frames and interprets reality

Mediation frames: how all knowledge is mediated in ways that frame perception of reality

Myth: a grand narrative that explains a society's origins and destinies; not the opposite of *truth*

Narrative: form of human rationality that is expressed in storytelling

Naturalization: when a belief or value comes to seem like the unquestionable, natural truth

Oppression: systemic, institutional and collective discrimination, disenfranchisement, dehumanization, and abuse of groups based on identity in the service of social division and scapegoating; includes racism, sexism, Islamophobia, the persecution of LGBTQ* persons, anti-immigrant sentiment and policy, and more

Paine, Thomas: American revolutionary whose pamphlet *Common Sense* influenced Americans to support the War for Independence

Pedagogy: the study and practice of methods of teaching

Plato: Ancient Greek realist who denounced rhetoric as relativist

Postmodernism: refusal of foundations in favor of recognizing that dominant reality is made up of fragmented language and images forming spectacles

Poststructuralism: camp of critical thought committed to relativist critique

Public intellectual: person with knowledge who shares that knowledge outside of the academy to promote public discussion and debate

Public sphere: domain of debate and deliberation without state interference

Punctum: concept defined by Roland Barthes about images; moment of interruption in the given meaning of an image, narrative, or myth

Queer: a term describing nonstandard gender identity, expression, or sexual practices; once pejorative, now embraced in many LGBTQ* contexts as capturing strategies of resistance to dominant gender/sex regimes

Radical pedagogy: methods of teaching that emphasize how knowledge is connected to power based on students' lived experience

Realism: the perspective that reality exists outside of human perception and that it is a knowable foundation for judgment and action

Reality: objective world independent of human perception or interpretation

Reflexivity: when rhetoric cues an audience to its own strategies, interrupting naturalization

Relativism: the perspective that challenges realist foundations in favor of views that locate reality in human perception and language without referent to an "outside" truth

Rhetoric: the study and practice of persuasion

Rhetoric of inquiry/science: body of scholarship exploring how scientific investigation is influenced by prevailing beliefs and values and how scientists use rhetoric to be persuasive

Snowden, Edward: whistleblower who exposed NSA spying on a mass scale

Sophists: Ancient Greek relativist teachers of rhetoric

Spectacle: the use of awe-inspiring, usually visual, methods to convey information

Standpoint epistemology: the idea that knowledge and truth vary according to where you stand in power relations in society

Stasis system: a set of concepts developed by the Ancient Greek rhetorician Hermagoras; the staseis are conjecture, definition, causation, evaluation, jurisdiction, and proposal

Structuralism: position that our social world is constructed in signs and symbols in such a way that human agency is constrained

Studium: concept defined by Roland Barthes about images, meaning standard cultural interpretation of a photographic image

Therapeutic rhetoric: the transforming of social problems that are most properly understood as political, collective, and structural into personal problems and the psychopathology of individuals

Truth: a belief about reality that is faithful to the interests and experiences of those whose worlds it organizes

Truthiness: when an idea is repeated so frequently or controlled by the powerful such that it comes to be naturalized truth

Tyson, Neil deGrasse: celebrity scientist and host of show *Cosmos: A Spacetime Odyssey*

Working class: people who, in capitalism, have to work for a wage

BIBLIOGRAPHY

Ackerman, Bruce. "Bradley Manning's Inhumane Treatment." *Guardian*, April 11, 2011. https://www
.theguardian.com/commentisfree/cifamerica/2011/apr/11/bradley-manning-julian-assange.

Adamson, Walter L. *Hegemony and Revolution: Antonio Gramsci's Political and Cultural Theory.*
Brattleboro, VT: Echo Point Books & Media, 2014.

Ahmed, Sara. *Cultural Politics of Emotion.* Edinburgh: Edinburgh University Press, 2014.

Alexander, Michelle, and Cornel West. *The New Jim Crow: Mass Incarceration in the Age of Color-
blindness.* New York: The New Press, 2012.

Allen, Samantha. "Planned Parenthood Smear Videos Caused Nine Times More Threats."
Daily Beast, December 2, 2015. http://www.thedailybeast.com/articles/2015/12/02/planned
-parenthood-vids-sparked-threats.html.

Althusser, Louis. "Ideology and Ideological State Apparatuses." In *Lenin and Philosophy and
Other Essays*, translated by Ben Brewster, 1970. https://www.marxists.org/reference/archive/
althusser/1970/ideology.htm.

"An Overview of Abortion Laws." Guttmacher Institute. August 1, 2017. Accessed August 6, 2017.
https://www.guttmacher.org/state-policy/explore/overview-abortion-laws.

Anderson, Monica, and Paul Hitlin. "The Hashtag #BlackLivesMatter Emerges: Social Activism on
Twitter." *Pew Research Center: Internet, Science & Tech*, August 15, 2016. http://www.pewinternet
.org/2016/08/15/the-hashtag-blacklivesmatter-emerges-social-activism-on-twitter/.

Andrejevic, Mark. *Infoglut: How Too Much Information Is Changing the Way We Think and Know.*
New York: Routledge, 2013.

Answers in Genesis. "Anisotropic Synchrony Convention—Distant Starlight Problem." September 22, 2010. Accessed January 7, 2017. https://answersingenesis.org/astronomy/starlight/
anisotropic-synchrony-convention-distant-starlight-problem/.

———. *"Cosmos* Review: 'Unafraid of the Dark.'" June 13, 2014. Accessed January 7, 2017.
https://answersingenesis.org/reviews/tv/cosmos-review-unafraid-of-the-dark/.

———. *"Cosmos: A SpaceTime Odyssey* Review." March 11, 2014. Accessed January 7, 2017.
https://answersingenesis.org/countering-the-culture/cosmos-a-spacetime-odyssey/.

———. "Creation for Kids." Accessed January 8, 2017. https://answersingenesis.org/kids/creation/.

———. "Kids Answers." Accessed January 8, 2017. https://answersingenesis.org/kids/answers/.

———. "Questioning Cosmos." November 1, 2014. Accessed January 8, 2017. https://answersingenesis .org/blogs/ken-ham/2014/11/01/questioning-cosmos/.

Aptheker, Herbert. *The American Revolution, 1763–1783: A History of the American People: An Interpretation*. New York: International Publishers, 1960.

Arel, Dan. "13 Ways Neil deGrasse Tyson's 'Cosmos' Sent the Religious Right off the Deep End," *Salon*, June 14, 2014. http://www.salon.com/2014/06/14/13_ways_neil_degrasse_tysons _cosmos_sent_the_religious_right_off_the_deep_end_partner/.

———. "Why Neil deGrasse Tyson Has Creationists so Thoroughly Petrified." *Salon*, May 22, 2014. Accessed January 9, 2017. http://www.salon.com/2014/05/22/why_neil_degrasse_has _creationists_so_thoroughly_petrified_partner/.

Aristotle. *Aristotle: Art of Rhetoric*. Translated by J. H. Freese. Vol. 22. Cambridge, MA: Harvard University Press, 1926.

Audiophile Vintage. *Famous Maxell Blown Away Guy over 500 Plays Tape C*. Accessed January 8, 2017. https://www.youtube.com/watch?v=Zjf5pdJJ44Q.

Aune, James Arnt. "Cultures of Discourse: Marxism and Rhetorical Theory." In *Argumentation Theory and the Rhetoric of Assent*, edited by David Williams and Michael David Hazen, 157–72. Tuscaloosa, AL: University of Alabama Press, 2006.

———. *Rhetoric and Marxism*. Boulder, CO: Westview Press, 1994.

Backer, David I. "Toward an Activist Theory of Language," in Hannan, 3–22.

Bale, Jeff, and Sarah Knopp. *Education and Capitalism: Struggles for Learning and Liberation*. Chicago: Haymarket Books, 2012.

Barak, Miri, and Yehudit J. Dori. "Science Education in Primary Schools: Is an Animation Worth a Thousand Pictures?" *Journal of Science Education and Technology* 20, no. 5 (October 1, 2011): 608. doi:10.1007/s10956-011-9315-2.

Barthes, Roland. *Image-Music-Text*. Translated by Stephen Heath. New York: Hill and Wang, 1978.

———. *Mythologies*. Translated by Annette Lavers. New York: Farrar, Straus and Giroux, 1972.

Baudrillard, Jean. *Simulacra and Simulation*. Translated by Sheila Faria Glaser. Ann Arbor: University of Michigan Press, 1994.

Bazerman, Charles. "Codifying the Social Scientific Style: The APA Publication Manual as a Behaviorist Rhetoric." In *The Rhetoric of the Human Sciences: Language and Argument in Scholarship and Public Affairs*, edited by John S. Nelson, Allan Megill, and Donald N. McCloskey, 125–44. Madison: University of Wisconsin Press, 1987.

Bell, Bethan. "Aww-Some Animals: Why Do Baby Mammals Melt Our Hearts?" *BBC News*, June 29, 2014, sec. England. http://www.bbc.com/news/uk-england-28036667.

Bennett, Beth. "Hermagoras of Temnos." In *Classical Rhetorics and Rhetoricians*, edited by Michelle Bailiff and Michael G. Moran, 186–93. Westport, CT: Praeger, 2005.

Bernick, Michael. "The Jobs Perplex: With U. S. Unemployment Low, Why Is Job Dissatisfaction and Anxiety So High?" *Forbes*, August 30, 2016. http://www.forbes.com/sites/michaelbernick/ 2016/08/30/the-jobs-perplex-labor-day-2016/.

Bernstein, Richard J. *Beyond Objectivism and Relativism: Science, Hermeneutics, and Praxis*. Philadelphia: University of Pennsylvania Press, 1983.

Bland, Mark W., and Elizabeth Morrison. "The Experimental Detection of an Emotional Response to the Idea of Evolution." *The American Biology Teacher* 77, no. 6 (August 1, 2015): 413–20. doi:10.1525/abt.2015.77.6.413.

Blankstein, Andrew, and Daniella Silva, "LeBron James' Los Angeles Home Vandalized with 'N-Word' Graffiti." NBC News, June 1, 2017. http://www.nbcnews.com/news/us-news/lebron-james-los-angeles-home-vandalized-n-word-graffiti-n766651.

Bonilla, Yarimar, and Jonathan Rosa. "#Ferguson: Digital Protest, Hashtag Ethnography, and the Racial Politics of Social Media in the United States." *American Ethnologist* 42, no. 1 (February 2015): 4–17. doi:10.1111/amet.12112.

Bourdieu, Pierre. *Outline of a Theory of Practice.* Cambridge: Cambridge University Press, 1977.

Bouton, Terry. *Taming Democracy.* New York: Oxford University Press, 2007.

Broder, John, and Ginger Thompson. "Loner Sought a Refuge, and Ended up in War." *New York Times,* July 31, 2013. http://www.nytimes.com/2013/07/31/us/loner-sought-a-refuge-and-chose-the-army.html.

Brummett, Barry. "The Representative Anecdote as a Burkean Method, Applied to Evangelical Rhetoric." *Southern Speech Communication Journal* 50, no. 1 (December 30, 1984): 1–23. doi: 10.1080/10417948409372619.

———. "Some Implications of 'Process' or 'Intersubjectivity': Postmodern Rhetoric." *Philosophy & Rhetoric* 9, no. 1 (1976): 21–51.

Brutus, Dennis. *Poetry and Protest: A Dennis Brutus Reader.* Edited by Aisha Karim and Lee Sustar. Chicago: Haymarket Books, 2006.

Burke, Kenneth. *Attitudes toward History.* Berkeley: University of California Press, 1984.

———. *A Grammar of Motives.* Berkeley: University of California Press, 1969.

———. *Language as Symbolic Action.* Berkeley: University of California Press, 1968.

———. *Permanence and Change: An Anatomy of Purpose.* Berkeley: University of California Press, 1984.

———. *The Philosophy of Literary Form: Studies in Symbolic Action.* Berkeley: University of California Press, 1974.

———. "Revolutionary Symbolism in America." In *The Legacy of Kenneth Burke,* edited by Herbert W. Simons and Trevor Melia, 267–80. Madison: University of Wisconsin Press, 1989.

———. *The Rhetoric of Religion: Studies in Logology.* Berkeley: University of California Press, 1970.

Bynum, Haywood, III. "TV Networks Refuse to Renew Neil deGrasse Tyson's Cosmos." *Topeka's News,* May 13, 2014. http://topekasnews.com/tv-networks-refuse-renew-neil-degrasse-tysons-cosmos-season-two.

Campbell, Hank. "Five Things Neil deGrasse Tyson's 'Cosmos' Gets Wrong." *Federalist,* March 13, 2014. http://thefederalist.com/2014/03/13/five-things-neil-degrasse-tysons-cosmos-gets-wrong/.

Campbell, Karlyn Kohrs. "Consciousness-Raising: Linking Theory, Criticism, and Practice." *Rhetoric Society Quarterly* 32 (2002): 45–64.

Carbonell, Curtis D. "Intelligent Design Creationism and the Mechanisms of Postmodernity." *Journal of Religion and Popular Culture* 23, no. 3 (September 22, 2011): 276.

Cashmore, Ellis. *Celebrity Culture.* Abingdon, UK: Routledge, 2006.

Cass, Connie. "Who Is Edward Snowden? Many Questions Remain." *Christian Science Monitor,* June 13, 2013. http://www.csmonitor.com/usA/Latest-News-Wires/2013/0613/Who-is-Edward-Snowden-Many-questions-remain.

Cauterucci, Christina. "The Women's March on Washington Has Released an Unapologetically Progressive Platform." *Slate, XXFactor,* January 12, 2017. http://www.slate.com/blogs/xx

_factor/2017/01/12/the_women_s_march_on_washington_has_released_its_platform_and_it
_is_unapologetically.html.

Ceccarelli, Leah. *On the Frontier of Science: An American Rhetoric of Exploration and Exploitation.* East Lansing: Michigan State University Press, 2013.

———. "Science and Civil Debate: The Case of E. O. Wilson's Sociobiology." In *Rhetoric and Incommensurability,* edited by Randy Allen Harris, 271–93. West Lafayette, IN: Parlor Press, 2005.

———. *Shaping Science with Rhetoric: The Cases of Dobzhansky, Schrodinger, and Wilson.* Chicago: University of Chicago Press, 2001.

Center for Medical Progress. "Human Capital." May 25, 2015. http://www.centerformedicalprogress.org/human-capital/.

Charland, Maurice. "Constitutive Rhetoric: The Case of the Peuple Québécois." *Quarterly Journal of Speech* 73, no. 2 (May 1987): 133.

Cherwitz, Richard A., ed. *Rhetoric and Philosophy.* Hillsdale, NJ: L. Erlbaum Associates, 1990.

Cherwitz, Richard A., and James W. Hikins. *Communication and Knowledge: An Investigation in Rhetorical Epistemology.* Studies in Rhetoric/Communication. Columbia: University of South Carolina Press, 1986.

———. "Rhetorical Perspectivism." *Quarterly Journal of Speech* 69, no. 3 (August 1983): 249.

Chokshi, Niraj. "How #BlackLivesMatter Came to Define a Movement." *New York Times,* August 22, 2016. http://www.nytimes.com/2016/08/23/us/how-blacklivesmatter-came-to-define-a-movement.html.

Cloud, Dana L. "Hegemony or Concordance? The Rhetoric of Tokenism in 'Oprah' Winfrey's Rags-to-Riches Biography." *Critical Studies in Mass Communication* 13, no. 2 (June 1, 1996): 115–37. doi:10.1080/15295039609366967.

———. "The Irony Bribe and Reality Television: Investment and Detachment in *The Bachelor.*" *Critical Studies in Media Communication* 27 (2010): 413–37.

———. "Materiality of Discourse as Oxymoron: A Challenge to Critical Rhetoric." *Western Journal of Communication* 58 (1994): 141–63.

———. "*The Matrix* and Critical Theory's Desertion of the Real." *Communication and Critical/Cultural Studies* 3, no. 4 (December 1, 2006): 329–54. doi:10.1080/14791420600984243.

———. "Shock Therapy: Oprah Winfrey, Celebrity Philanthropy, and Disaster 'Relief' in Haiti." *Critical Studies in Media Communication* 31, no. 1 (March 2014): 42–56. doi:10.1080/15295036.2013.864047.

Cloud, Dana L., and Kathleen Eaton Feyh. "Reason in Revolt: Emotional Fidelity and Working Class Standpoint in the 'Internationale.'" *Rhetoric Society Quarterly* 45, no. 4 (August 8, 2015): 300–323. doi:10.1080/02773945.2014.965338.

Cloud, Dana L., Kathleen E. Feyh, and Bryan McCann. "Kairos of the Vanguard." In *Concerning Argument,* edited by Scott Jacobs. Washington, DC: National Communication Association and the American Forensics Association, 2007.

Cloud, Dana L., and Amanda Davis Gatchet. "David, Goliath, and the Black Panthers: The Paradox of the Oppressed Militant in Rhetoric of Self-Defense." *Journal of Communication Inquiry* 37, no. 1 (2012): 5–25.

Cohen, Cathy J., and Sarah J. Jackson. "Ask a Feminist: A Conversation with Cathy J. Cohen on Black Lives Matter, Feminism, and Contemporary Activism." *Signs: Journal of Women in Culture and Society* 41, no. 4 (June 1, 2016): 775–92. doi:10.1086/685115.

Colbert, Stephen. "The Word—'Truthiness.'" *The Colbert Report,* 2005. http://www.cc.com/video -clips/63ite2/the-colbert-report-the-word—truthiness.

Cole, Mike. *Marxism and Educational Theory: Origins and Issues.* Abingdon, UK: Routledge, 2008.

Collins, Patricia Hill. "Black Public Intellectuals: From Du Bois to the Present." *Contexts* 4, no. 4 (November 1, 2005): 22–27. doi:10.1525/ctx.2005.4.4.22.

Condit, Celeste. *Decoding Abortion Rhetoric.* Urbana: University of Illinois Press, 1990.

Connolly, Marshall. "Is It Okay for Catholics to Watch Cosmos: A Spacetime Odyssey?" *Catholic Online,* May 3, 2014. http://www.catholic.org/news/ae/tv/story.php?id=55228.

Cook, John, Dana Nuccitelli, Sarah A. Green, Mark Richardson, Bärbel Winkler, Rob Painting, Robert Way, Peter Jacobs, and Andrew Skuce. "Quantifying the Consensus on Anthropogenic Global Warming in the Scientific Literature." *Environmental Research Letters* 8, no. 2 (2013): 24024. doi:10.1088/1748–9326/8/2/024024.

Coppola, Al. "Science Hasn't Been This Controversial Since 1676." *Quartz,* April 22, 2017, https://qz .com/966053/science-hasnt-been-this-controversial-since-1676/.

"*Cosmos: A Personal Voyage.*" *Wikipedia,* January 6, 2017. https://en.wikipedia.org/w/index.php ?title=Cosmos:_A_Personal_Voyage&oldid=758633133.

Cosmos: A Personal Voyage. Written by Carl Sagan, Ann Druyan, and Steven Soter. Public Broadcasting System, 1980.

Cosmos: A Spacetime Odyssey. Produced and written by Neil deGrasse Tyson, Ann Druyan, Brannon Braga, Mitchell Canold, and Steven Soter. Fox and National Geographic Channel, 2014.

"*Cosmos: A Spacetime Odyssey.*" *Wikipedia,* December 31, 2016. https://en.wikipedia.org/w/index .php?title=Cosmos:_A_Spacetime_Odyssey&oldid=757594804.

"Cosmos: A Spacetime Odyssey on FOX." *Canceled TV Shows—TV Series Finale,* June 10, 2015. http://tvseriesfinale.com/tv-show/cosmos-a-spacetime-odyssey/.

Coupe, Laurence. *Kenneth Burke on Myth: An Introduction.* Psychology Press, 2005.

Creation Ministries International. "About Us—Creation.com." Accessed January 7, 2017. http:// creation.com/about-us.

———. "Cosmos Neil deGrasse Tyson Review—Creation.com." Accessed January 7, 2017. http:// creation.com/cosmos-neil-degrasse-tyson-review.

Creation Museum. "Prepare to Believe." Accessed May 28, 2013. https://creationmuseum.org/.

Crugnale, James. "'Cosmos' Evolution Segment Cut Out of Fox Affiliate Broadcast." *TheWrap,* March 13, 2014. http://www.thewrap.com/evolution-segment-cut-oklahoma-affiliate -broadcast-cosmos/.

Davidson, Neil. *How Revolutionary Were the Bourgeois Revolutions?* Chicago: Haymarket Books, 2012.

Davies, William. "The Age of Post-Truth Politics." *New York Times,* August 24, 2016. http://www.nytimes.com/2016/08/24/opinion/campaign-stops/the-age-of-post-truth-politics .html.

Debord, Guy. *Society of the Spectacle.* New York: Zone Books, 1995.

Dennehy, Robert F., Sandra Morgan, and Pauline Assenza. "Thomas Paine: Creating the New Story for a New Nation." *Tamara Journal of Critical Organisation Inquiry* 5, no. 3/4 (2006): 183–92.

Dewey, John. *Democracy and Education.* New York: Free Press, 1997.

Dewey, John, and Melvin L. Rogers. *The Public and Its Problems: An Essay in Political Inquiry.* University Park, PA: Penn State Press, 2012.

Dowling, Sarah, Marcus Johnson, and Ron Krabill. "Teaching Ferguson: Can #BlackLivesMatter in the Neoliberal University?" *Rethinking Marxism* 28, no. 2 (April 2, 2016): 295–305. doi:10 .1080/08935696.2016.1168245.

Druyan, Ann. "Quest for Students, Episode 1." *Static Media,* n.d. http://static-media.fox.com/ cosmos/Cosmos_Quest_Episode_1.pdf.

Eagleton, Terry. *Ideology: An Introduction.* London: Verso, 1991.

Eberly, Rosa A. *Citizen Critics: Literary Public Spheres.* Urbana: University of Illinois Press, 2000.

Economic Policy Institute. "The Top Charts of 2016: 13 Charts That Show the Difference between the Economy We Have Now and the Economy We Could Have." December 22, 2016. http://www.epi.org/publication/the-top-charts-of-2016–13-charts-that-show-the-difference -between-the-economy-we-have-now-and-the-economy-we-could-have/.

Edelman, Murray. *Constructing the Political Spectacle.* Chicago: University of Chicago Press, 1988.

Egan, Timothy. "Lord of the Lies." *New York Times,* June 9, 2016. http://www.nytimes.com/2016/ 06/10/opinion/lord-of-the-lies.html.

Eilperin, Juliet. "The Public's Interest in Climate Change Is Waning." *Washington Post,* April 2, 2013, sec. The Fix. https://www.washingtonpost.com/news/the-fix/wp/2013/04/02/polls -suggest-publics-interest-in-climate-change-is-waning/.

Elliott, Larry. "Richest 62 People as Wealthy as Half of World's Population, Says Oxfam." *Guardian,* January 18, 2016, sec. Business. https://www.theguardian.com/business/2016/jan/18/richest-62 -billionaires-wealthy-half-world-population-combined.

Elster, Jon. *Making Sense of Marx.* Cambridge: Cambridge University Press, 1985.

Engster, Frank. "Subjectivity and Its Critics: Commodity Mediation and the Economic Constitution of Objectivity and Subjectivity." *History of the Human Sciences* 29 (2016): 77–95.

Enns, Peter. "'Cosmos' and Christianity (or Any Religion, for That Matter)." *Patheos,* June 10, 2014. http://www.patheos.com/blogs/peterenns/2014/06/cosmos-and-christianity-or-any-religion -for-that-matter/.

Entman, Robert. "Framing: Toward Clarification of a Fractured Paradigm." *Journal of Communication* 43 (1993): 51–60.

Epic Step. *Cosmos: A Spacetime Odyssey—Alan Silvestri—Soundtrack.* Accessed January 8, 2017. https://www.youtube.com/watch?v=2D5ZGxuAGSc&list=RD2D5ZGxuAGSc#t=111.

Fahy, Declan. *The New Celebrity Scientists: Out of the Lab and into the Limelight.* Lanham, MD: Rowman & Littlefield Publishers, 2015.

Finnegan, Cara. *Making Photography Matter: A Viewer's History from the Civil War to the Great Depression.* Champaign-Urbana: University of Illinois, 2015.

Fisher, Dana R., Dawn Marie Down, and Rashawn Ray. "The Demographics of the #Resistance." *The Conversation,* May 31, 2017. https://theconversation.com/the-demographics-of-the -resistance-77292.

Fishman, Steve. "Bradley Manning's Army of One." *NYMag.com,* July 3, 2011. Accessed December 29, 2016. http://nymag.com/news/features/bradley-manning-2011-7/.

Foner, Eric. *Reconstruction: America's Unfinished Revolution, 1863–1877.* New York: Harper Collins, 2011.

———. *Slavery, the Civil War, and Reconstruction.* Washington, DC: American Historical Association, 1997.

———. *Tom Paine and Revolutionary America.* Updated ed. New York: Oxford University Press, 2004.

Foster, Alice. "What is Covfefe? Donald Trump's Bizarre Tweet Confuses the World as Typo Mocked Online." *Express,* May 31, 2017. http://www.express.co.uk/news/politics/811350/Covfefe-what-is-Donald-Trump-tweet-explanation-Twitter.

Foucault, Michel. *Discipline & Punish: The Birth of the Prison.* Translated by Alan Sheridan. 2nd Vintage Books ed., 1995. New York: Random House, 1975.

———. *The History of Sexuality: An Introduction.* Translated by Robert Hurley. Vintage Books ed., 1990. Vol. 1. 3 vols. *History of Sexuality.* New York: Random House, 2012.

———. "Two Lectures." In *Power/Knowledge: Selected Interviews and Other Writings,* edited by Colin Gordon. New York: Pantheon, 1980.

Fraser, Nancy. "Rethinking the Public Sphere: A Contribution to the Critique of Actually Existing Democracy." *Social Text,* no. 25/26 (1990): 56–80. doi:10.2307/466240.

Freire, Paulo. *Paulo Freire: A Critical Encounter.* Edited by Peter Leonard and Peter McLaren. London: Routledge, 1992.

Freire, Paulo, and Donaldo Macedo. *Pedagogy of the Oppressed, 30th Anniversary Edition.* Translated by Myra Bergman Ramos. New York: Bloomsbury Academic, 2000.

Friedland, Lewis, and Thomas B. Hove. "Habermas' Account of Truth in Political Communication." In *Truth in the Public Sphere,* edited by Jason Hannan. Lanham. MD: Lexington Books, 2013.

Fuglei, Monica. "Five Ways Neil deGrasse Tyson and Bill Nye Can Help Teachers Improve Science Literacy." *Hot Chalk Lesson Plans.* Accessed August 12, 2017. http://lessonplanspage.com/five-ways-neil-degrasse-tyson-and-bill-nye-can-help-teachers-improve-science-literacy/.

Gabler, Neal. "Toward a New Definition of Celebrity." Working paper, *Norman Lear Center of the Annenberg School for Communications,* 2016. https://learcenter.org/pdf/Gabler.pdf.

Gajanan, Mahita. "Colin Kaepernick and a Brief History of Protest in Sports." *Time,* August 29, 2016. http://time.com/4470998/athletes-protest-colin-kaepernick/.

Gallagher, Edward J. "Thomas Paine's CRISIS 1 and the Comfort of Time." *The Explicator* 68, no. 2 (March 31, 2010): 87–89. doi:10.1080/00144941003723717.

Gallagher, Ryan J., Andrew J. Reagan, Christopher M. Danforth, and Peter Sheridan Dodds. "Divergent Discourse between Protests and Counter-Protests: #BlackLivesMatter and #AllLivesMatter." Cornell University Library, submitted June 22, 2016, last revised May 20, 2017. http://arxiv.org/abs/1606.06820.

Gaonkar, Dilip Parameshwar. "The Idea of Rhetoric in the Rhetoric of Science." *Southern Communication Journal* 58, no. 4 (November 1, 1993): 258–95. doi:10.1080/10417949309372909.

Garrison, Jim, Stefan Neubert, and Kersten Reich. *Democracy and Education Reconsidered: Dewey after One Hundred Years.* Reprint ed. New York: Routledge, 2015.

Garza, Alicia. "A Herstory of the #BlackLivesMatter Movement by Alicia Garza." *The Feminist Wire,* October 7, 2014. http://www.thefeministwire.com/2014/10/blacklivesmatter-2/.

Gellman, Barton. *Dark Mirror: Edward Snowden and the American Surveillance State.* New York: Penguin Press, 2017.

German, Lindsay. *A Question of Class.* London: Bookmarks, 1973.

Geuss, Raymond. *Philosophy and Real Politics*. Princeton: Princeton University Press, 2008.

Gilbert, Christopher J. "#NotIntendedToBeAFactualStatement: On Truth and Lies in an Affective Sense," in Hannan, 93–114.

Giroux, Henry A. *On Critical Pedagogy*. New York: Bloomsbury Academic, 2011.

———. *Schooling and the Struggle for Public Life: Democracy's Promise and Education's Challenge*. 2nd ed. Boulder, CO: Routledge, 2005.

Gitlin, Todd. *The Whole World Is Watching: Mass Media in the Making & Unmaking of the New Left*. Berkeley: University of California Press, 1980.

Goetzmann, William. *Beyond the Revolution: A History of American Thought from Paine to Pragmatism*. New York: Basic Books, 2009.

Goffman, Erving. *Frame Analysis: An Essay on the Organization of Experience*. Boston: Northeastern University Press, 1986.

Gramsci, Antonio. *An Antonio Gramsci Reader*. Edited by David Forgacs. New York: Schocken Books, 1988.

———. *Selections from the Prison Notebooks of Antonio Gramsci*. Edited by Quintin Hoare and Geoffrey Nowell-Smith. London: Lawrence & Wishart, 1971. http://www.marxists.org/archive/gramsci/editions/spn/modern_prince/ch15.htm.

Graves, Lucas, Brendan Nyhan, and Jason Reifler. "The Diffusion of Fact-Checking: Understanding the Growth of a Journalistic Innovation." American Press Institute, April 22, 2015. http://www.americanpressinstitute.org/wp-content/uploads/2015/04/The-Growth-of-Fact-Checking.pdf.

Greene, Ronald Walter. "Another Materialist Rhetoric." *Critical Studies in Mass Communication* 15, no. 1 (March 1, 1998): 21–40. doi:10.1080/15295039809367031.

———. "Rhetoric and Capitalism: Rhetorical Agency as Communicative Labor." *Philosophy & Rhetoric* 37, no. 3 (2004): 188–206.

Greenwald, Glenn. *No Place to Hide: Edward Snowden, the NSA, and the U. S. Surveillance State*. New York: Metropolitan Books, 2014.

Gross, Alan. *Starring the Text: The Place of Rhetoric in Science Studies*. Carbondale: Southern Illinois University Press, 2006.

Guardian Editorial Board. "Edward Snowden: More Conscientious Objector than Common Thief." *Guardian*, June 9, 2013, sec. Opinion. https://www.theguardian.com/commentisfree/2013/jun/10/edward-snowden-conscientious-objector.

Gunn, Joshua. "Review Essay: Mourning Humanism, or, the Idiom of Haunting." *Quarterly Journal of Speech* 92, no. 1 (February 2006): 77–102.

Gunn, Ricard. "Marxism and Mediation." *Common Sense*, no. 2 (July 1987): 1–11.

Habermas, Jürgen. *The Structural Transformation of the Public Sphere: An Inquiry into a Category of Bourgeois Society*. 6th ed. Cambridge, MA: MIT Press, 1991.

Hall, Stuart. "The Problem of Ideology." In *Critical Dialogues in Cultural Studies*, edited by David Morley and Kuan-Hsing Chen, 24–45. London: Verso, 1996.

Hall, Stuart, Chas Critcher, Tony Jefferson, John Clarke, and Brian Roberts. *Policing the Crisis: Mugging, the State, and Law and Order*. New York: Palgrave, 1978.

Ham, Paul. "As Hiroshima Smouldered, Our Atom Bomb Scientists Suffered Remorse." *Newsweek*, August 5, 2015, sec. World. http://www.newsweek.com/hiroshima-smouldered-our-atom-bomb-scientists-suffered-remorse-360125.

Hannan, Jason, ed. *Truth in the Public Sphere*. Lanham, MD: Lexington Books, 2016.

Harding, Luke. *The Snowden Files: The Inside Story of the World's Most Wanted Man*. New York: Vintage, 2014.

Hariman, Robert, and John Lucaites. *No Caption Needed: Iconic Photographs, Public Culture, and Liberal Democracy*. Chicago: University of Chicago, 2007.

Harris, Elizabeth A. "Where Nearly Half of Pupils Are Homeless, School Aims to Be Teacher, Therapist, Even Santa." *New York Times*, June 6, 2016. http://www.nytimes.com/2016/06/07/nyregion/public-school-188-in-manhattan-about-half-the-students-are-homeless.html.

Hartsock, Nancy. *Money, Sex, and Power: Toward a Feminist Historical Materialism*. Boston: Northeastern University Press, 1985.

———. *Standpoint Theory Revisited*. New York: Basic Books, 1999.

Haskins, Ekaterina V. *Logos and Power in Isocrates and Aristotle*. Columbia: University of South Carolina Press, 2004.

Hawhee, Debra. *Bodily Arts: Rhetoric and Athletics in Ancient Greece*. Austin: University of Texas Press, 2013.

Head, B. W. *Ideology and Social Science: Destutt de Tracy and French Liberalism*. Springer Science & Business Media, 2012.

Hedges, Chris. *Empire of Illusion: The End of Literacy and the Triumph of Spectacle*. New York: Nation Books, 2014.

———. "Shooting the Messenger." *truthdig*, December 8, 2013. https://www.truthdig.com/articles/shooting-the-messenger/.

Henley, Jon. "White and Wealthy Voters Gave Victory to Donald Trump, Exit Polls Show." *Guardian*, November 9, 2016. https://www.theguardian.com/us-news/2016/nov/09/white-voters-victory-donald-trump-exit-polls.

Hesford, Wendy. *Spectacular Rhetorics: Human Rights Visions, Recognitions, Feminisms*. Durham, NC: Duke University Press, 2011.

Hesk, Jon. *Deception and Democracy in Classical Athens*. Cambridge: Cambridge University Press, 2001.

Hess, Amanda. "That Cute Whale You Clicked On? It's Doomed." *New York Times*, September 14, 2016. http://www.nytimes.com/2016/09/15/arts/design/that-cute-whale-you-clicked-on-its-doomed.html.

Hill, Dave, ed. *Contesting Neoliberal Education: Public Resistance and Collective Advance*. New York: Routledge, 2008.

Hodson, Jane. *Language and Revolution in Burke, Wollstonecraft, Paine, and Godwin*. Hampshire, UK: Ashgate, 2007.

Hoffman, David C. "Paine and Prejudice: Rhetorical Leadership through Perceptual Framing in 'Common Sense.'" *Rhetoric and Public Affairs* 9, no. 3 (2006): 373–410.

Hogan, J. Michael, and Glen Williams. "Republican Charisma and the American Revolution: The Textual Persona of Thomas Paine's Common Sense." *Quarterly Journal of Speech* 86, no. 1 (February 1, 2000): 1–18. doi:10.1080/00335630009384276.

Holton, Woody. *Forced Founders*. Charlotte, NC: University of North Carolina Press, 1999.

Horst, Carole. "'Cosmos' Writer Ann Druyan on Science and Seth MacFarlane." *Variety*, August 5, 2014. http://variety.com/2014/tv/awards/cosmos-writer-ann-druyan-on-science-and-seth-macfarlane-1201275597/.

Hoyt, Sarah F. "The Etymology of Religion." *Journal of the American Oriental Society*, 1912. http://archive.org/details/jstor-3087765.

Humes, Edward. *Monkey Girl: Evolution, Education, Religion, and the Battle for America's Soul.* Reprint ed. New York: Harper Perennial, 2008.

Institute for Creation Research. "Guide to the Universe, by Institute for Creation Research." Accessed January 7, 2017. http://store.icr.org/guide-to-the-universe.html?source=facebook.

———. "Who We Are." http://www.icr.org/who-we-are.

Irwin, Jones. *Paulo Freire's Philosophy of Education: Origins, Developments, Impacts and Legacies.* London: Bloomsbury Academic, 2012.

Isocrates. *Isocrates II: On the Peace. Areopagiticus. Against the Sophists. Antidosis. Panathenaicus.* Translated by George Norlin. Vol. 2. Loeb Classic Library—Isocrates. Cambridge, MA: Harvard University Press, 1929.

Iyengar, Shanto. *Is Anyone Responsible? How Television Frames Political Issues.* Chicago: University of Chicago Press, 1994.

Jackson, Sarah J., and Brooke Foucault Welles. "#Ferguson is Everywhere: Initiators in Emerging Counterpublic Networks." *Information, Communication & Society* 19 (2016): 397–418.

———. "Hijacking #MyNPD: Social Media Dissent and Networked Counterpublics." *Journal of Communication* 65 (2015): 932–52.

Jacoby, Russell. *The Last Intellectuals: American Culture in the Age of Academe.* New York: Basic Books, 2000.

Jameson, Fredric. *The Political Unconscious.* Ithaca: Cornell University Press, 1982.

Jarman, Jeffery W. "Motivated to Ignore the Facts: The Inability of Fact-Checking to Promote Truth in the Public Sphere." In Hannan, 115–30.

Jarratt, Susan C. *Rereading the Sophists: Classical Rhetoric Refigured.* Carbondale: Southern Illinois University Press, 1998.

Jenkins, Nash. "After One Brief Season, Cosmos Makes Its Final Voyage." *Time,* June 9, 2014. http://time.com/2846928/cosmos-season-finale/.

Jenlink, Patrick M. *Dewey's Democracy and Education Revisited: Contemporary Discourses for Democratic Education and Leadership.* Lanham, MD: Rowman & Littlefield, 2009.

Johnson, David K. *The Lavender Scare: the Cold War Persecution of Gays and Lesbians in the Federal Government.* Chicago: University of Chicago, 2006.

Johnston, James Scott. *Deweyan Inquiry: From Education Theory to Practice.* Albany: State University of New York Press, 2009.

Kahn, Brian. "The World Passes 400 PPM Threshold. Permanently." Climate Central, September 27, 2016. Accessed January 13, 2017. http://www.climatecentral.org/news/world-passes-400-ppm-threshold-permanently-20738.

Kellner, Douglas. *Media Spectacle.* Psychology Press, 2003.

Kelly, Casey Ryan, and Kristen E. Hoerl. "Genesis in Hyperreality: Legitimizing Disingenuous Controversy at the Creation Museum." *Argumentation and Advocacy* 48, no. 3 (January 1, 2012): 123.

Kennedy, George A. *A New History of Classical Rhetoric.* New Brunswick: Princeton University Press, 2011.

Kennerly, Michele. "Getting Carried Away: How Rhetorical Transport Gets Judgment Going." *Rhetoric Society Quarterly* 40, no. 3 (June 1, 2010): 269–91. doi:10.1080/02773941003785678.

Kingkade, Tyler. "Prosecutors Rarely Bring Charges in College Rape Cases." *Huffington Post,* June 17, 2014, sec. College. http://www.huffingtonpost.com/2014/06/17/college-rape-prosecutors-press-charges_n_5500432.html.

Kinneavy, James L., and Catherine R. Eskin. "Kairos in Aristotle's Rhetoric." *Written Communication* 17, no. 3 (July 1, 2000): 432–44. doi:10.1177/0741088300017003005.

Klinghoffer, David. "There's No Question that *Cosmos* Is Coming to Public School Science Classrooms." *Evolution News,* May 19, 2014. https://evolutionnews.org/2014/05/theres_no_quest/.

Kuhn, Thomas S. *The Structure of Scientific Revolutions.* 3rd ed. Chicago: University of Chicago Press, 1996.

Kuypers, Jim A. "Framing Analysis from a Rhetorical Perspective," In *Doing News Framing: Empirical and Theoretical Perspectives,* edited by Paul D'Angelo and Jim. A Kuypers, 286–311. New York: Routledge, 2010.

Laclau, Ernesto. *On Populist Reason.* London: Verso, 2005.

Laclau, Ernesto, and Chantal Mouffe. *Hegemony and Socialist Strategy.* London: Verso, 1987.

LaFrance, Adrienne. "What Makes the Stanford Rape Case So Unusual." *The Atlantic,* June 9, 2016. http://www.theatlantic.com/politics/archive/2016/06/what-makes-the-stanford-rape-case-so-unusual/486374/.

Lakoff, George. *Moral Politics: How Liberals and Conservatives Think.* Chicago: University of Chicago Press, 2002.

Larkin, Edward. *Thomas Paine and the Literature of Revolution.* New York: Cambridge University Press, 2005.

Larrain, Jorge. "Stuart Hall and the Marxist Conception of Ideology." In *Stuart Hall: Critical Dialogues in Cultural Studies,* edited by David Morely and Huan-Hsing Chen, 46–70. London: Verso, 1996.

Leff, Michael. "Modern Sophistic and the Unity of Rhetoric." In *The Rhetoric of the Human Sciences: Language and Argument in Scholarship and Public Affairs,* edited by John S. Nelson, Allan Megill, and Donald N. McCloskey, 19–37. Madison: University of Wisconsin Press, 1987.

Lemonick, Michael D. "Global Warming: Beyond the Tipping Point." *Scientific American,* September 1, 2008. https://www.scientificamerican.com/article/global-warming-beyond-the-co2/.

Levy, Sarah. *Bloody Trump.* Menstrual blood on canvas, 2017.

Lewis, Shantrelle. "'Formation' Exploits New Orleans' Trauma." *Slate,* February 10, 2016. http://www.slate.com/articles/double_x/doublex/2016/02/beyonc_s_formation_exploits_new_orleans_trauma.html.

Lindsey, Treva B. "Post-Ferguson: A 'Herstorical' Approach to Black Violability." *Feminist Studies* 41, no. 1 (2015): 232–37. doi:10.15767/feministstudies.41.1.232.

Lipstadt, Deborah E. *Denying the Holocaust: The Growing Assault on Truth and Memory.* New York: Simon and Schuster, 2012.

Londoño, Ernesto. "Chelsea Manning Wins Change of Legal Name to Chelsea Elizabeth Manning." *Washington Post,* April 24, 2014. https://www.washingtonpost.com/world/national-security/convicted-leaker-bradley-manning-changes-legal-name-to-chelsea-elizabeth-manning/2014/04/23/e2a96546-cb1c-11e3-a75e-463587891b57_story.html?utm_term=.d29583124958.

Loughran, Trish. "Disseminating Common Sense: Thomas Paine and the Problem of the Early National Bestseller." *American Literature* 78, no. 1 (March 1, 2006): 1–28. doi:10.1215/00029831-78-1-1.

Lucas, Edward. *The Snowden Operation: Inside the West's Greatest Intelligence Disaster.* Seattle: Amazon Digital Services, 2014. Kindle edition.

Lukács, Georg. *History and Class Consciousness: Studies in Marxist Dialectics.* Cambridge, MA: MIT Press, 1971.

Lynch, John. "'Prepare to Believe': The Creation Museum as Embodied Conversion Narrative." *Rhetoric & Public Affairs* 16, no. 1 (March 31, 2013): 1–27.

Lyotard, Jean-François. *The Postmodern Condition: A Report on Knowledge.* Translated by Geoff Bennington and Brian Massumi. Minneapolis: University of Minnesota Press, 1984.

Mackin, Glenn. "Black Lives Matter and the Concept of the Counterworld." *Philosophy & Rhetoric* 49, no. 4 (2016): 459–81. doi:10.5325/philrhet.49.4.0459.

Macrine, Sheila, Peter McLaren, and Dave Hill. *Revolutionizing Pedagogy: Education for Social Justice within and beyond Global Neo-Liberalism.* 2010 ed. New York: Palgrave Macmillan, 2009.

Madar, Chase. *The Passion of Bradley Manning: The Story Behind the Wikileaks Whistleblower.* London: Verso, 2013.

Manning, Chelsea. "The Fog Machine of War: Chelsea Manning on the U. S. Military and Media Freedom." *New York Times,* June 14, 2014. https://www.nytimes.com/2014/06/15/opinion/sunday/chelsea-manning-the-us-militarys-campaign-against-media-freedom.html.

Mantzarlis, Alexios. "No, We're Not in a 'Post-Fact' Era." Poynter, *Fact Checking,* July 21, 2016. http://www.poynter.org/2016/no-were-not-in-a-post-fact-era/421582/.

Marshall, P. David, ed. *The Celebrity Culture Reader.* New Ed ed. London: Routledge, 2006.

Marx, Karl. "Commodities." *Capital, Volume I.* 1867.

Marx, Karl. "The German Ideology." Accessed August 6, 2017. https://www.marxists.org/archive/marx/works/1845/german-ideology/.

Marx, Karl, and Frederick Engels. "Manifesto of the Communist Party." Accessed January 13, 2017. https://www.marxists.org/archive/marx/works/1848/communist-manifesto/.

McClure, Kevin. "Resurrecting the Narrative Paradigm: Identification and the Case of Young Earth Creationism." *Rhetoric Society Quarterly* 39, no. 1 (2009): 189–211.

McGee, Michael C. "A Materialist's Conception of Rhetoric." In *Explorations in Rhetoric,* edited by Raymie McKerrow, 23–48. Glenview, IL: Scott, Foresman, and Company., 1982.

———. "In Search of 'the People': A Rhetorical Alternative." *Quarterly Journal of Speech* 61, no. 3 (October 1975): 235.

McGee, Michael C., and John R. Lyne. "What Are Nice Folks Like You Doing in a Place Like This? Some Entailments of Treating Knowledge Claims Rhetorically." In *The Rhetoric of the Human Sciences: Language and Argument in Scholarship and Public Affairs,* edited by John S. Nelson, Allan Megill, and Donald N. McCloskey, 381–406. Madison: University of Wisconsin Press, 1987.

McKerrow, Raymie E. "Critical Rhetoric: Theory and Praxis." *Communication Monographs* 56, no. 2 (June 1989): 91.

Merriam-Webster. "2006 Word of the Year: Merriam-Webster Announces 'Truthiness' as 2006 Word of the Year." News release. Accessed December 20, 2016. https://www.merriam-webster.com/press-release/2006-word-of-the-year.

Miller, Kenneth R. *Only a Theory: Evolution and the Battle for America's Soul.* Reprint ed. New York: Penguin Books, 2009.

Mishra, Pankaj. "The Anti-Élite, Post-Fact Worlds of Trump and Rousseau." *New Yorker, Culture Desk,* November 14, 2016. http://www.newyorker.com/culture/culture-desk/for-the-love-of -the-poorly-educated.

Mitchell, Greg, and Kevin Gosztola. *Truth and Consequences: The U. S. vs. Bradley Manning.* New York: Sinclair Books, 2012.

Monahan, Sean. "Reading Paine from the Left." *Jacobin,* March 6, 2015. https://www.jacobinmag .com/2015/03/thomas-paine-american-revolution-common-sense/.

Moore, Randy, Murray Jensen, and Jay Hatch. "Twenty Questions: What Have the Courts Said about the Teaching of Evolution and Creationism in Public Schools?" *BioScience* 53, no. 8 (August 1, 2003): 766–71. doi:10.1641/0006–3568(2003)053[0766:TQWHTC]2.0.CO;2.

Moran, Jeffrey P. *American Genesis: The Evolution Controversies from Scopes to Creation Science.* New York: Oxford University Press, 2012.

Nadeau, Ray. "Classical Systems of Stases in Greek: Hermagoras to Hermogenes." *Greek, Roman and Byzantine Studies* 2, no. 1 (1959): 51–71.

Nakashima, Ellen, and Peter Finn. "Lawyer: Leaks Suspect's Mental Health Doubted." *Washington Post,* September 2, 2010. http://www.washingtonpost.com/wp-dyn/content/article/2010/09/ 01/AR2010090106707.html.

Nash, Gary. *The Unknown American Revolution.* New York: Viking Press, 2005.

National Alliance to End Homelessness. "The State of Homelessness in America 2016." April 6, 2016. http://www.endhomelessness.org/library/entry/SOH2016.

National Center for Science Education. "Ten Major Court Cases about Evolution and Creationism." Accessed May 28, 2013. https://ncse.com/library-resource/ten-major-court-cases -evolution-creationism.

National Public Radio. "Bradley Manning Had Long Been Plagued by Mental Health Issues." *All Things Considered,* July 31, 2013. Accessed December 29, 2016. http://www.npr.org/templates/ story/story.php?storyId=207458025.

National Sexual Violence Resource Center. "Statistics About Sexual Violence." 2015. https://www.nsvrc.org/sites/default/files/publications_nsvrc_factsheet_media-packet _statistics-about-sexual-violence_0.pdf.

Nayar, Pramod K. *Seeing Stars: Spectacle, Society and Celebrity Culture.* New Delhi: Sage Publications, 2009.

Neate, Rupert. "Scandal of Europe's 11m Empty Homes." *Guardian,* February 23, 2014, sec. Society. https://www.theguardian.com/society/2014/feb/23/europe-11m-empty-properties-enough -house-homeless-continent-twice.

Negt, Oskar, and Alexander Kluge. *Public Sphere and Experience: Toward an Analysis of the Bourgeois and Proletarian Public Sphere.* Translated by Assenka Oksiloff and Peter Labanyo. Minneapolis: University of Minnesota Press, 1993.

Nelson, Craig. "Thomas Paine and the Making of 'Common Sense.'" *New England Review* 27, no. 3 (2006): 228–50.

Nelson, John S., Allan Megill, and Donald N. McCloskey. *The Rhetoric of the Human Sciences: Language and Argument in Scholarship and Public Affairs.* Madison: University of Wisconsin Press, 1987.

Nelson, Steven. "Edward Snowden Unpopular at Home, A Hero Abroad, Poll Finds." *US News & World Report,* April 21, 2015. Accessed January 3, 2017. http://www.usnews.com/news/articles/ 2015/04/21/edward-snowden-unpopular-at-home-a-hero-abroad-poll-finds.

Nicks, Denver. *Private: Bradley Manning, WikiLeaks, and the Biggest Exposure of Official Secrets in American History.* Chicago: Chicago Review Press, 2012.

Nietzsche, Friedrich. *Will to Power.* Translated by Anthony M. Ludovici. https://en.wikisource.org/wiki/The_Will_to_Power.

Paine, Thomas. *Common Sense.* Mineola, NY: Dover Publications, 1997.

Park, Haeyoun, and Iaryna Mykhyalyshyn. "L.G.B.T. People Are More Likely to Be Targets of Hate Crimes Than Any Other Minority Group." *New York Times,* June 16, 2016. http://www.nytimes.com/interactive/2016/06/16/us/hate-crimes-against-lgbt.html.

Pew Research Center. "Keystone XL Pipeline Draws Broad Support." April 2, 2013. http://www.people-press.org/2013/04/02/keystone-xl-pipeline-draws-broad-support/.

Pilkington, Ed. "Chelsea Manning Allowed to Have Hormone Therapy." *Guardian,* February 13, 2015. https://www.theguardian.com/us-news/2015/feb/13/chelsea-manning-allowed-to-have-hormone-therapy.

———. "Chelsea Manning May Face Solitary Confinement for Having Jenner Vanity Fair Issues." *Guardian,* August 13, 2015. https://www.theguardian.com/us-news/2015/aug/12/chelsea-manning-solitary-confinement-toothpaste-army.

———. "Manning Chose Leaks That Would Not Harm US, Lawyer Says." *Guardian,* January 8, 2013. https://www.theguardian.com/world/2013/jan/08/bradley-manning-hearing-fort-meade-lawyer.

Plato. *Gorgias.* Translated by Robin Waterfield. Oxford: Oxford University Press, 2008.

———. *Phaedrus.* Translated by Robin Waterfield. Oxford: Oxford University Press, 2009.

———. *Sophist.* Translated by Nicholas P. White. Indianapolis: Hackett Publishing Company, 1993.

Posner, Richard A. *Public Intellectuals: A Study of Decline, with a New Preface and Epilogue.* Revised ed. Cambridge, MA: Harvard University Press, 2003.

Powell, Kashif Jerome. "Making #BlackLivesMatter: Michael Brown, Eric Garner, and the Specters of Black Life—Toward a Hauntology of Blackness." *Cultural Studies ☒ Critical Methodologies* 16, no. 3 (June 1, 2016): 253–60. doi:10.1177/1532708616634770.

Qiu, Linda. "Fact-Checking Trump Through His First 100 Days." *New York Times,* April 27, 2017. https://www.nytimes.com/2017/04/29/us/politics/fact-checking-president-trump-through-his-first-100-days.html.

Rall, Ted. *Snowden.* New York: Seven Stories Press, 2015.

Rancid Honeytrap. "Confronting Edward Snowden's Remarks on Bradley Manning." June 10, 2013. http://ohtarzie.wordpress.com/2013/06/10.

Raphael, Ray. *The First American Revolution.* New York: New Press, 2002.

———. *Founding Myths: Stories That Hide Our Patriotic Past.* 2nd ed. New York: New Press, 2014.

———. *A People's History of the American Revolution.* New York: New Press, 2001.

Ravitz, Jessica. "Before Orlando: The (Former) Deadliest LGBT Attack in U. S. History." *CNN Health,* June 19, 2016. http://www.cnn.com/2016/06/16/health/1973-new-orleans-gay-bar-arson-attack/index.html.

Reader, Ruth. "How We Got to Post-Truth." *Fast Company,* November 18, 2016. https://www.fastcompany.com/3065580/how-we-got-to-post-truth.

Requarth, Tim. "Scientists, Stop Thinking Explaining Science Will Fix Things." *Slate,* April 19, 2017. http://www.slate.com/articles/health_and_science/science/2017/04/explaining_science_won_t_fix_information_illiteracy.html.

Richards, Jay. "How *Cosmos* Does Religious History Badly." *Federalist,* April 30, 2014. http://thefederalist.com/2014/04/30/how-cosmos-does-religious-history-badly/.

Riese. "Homophobic Man Beats Lesbian Unconscious on Brooklyn-Bound Q Train." *Autostraddle,* May 31, 2017. https://www.autostraddle.com/man-beats-lesbian-unconscious-on-brooklyn -bound-q-train-a-381036/.

Rorty, Richard. "Science as Solidarity." In *The Rhetoric of the Human Sciences: Language and Argument in Scholarship and Public Affairs,* edited by John S. Nelson, Allan Megill, and Donald N. McCloskey, 38–52. Madison: University of Wisconsin Press, 1987.

Rosaldo, Renato. "Where Objectivity Lies: The Rhetoric of Anthropology." In *The Rhetoric of the Human Sciences: Language and Argument in Scholarship and Public Affairs,* edited by John S. Nelson, Allan Megill, and Donald N. McCloskey, 87–110. Madison: University of Wisconsin Press, 1987.

Rosenfeld, Sophia. *Common Sense: A Political History.* Cambridge, MA: Harvard University Press, 2011.

Rusbridger, Alan, and Ewen MacAskill. "I, Spy: Edward Snowden in Exile." *Guardian,* July 19, 2014, sec. World news. https://www.theguardian.com/world/2014/jul/18/-sp-edward-snowden -interview-rusbridger-macaskill.

Rutenberg, Jim. "Data Breaches Change the Rules." *New York Times,* April 11, 2016.

Santorsola, Salvador. *Carl Sagain-Cosmos-Evolution into 40 Seconds.* Accessed January 8, 2017. https://www.youtube.com/watch?v=MvG-Aob_fJc.

Saussure, Ferdinand de. *Course in General Linguistics.* Edited by Perry Meisel and Haun Saussy. Translated by Wade Baskin. New York: Columbia University Press, 2011.

Savage, Charlie. "Bradley Manning Admits Providing Files to WikiLeaks." *New York Times,* February 28, 2013. http://www.nytimes.com/2013/03/01/us/bradley-manning-admits-giving-trove -of-military-data-to-wikileaks.html.

Savali, Kirsten West. "Princeton Professor Keeanga-Yamahtta Taylor Cancels Public Appearances after Death Threats." *The Root,* June 1, 2017. http://www.theroot.com/princeton-professor -keeanga-yamahtta-taylor-cancels-pub-1795719438.

Scheufele, Deitram A., and Shanto Iyengar. "The State of Framing Research: A Call for New Directions." Political Communication Lab, Stanford University, 2011.

Schiappa, Edward. *Defining Reality: Definitions and the Politics of Meaning.* Carbondale: Southern Illinois University Press, 2003.

Schmid, Thacher. "White Supremacist Arrested in Fatal Stabbing of Two Men after Anti-Muslim Rant in Portland." *Los Angeles Times,* May 25, 2017. http://www.latimes.com/nation/ nationnow/la-na-portland-stabbing-20170527-story.html.

Scott, Robert L. "On Viewing Rhetoric as Epistemic." *Central States Speech Journal* 18, no. 1 (February 1, 1967): 9–17. doi:10.1080/10510976709362856.

Selfa, Lance. "Trump's Middle Class Army." *Jacobin,* September 7, 2016. https://www.jacobinmag .com/2016/09/trump-voters-populism-middle-class-education-gop/.

Shapiro, Adam R. *Trying Biology: The Scopes Trial, Textbooks, and the Antievolution Movement in American Schools.* Chicago: University of Chicago Press, 2013.

Shapiro, Mike. "The Rhetoric of Social Science: The Political Responsibilities of the Scholar." In *The Rhetoric of the Human Sciences: Language and Argument in Scholarship and Public Affairs,* edited by John S. Nelson, Allan Megill, and Donald N. McCloskey, 363–80. Madison: University of Wisconsin Press, 1987.

Smith, Page. *A People's History of the United States*. New York: McGraw Hill, 1976.

Snowden, Edward James. *Everything You Know about the Constitution Is Wrong*. CreateSpace Independent Publishing Platform, 2013.

Sontag, Susan. *On Photography*. New York: Macmillan, 2011.

Spanos, Brittany. "Beyoncé: 'The War on People of Color Needs to Be Over.'" *Rolling Stone,* July 7, 2016. Accessed December 15, 2016. http://www.rollingstone.com/music/news/beyonce-the -war-on-people-of-color-and-all-minorities-needs-to-be-over-20160707.

Stabile, Carol. *Prime Time Animation: Television Animation and American Culture*. London: Routledge, 2003.

Stack, Liam. "Yes, Trump Really Is Saying 'Big League,' not 'Bigly,' Linguists Say." *New York Times,* October 24, 2016. https://www.nytimes.com/2016/10/25/us/politics/trump-bigly-big-league -linguists.html?

"Stalking the Wild Neutrino." *National Geographic Video*. Accessed August 12, 2017. https://www .youtube.com/watch?v=EY-WH62IXbM.

Stein, Perry, and Sandhya Somashekhar. "Women's March on Washington Is Poised to Be the Biggest Anti-Trump Demonstration." *Houston Chronicle,* January 4, 2017. http://www.chron.com/ national/article/Women-s-March-on-Washington-is-poised-to-be-the-10833059.php.

Stoeckley, Clark, and Julian Assange. *The United States vs. Private Chelsea Manning: A Graphic Account from inside the Courtroom*. New York: OR Books, 2014.

Stopera, Matt. "The Pepper Spraying Cop Meme." *BuzzFeed,* November 21, 2011. https://www.buzzfeed.com/mjs538/the-pepper-spraying-cop-meme?utm_term=.ftevqeLbly #.rynRBxl1QL.

Suskind, Ron. "Faith, Certainty and the Presidency of George W. Bush." *New York Times,* October 17, 2004. http://www.nytimes.com/2004/10/17/magazine/faith-certainty-and-the-presidency -of-george-w-bush.html.

Tavernise, Sabrina. "As Fake News Spreads Lies, More Readers Shrug at the Truth." *New York Times,* December 6, 2016. https://www.nytimes.com/2016/12/06/us/fake-news-partisan -republican-democrat.html.

Tavernise, Sabrina, and Andrew Lehren. "A Grim Portrait of Civilian Deaths in Iraq." *New York Times,* October 22, 2010. http://www.nytimes.com/2010/10/23/world/middleeast/23casualties .html. *An index to the Iraq logs and Afghanistan logs can be found at http://www.nytimes .com/interactive/world/war-logs.html.

Taylor, Keeanga-Yamahtta. *From #BlackLivesMatter to Black Liberation*. Chicago: Haymarket Books, 2016.

Thomas, Brian. "Cosmos: A Series Created to Counter Creation." *Institute for Creation Research.* Accessed August 12, 2017. http://www.icr.org/article/cosmos-series-created-counter-creation/.

Thompson, Ginger. "Early Struggles of Soldier Charged in Leak Case." *New York Times,* August 8, 2010. http://www.nytimes.com/2010/08/09/us/09manning.html.

Tierney, William G., and Karri A. Holley. "Intelligent Design and the Attack on Scientific Inquiry." *Cultural Studies* ↔ *Critical Methodologies* 8, no. 1 (February 1, 2008): 39–49. doi:10.1177/ 1532708607305125.

Tracy, Marc. "Is Edward Snowden the Anti-Bradley Manning?" *New Republic,* June 10, 2013. https://newrepublic.com/article/113429/nsa-leaker-edward-snowden-reminiscent-wikileaks -source-manning.

Treichler, Paula A. *How to Have Theory in an Epidemic: Cultural Chronicles of AIDS.* Durham, NC: Duke University Press Books, 1999.

Triece, Mary E. *Tell It Like It Is: Women in the National Welfare Rights Movement.* Columbia: University of South Carolina Press, 2013.

Vincent, Rickey. *Party Music: The Inside Story of the Black Panthers' Band and How Black Power Transformed Soul Music.* Foreword by Boots Riley. Chicago: Chicago Review Press, 2013.

Vogel, Lisa. *Marxism and the Oppression of Women.* Chicago: Haymarket, 2014.

Wachowski, Lana, and Lilly Wachowski. *The Matrix.* Warner Bros., 1999.

———. *The Matrix Reloaded.* Warner Bros., 2003.

———. *The Matrix Revolutions.* Warner Bros., 2003.

Wang, Amy. "'Post-Truth' Named 2016 Word of the Year by Oxford Dictionaries." *Washington Post, The Fix,* November 16, 2016. https://www.washingtonpost.com/news/the-fix/wp/2016/11/16/post-truth-named-2016-word-of-the-year-by-oxford-dictionaries/.

Warner, Michael. *Publics and Counterpublics.* New York: Zone Books, 2005.

Washington Post Editorial Board. "The Manning Moment." *Washington Post,* September 2, 2013.

Wayne, Mike. *Marxism and Media Studies.* New York: Pluto Press, 2015.

Wiener-Bronner, Danielle, and Abby Ohlheiser. "What Does Neil deGrasse Tyson's 'Cosmos' Say about Religion?" *The Atlantic,* March 10, 2014. http://www.theatlantic.com/entertainment/archive/2014/03/what-does-neil-degrasse-tysons-cosmos-say-about-religion/358979/.

Williams, Clarence, and Peggy McGlone, "Noose Found at Exhibit in African American Smithsonian Museum," *Washington Post,* June 1, 2017. https://www.washingtonpost.com/local/public-safety/noose-found-at-exhibit-in-african-american-smithsonian-museum/2017/05/31/ceoeccf6–464e-11e7-a196-a1bb629f64cb_story.html?utm_term=.29025f672ad4.

Yan, Holly, Darran Simon, and Aileen Graef. "Campus Killing: Suspect Is a Member of 'Alt-Reich' Facebook Group, Police Say." CNN, May 22, 2017. http://www.cnn.com/2017/05/22/us/university-of-maryland-stabbing/.

Yang, Guobin. "Narrative Agency in Hashtag Activism: The Case of #BlackLivesMatter." *Media and Communication* 4, no. 4 (2016): 13–17. doi:http://dx.doi.org.libezproxy2.syr.edu/10.17645/mac.v4i4.692.

Young, Anna M. *Prophets, Gurus, and Pundits: Rhetorical Styles and Public Engagement.* Carbondale: Southern Illinois University Press, 2014.

Younge, Gary. "Donald Trump Is Not Too Big to Fail." *The Nation,* January 6, 2017. https://www.thenation.com/article/donald-trump-is-not-too-big-to-fail/.

Zimdars, Melissa. "False, Misleading, Clickbait-y, and Satirical 'News' Sources." Creative Commons, 2016. https://docs.google.com/document/d/10eA5-mCZLSS4MQY5QGb5ewC3VAL6pLkT53V_81ZyitM/preview.

Zimmer, Ben. "Truthiness." *New York Times,* October 13, 2010. http://www.nytimes.com/2010/10/17/magazine/17FOB-onlanguage-t.html.

Zirin, Dave. *Brazil's Dance with the Devil: The World Cup, the Olympics, and the Fight for Democracy.* Updated Olympics ed. Chicago: Haymarket Books, 2016.

———. *People's History of Sports in the United States: 250 Years of Politics, Protest, People, and Play.* New York: The New Press, 2009.

Zweig, Michael. *The Working Class Majority: America's Best-Kept Secret.* Ithaca, NY: ILR Press, 2001.

INDEX

abortion: anti-, 53, 56, 68–69, 71; clinic(s)/ clinician(s), 52, 57; opponent(s), 70–71; provider(s), 53, 64–66, 70–71, 160, 163; rights, 52–53, 69–72, 160; video controversy, 28, 54, 56, 64

activism, 10, 20, 152–53, 167–68; activist(s), xiii, xv, 2–4, 15, 18, 28, 31, 35, 39, 43, 48, 68, 70, 83, 89, 137, 139–40, 148, 150–54, 164–65, 168; scholar–activist, 150

affect, 3–4, 9, 11, 27, 35–36, 38, 40–42, 47, 51, 53, 68, 72–73, 76, 100, 105, 108, 112, 118, 146, 149, 154, 160–61, 187. *See also* feeling(s)

agency, 10, 30, 32, 85, 91, 94, 98–100, 132, 155, 187, 189; agent(s), 16, 32, 66, 76–77, 81, 84–85, 87–90, 98–99, 113; agent/victim, 77, 84, 97; narrative, 153; personal, 91; political, 92, 98; public, 98; rhetorical, 80; secret, 75, 77, 85

Ahmed, Sarah, 41

Althusser, Louis, 17

American Legislative Exchange Council (ALEC), 71

American Press Institute, 54, 57

American Revolution, 11, 139–40, 156, 187

Andrejevic, Mark, 56

animation, 109, 112, 120, 123–25, 161, 182n53

antifoundationalism/ist, 5, 35

argument, xii, xiv, 3, 9–11, 14, 16, 18, 20–22, 34, 37–38, 42, 46–47, 54, 57, 59, 61, 70, 72, 78, 87–88, 90, 108, 111–12, 118, 122, 127, 130–31, 133, 135, 138–39, 143–44, 146, 148–49, 151, 159, 162–64, 167, 172n60, 174n13, 182n63, 182n64, 183n8, 187

Aristotle, 21, 50, 187

Assange, Julian, 94, 96, 102

Barthes, Roland, 123–24, 161–62, 189

Baudrillard, Jean, 19

Bazerman, Charles, 25

belief, rhetoric of, 5

Bernstein, Richard, 24, 35, 171n28

Bible, 110, 136; biblical, 110–12, 130, 135; anti-, 135

Big Bang, 110, 120, 135

"big five," 9, 11, 53–54, 76, 105, 111, 138

black(s), 39, 44–46, 64, 83, 122, 150–52, 154, 156, 160, 163, 166, 187

#BlackLivesMatter, 138, 140, 149, 151–53, 155–56, 184, 187; Black Lives Matter, 7, 12, 40, 83, 151, 154–55, 162–63, 166, 187

bodies, 3, 17, 42–43, 45, 118, 121, 131, 133, 154, 156

Bourdieu, Pierre, 8

Burke, Kenneth, 9, 43–44, 54, 59, 61, 72, 112, 128, 136, 174n18, 187

capitalism, xi, 28–29, 31–32, 50, 129, 146–47, 156, 164, 172n62, 187, 189; pro-capitalism, 100

cartoon(s), 79, 123–24; cartoonish, 123

causal(ity), 17, 62, 101, 135

Ceccarelli, Leah, 26

celebrity(ies), 9, 11, 45, 48, 83, 101, 111, 121–22, 150, 162, 187, 189

Center for Medical Progress, 52, 64

Cherwitz, Richard, 6, 22